LIFE, LIBERTY, AND THE PURSUIT OF HAPPINESS

FOURTH OF JULY STORIES

THOMAS K. CLANCY

Mechanicsburg, PA USA

Published by Sunbury Press, Inc.
Mechanicsburg, Pennsylvania

SUNBURY PRESS
www.sunburypress.com

For information about special discounts for bulk purchases, please contact Sunbury Press Orders Dept. at (855) 338-8359 or orders@sunburypress.com.

To request one of our authors for speaking engagements or book signings, please contact Sunbury Press Publicity Dept. at publicity@sunburypress.com.

FIRST SUNBURY PRESS EDITION: January 2025

Set in Adobe Garamond | Interior design by Crystal Devine | Cover by Lawrence Knorr | Edited by Sarah Peachey.

Publisher's Cataloging-in-Publication Data
Names: Clancy, Thomas K., author.
Title: Life, liberty, and the pursuit of happiness : Fourth of July stories / Thomas K. Clancy.
Description: First trade paperback edition. | Mechanicsburg, PA : Sunbury Press, 2025.
Summary: This book tells American stories occurring on one day—the Fourth of July—throughout our 250-year history. Beginning with the founders and carrying through generations fighting for freedom and equality or military victories, these stories show how worthy America is to be our honoree.
Identifiers: ISBN 979-8-88819-254-2 (softcover).
Subjects: HISTORY / United States / General | HISTORY / United States / Revolutionary Period | POLITICAL SCIENCE / Political Ideologies / Democracy.

Designed in the USA
0 1 1 2 3 5 8 13 21 34 55

For the Love of Books!

To my family
Sally, Kevin, & Brian

CONTENTS

CONTENTS

Preface

The shooting started on Lexington Green on April 19, 1775. The British regulars killed eight colonial militia and wounded ten others. The militia scattered and the British marched on to Concord, seeking to capture Samuel Adams and John Hancock, who were leaders of colonial opposition, and to seize the munitions that were said to be stored there. The day did not end as the British had expected. The men of Massachusetts had been forming companies of volunteers—Minutemen and militia—for years, who had been drilling and preparing. Upon learning of the British advance, volunteer companies came from villages near and far, turning the British advance into a rout, with the regulars suffering disproportionate casualties inflicted by the untried colonial militias. The events that day seem almost mythical but are true enough: "If the battle's importance were to be measured by its casualties, Concord and Lexington would have been trifling indeed. But the shots 'heard round the world' had been fired, and the Revolutionary War—one of the most momentous in history—had started."[1] It would take eight years to complete the task of being recognized by Great Britain as a separate country—the United States of America.

It would also take Americans fifteen months after Lexington and Concord to decide that they were independent, which occurred on July 4, 1776. That day is celebrated as America's birthday. On July 4, 2026, there will have been 250 celebrations of that birth and 91,309 days in between those dates. To state the obvious, most of American history has occurred on days that are not July 4. But there are many July Fourths that have seen more than their share of important events, adding disproportionately to the concept of freedom, making the Fourth of July worthy to be our only federal holiday with America as the honoree. The Declaration of Independence, announced that day, detailed the reasons for the separation from Great Britain and announced that the new nation was grounded in an idea: "all Men are created equal, that they are endowed by their Creator with certain unalienable Rights, that among these are Life, Liberty, and the Pursuit of Happiness." That idea has evolved to include more people, and what constitutes liberty is viewed much more expansively than what the Founders believed when Jefferson wrote those words. On that Fourth of July and many subsequent ones, Americans have had to exhibit extraordinary courage, dedication, perseverance, and bravery to make that idea a reality. That is what gives us a reason to celebrate the day every year. It has been a long journey to a more perfect Union and to a better understanding of the idea that animates America. This book tells those stories.

The book is divided into three parts. Part I, *The Founding*, focuses on the people, reasons, and events that shaped the decision to separate from Great Britain. Those who shaped that decision have been called the *Founders* for their instrumental role in achieving independence and sustaining it in the early years after the separation. The day independence was announced, July 4, 1776, and how the decision was reached is the subject of Chapter One, with a particular focus on the central role of John Adams. The Declaration of Independence detailed the reasons for the separation. John Adams, a chief agitator for independence, traveled the road from British subject to free American, and his journey illuminates the path that many Americans took. He predicted that the road to independence would be hard, and the three chapters in this part shed light on that observation. George Washington, one of those instrumental Founders, is the subject of the second chapter; he had many remarkable Fourth of Julys in his lifetime, both predating and following July 4, 1776. The Founding Era closed with the deaths of John Adams and Thomas Jefferson on July 4, 1826, exactly fifty years to the day from when the Declaration of Independence was issued. Their complex relationship, culminating in their deaths on that day, is discussed in Chapter Three.

Part II, *The Evolution of the Promises of Freedom and Equality*, examines the enduring aspects of the Declaration of Independence, which offer the promise of created equality and fundamental rights to life, liberty, and the pursuit of happiness. The equality principle now includes more people than when Jefferson wrote those words, and what constitutes liberty and the pursuit of happiness are viewed much more expansively. Chapter Four sets forth the Declaration's words and the restrictive original meaning of those words. Missing from that view were blacks and women.

Chapter Five examines the sentiments of one agitator for freedom, Frederick Douglass, and his powerful indictment of slavery prior to the Civil War in his famous Fourth of July speech. Douglass, after physically freeing himself from slavery, used his voice to point to the vast number of Americans who were not free and to underscore the hypocrisy of the promise of the Declaration of Independence. He pursued a life of agitating for freedom and equality for his race.

Chapter Six looks at the costs of freedom, underlined by two important Union victories—Vicksburg and Gettysburg—on July 4, 1863, which are framed by words of affirmation and dissent that day. The determination of General Ulysses S. Grant to take Vicksburg and the steadiness of the Union lines at Gettysburg are underlined examples of the importance of the date in American history and how things could have turned out very differently. They highlight the extraordinary dedication and sacrifices of so many in the Civil War to further the promises of the Declaration. Abraham Lincoln, speaking of those victories, gave modern meaning to the promise of the Declaration of Independence, eventually polishing his views in his memorable speech at Gettysburg, dedicating the National Cemetery. He sought a new birth to the idea of equality and liberty within an enduring Union.

The long road women took to change their omission from the Declaration (and the Constitution) is discussed in Chapter Seven, with a focus on their protest at the Nation's Centennial celebration on July 4, 1876. Susan B. Anthony and her fellow suffragettes used the day to protest the unequal treatment of their gender. Anthony, the drafter of the Nineteenth Amendment guaranteeing women the right to vote, did not live to see it adopted.

Chapter Eight looks at the extension of liberty to other peoples who have come within the jurisdiction of the United States. The aftermath of the Spanish-American War saw the country in possession of new lands and new peoples. It took many years and much conflict before acknowledging the independence of the Philippines on July 4, 1946, and granting self-determination to Puerto Rico on July 3, 1952. The promises of the Declaration, long delayed, were finally extended to each, formally decreed on those two July days.

Part III is called *Pursuing Happiness*. The Declaration of Independence claims for Americans the inalienable right to the "pursuit of happiness." The chapters in this part set forth some of the myriad ways in which Americans *have* pursued happiness on the Fourth of July. Those pursuits have been, in ways large and small, peculiar to the individual and national in scope. Some have been quiet, others loud celebrations. Henry David Thoreau merely walked to his cabin at Walden Pond that day to begin his quiet quest for independence. A Union private suffered through two terrible Fourth of Julys during the Civil War but could still celebrate. A young man, Teddy Roosevelt, reminded Americans of their obligations in a memorable speech as the frontier closed in Dakota Territory. Lou Gehrig gave his famous speech at Yankee Stadium that day, suffering from the disease named after him, but described himself as the luckiest man. And, of course, some of the many ways Americans celebrated over the past 250 years are recounted.

There are deep flaws in our history, and this book does not ignore them. George Washington was one of Virginia's largest slaveholders, growing his plantation throughout his life through slave labor. So did Thomas Jefferson. The deaths, injuries, and sufferings of hundreds of thousands of Americans—North and South—occurred within the span of time that included the four July Fourths of the Civil War. Slavery and the denial of equal rights based on race and gender were highlighted by Frederick Douglass in one great Fourth of July speech and in the actions of Susan B. Anthony and her fellow suffragettes at the Centennial. Nonetheless, freedom has expanded, and that expansion has often coincided with the fourth day of the seventh month.

We may celebrate the date, but we should celebrate the ideas and the ideals represented by what occurred that day and on many subsequent

Fourth of Julys. The success of those ideas and ideals was the result of many individuals persevering and striving, sometimes for decades, sometimes for centuries, to expand the concept of freedom. There have been landmarks along the way; words, actions, people, and events that underscore the day's importance. This book, in fourteen chapters, tells many of those stories.

PART I

The Founding

As noted in the preface, this part focuses on the people, reasons, and events that shaped the decision to separate from Great Britain. The Founders were instrumental in achieving independence and sustaining it in the early years. Chapter One discusses the first Independence Day—July 4, 1776—and how the decision to declare independence was reached. George Washington and the remarkable number of Fourth of Julys he had is the subject of the second chapter. The Founding Era closed with the deaths of John Adams and Thomas Jefferson exactly fifty years to the day from when independence was declared. Their complex relationship, culminating in their deaths on that day, is discussed in Chapter Three.

CHAPTER 1

The Separation from Great Britain

> *When in the Course of human Events, it becomes necessary for one People to dissolve the Political Bands which have connected them with another, and to assume among the Powers of the Earth, the separate and equal Station to which the Laws of Nature and of Nature's God entitle them, a decent Respect to the Opinions of Mankind requires that they should declare the causes which impel them to the Separation.*

So begins the Declaration of Independence, the text of which was agreed to on July 4, 1776, by the delegates to the Second Continental Congress, meeting in Philadelphia, Pennsylvania. There are two aspects to that document. The first, treated in this chapter, is the formal statement of the separation of the colonies from Great Britain and the reasons for doing so. The second aspect, treated in Chapter Four, is the language that promises liberty and freedom to the inhabitants of the newly independent states. Those two aspects—the announcement of the Revolution and the assertion of individual rights—have assumed different importance over time.

Most of the document is a list of grievances detailing the reasons for the separation. The Declaration rejected independence for "light and transient Causes" but viewed the "Evils" suffered by the colonies as "a long Train of Abuses and Usurpations" that sought "to reduce them under absolute Despotism." It asserted that the King of Great Britain had "a History of repeated Injuries and Usurpations, all having in direct

Object the Establishment of an absolute Tyranny over these States." The list is long and included the king's interference with colonial legislatures and laws, his dissolution and suspension of colonial assemblies and charters, restricting immigration and limiting migration to new lands, obstructing justice and eliminating judicial independence, and creating offices "to harass our People, and eat out their Substance." The king kept large armies "among us, in Times of Peace" and protected those soldiers through mock trials. He cut off trade with the world, imposed taxes without consent, and deprived the colonies "in many Cases, of the Benefits of Trial by Jury." The king waged war against the colonies, "plundered our Seas, ravaged our Coasts, burnt our Towns, and destroyed the Lives of our People." He was, at that time, "transporting large Armies of foreign Mercenaries to compleat the Works of Death, Desolation and Tyranny." The king impressed colonial sailors to fight against their own colonies and employed Native people to wage war against the colonies. Although the colonies had repeatedly petitioned for redress, those "Petitions have been answered only by repeated Injury. A Prince, whose Character is thus marked by every act which may define a Tyrant, is unfit to be the Ruler of a free People."

The Declaration was the end of a series of legal measures. Its attack on the king "was a constitutional form. It was the way Englishmen announced revolution."[1] Petitioning the king for redress was the established way of addressing issues involving fundamental law, and that was the initial purpose of the Continental Congress—to petition for redress of grievances.[2] Congress did so in 1774 and 1775, but those petitions were refused consideration or rejected by the king; hence, the Declaration of 1776 signified the end of that process.[3] The Declaration appealed to "the Supreme Judge of the World for the Rectitude of our Intentions," and announced that the "United Colonies are, and of Right ought to be FREE AND INDEPENDENT STATES; that they are absolved from all Allegiance to the British Crown, and that all political Connection between them and the State of Great-Britain, is and ought to be totally dissolved; and that as FREE AND INDEPENDENT STATES, they have full Power to levy War, conclude Peace, contract Alliances, establish Commerce, and to do all other Acts and Things which INDEPENDENT

STATES may of right do. And for the support of this Declaration, with a firm Reliance on the protection of divine Providence, we mutually pledge to each other our Lives, our Fortunes, and our sacred Honor."

Historians estimate that only between 15% and 20% of the two million whites in the colonies in 1775 were Loyalists.[4] This means that a lot of minds and hearts had changed prior to the Declaration. Why did this happen? When did the people inhabiting the colonies stop thinking of themselves as British and start thinking of themselves as American? This is a complex and unanswerable question: Many minds and hearts were affected and changed over time. Surely, as historians have detailed, different colonists at different times began to view themselves as Americans and to question their relationship with Great Britain.

Here, the focus is on the evolution of thoughts and beliefs that led to the momentous decision to separate from Great Britain, as seen primarily through the lens of John Adams's own evolution. Adams had a remarkable opportunity to be involved in many of the events leading to the separation, and he left a detailed record of his thoughts and actions; thus, the evolution of his thoughts sheds much light on the broader change in the colonists' minds. Adams distinguished between the war and the Revolution.[5] He saw the "the real American Revolution" as a "radical change in the principles, opinions, sentiments and affections of the people" and "in the minds and hearts of the people."[6] In a letter to Thomas Jefferson, Adams offered this: "What do we mean by the revolution? The war? That was no part of the revolution: it was only an effect and consequence of it. The revolution was in the minds of the people, and this was affected from 1760 to 1775 . . . before a drop of blood was shed at Lexington."[7] He found the change in such a short period of time "a singular event in the history of mankind. Thirteen clocks were made to strike together—a perfection of mechanism, which no artist had ever before effected."[8]

To start at the beginning, Virginia was first successfully settled in 1607 at Jamestown, followed by Plymouth Colony in Massachusetts in 1620. The number of colonies and people in each grew rapidly for the next century and a half. For most of that time, the British government's impact was slight.[9] Each of the colonies had a form of government that fostered the development of a democratic experience in much of the white male populace. Women could not vote, and slaves were denied any semblance of rights. Those glaring exclusions were little noticed at the time. (More on this throughout this book.)

John Adams always marked the beginning of the change in how the populace viewed themselves as the *Writs of Assistance* case in Boston. Smuggling was a widespread practice in the American colonies, and writs of assistance were a principal means of combating the practice, at least in Massachusetts.[10] Writs of assistance—considered general warrants by the colonists—permitted officials unlimited searches. Authorities could search anywhere they wanted without any showing of justification, and the writs were issued permanently for the life of the king. Officials could be as intrusive and arbitrary as they wanted. In 1760, new writs of assistance were requested following the expiration of the previously issued writs due to the death of the king. A group of Boston merchants opposed the proposed writs, retaining James Otis to represent their cause. The key issue at the first hearing on the proposed writs, and the question upon which the case ultimately turned, was whether the Superior Court in Massachusetts should continue to grant the writs in general and open-ended form or whether it should limit the writs to a single occasion and location based on particularized suspicion given under oath.

Otis's argument has often been cited by the Supreme Court and many others as reflecting the Framers' intent and as an exposition of proper search and seizure practices. Indeed, no authority preceding Otis had articulated so completely the framework for proper search and seizure practices that was ultimately embodied in the Fourth Amendment's warrant clause.[11] Yet Otis lost, with the court ruling against the merchants and permitting broad, suspicionless searches and seizures.[12] Otis, writing about the importance of that decision, wrote:

> [E]very householder in this province, will necessarily become *less secure* than he was before this writ had any existence among us; for by it, *a custom house officer* or ANY OTHER PERSON *has a power given*

> *him, with the assistance of a peace officer,* TO ENTER FORCEFULLY *into a* DWELLING HOUSE, *and rifle every part of it where he shall* PLEASE *to suspect uncustomed goods are lodged*! — Will any man put so great a value on his freehold, after such a power commences as he did before? — every man in this province, will be liable to be insulted, by a *petty officer*, and threatened to have his house *ransacked*, unless he will comply with his unreasonable and *imprudent* demands: Will anyone under *such* circumstance, ever again boast of *british* honor or *british* privilege?[13]

His article acknowledged that a person's security in his home is sometimes "forfeited," but those instances were "in cases of the most urgent necessity and importance; and this necessity and importance is, and always ought to be determined by *adequate* and *proper* judges." The writs procedure, Otis maintained, stood in sharp contrast, with each person subject to "*petty tyrants*." After arguing that there was no necessity for the writs, Otis concluded by emphasizing the uncontrolled discretion of the customs officials: "can a community be safe with an uncontrolled power lodged in the hands of *such* officers, some of whom have given abundant proofs of the danger there is in trusting them with ANY?"

Sitting in the audience listening to Otis's arguments in the *Writs* case was a young lawyer named John Adams, who, in his turn, became a cornerstone in the struggle against Great Britain and later served as our second president. Adams left a long record regarding the importance of the *Writs of Assistance Case* to him. In his *Autobiography*, Adams wrote: "A contest appeared to me to be opened, to which I could foresee no end, and which would render my life a burden and property, industry and everything insecure. There was no alternative left, but to take the side, which appeared to be just, to march intrepidly forward in the right path, to trust in providence for the protection of truth and right, and to die with a good conscience and a decent grace, if that trial should become indispensable."[14]

Without a doubt, however, the most telling of Adams's comments occurred on July 3, 1776, the day after independence had been agreed to by Adams and the other delegates at the Continental Congress in

Philadelphia. In a letter to his wife, Abigail, reflecting on the moment, Adams wrote:

> Yesterday the greatest Question was decided, which ever was debated in America, and a greater perhaps, never was or will be decided among Men. A Resolution was passed without one dissenting Colony "that these united Colonies, are, and of right ought to be free and independent States, and as such, they have, and of Right ought to have full Power to make War, conclude Peace, establish Commerce, and to do all the other Acts and Things, which other States may rightfully do." You will see in a few days a Declaration setting forth the Causes, which have impelled Us to this mighty Revolution, and the Reasons which will justify it, in the Sight of God and Man.
>
> When I look back to the Year 1761, and recollect the Argument concerning Writs of Assistance, in the Superior Court, which I have hitherto considered as the Commencement of the Controversy, between Great Britain and America, and run through the whole Period from that Time to this, and recollect the series of political Events, the Chain of Causes and Effects, I am surprised at the Suddenness, as well as Greatness of this Revolution.[15]

Throughout his life, Adams repeatedly made similar statements. For example, in 1780, Adams marked 1761 as the beginning of the dispute with Great Britain,

> when orders were sent from the board of trade in England to the custom-house officials in America, to apply to the supreme courts of justice for writs of assistance to enable them to carry into a more rigorous execution of certain acts of parliament called the acts of trade . . . by breaking open houses, ships, or cellars, chests, stores, and magazines, to search for uncustomed goods. In most of the Colonies these writs were refused. In Massachusetts Bay the question, whether the writs were legal and constitutional, was solemnly and repeatedly argued before the supreme court by

> the most learned counsel in the Province. . . . [T]he arguments advanced upon that occasion by the bar and the bench, opened to the people such a view of the designs of the British government against their liberties and the danger they were in, as made a deep impression upon the public, which never wore out.[16]

Similarly, in a famous letter to William Tudor in 1817, Adams wrote about the impact of Otis's argument: "Every man of an immense crowded audience appeared to me to go away, as I did, ready to take arms against Writs of Assistance. Then and there was the first scene of the first act of opposition to the arbitrary claims of Great Britain. Then and there the child Independence was born."[17] The writs, Adams believed, were "illegal, unconstitutional, [and] destructive of the liberties of [the] country," and were "intended as an entering wedge to introduce unlimited taxation and legislation by authority of Parliament."[18]

As noted above, the Declaration of Independence itself lists many of the events and actions that occurred after 1760 that ultimately resulted in its issuance. Yet, those events and actions, as Adams's statements teach us, did a more; they served—at least in large part—as the catalyst for more important change, from being British to being American. Adams traveled that same road. In his diary on February 9, 1761, he welcomed a speech by the new king, George III, stating that it was "proofs of his piety" and "are the sentiments worthy of a King–a Patriot King."[19] Yet, only fifteen years later, he was a leading advocate in the struggle for independence and a proud signatory of the Declaration of Independence.

After the *Writs* case, Otis was wildly proper and became an early leader in the colonies against British overreaching. John Adams reflected that, for the following ten years, Otis's "tongue and his pen were incessantly employed in enlightening his fellow-citizens and countrymen in the knowledge of their rights, and developing and opposing the designs of Great Britain."[20] Adams always viewed Otis, whom he loved as a friend and patron, as a central figure in the fight for liberty.[21] Looking back late in life, he wrote: "I have been young, and now I am old, and I solemnly say, I have never known a man whose love of his country was more ardent or sincere; never one, who suffered so much; never one, whose services for any ten years of his life were so important and essential to the cause of his country, as those of Mr. Otis from 1760 to 1770."[22]

There were many other voices leading the way: Patrick Henry and Richard Henry Lee in Virginia, John Dickinson in Pennsylvania, and Isaac Sears and others in New York, to mention only a few. But perhaps the single most important leader was Samuel Adams, a mastermind—or at least master organizer and propagandist—who exercised outsized influence during that period in Massachusetts and throughout the colonies.[23] He was then seen as the "foremost revolutionist" in America and is now seen as the "prime mover" of the Revolution.[24] Samuel Adams, John Adams's cousin, was thirteen years older. He was a failed brewer and an indifferent tax collector. His real passion and full-time employment was politics, and his role cannot be overstated. Samuel Adams and Otis worked closely together for many years until Otis's mental health became so pervasive that he became incapacitated or ineffective. Samuel Adams, a tireless newspaper and pamphlet writer, used pseudonyms[25] to relentlessly pursue his agenda, regardless of the facts or contrary evidence.[26] He turned every event, every response by the colonial government, and Act of Parliament into a threat to colonial liberty. "[Samuel] Adams had at this disposal a single weapon: the word 'liberty.'"[27] He also knew how to turn out a crowd, working with various groups, including the Sons of Liberty, and he was a member of "almost every liberal political club in Boston."[28] "Under Sam Adams, Boston taverns became nurseries of revolution as well as nurseries of legislators."[29] Boston in 1770 had 15,520 inhabitants, but, for example, the meeting preceding the Boston Tea Party had an estimated 6,000 attendees. Finally, he worked tirelessly to paralyze the colonial administration and isolate the royal governor.

Otis burned his private letters[30] as did Samuel Adams (at least in part with other documents lost through neglect), with the latter stating that he destroyed his papers to protect his numerous confederates.[31] Although Otis's and Samuel Adams's numerous public documents and newspaper articles survived, much of their private thoughts did not. John Adams, in contrast, was a prolific diarist, letter writer, book author, autobiographer, and constitutional and legal theorist. He had a sense of history—and his role in it—and wrote about persons and events throughout the era, including the extraordinary number of events that he actually witnessed and participated in, beginning with the *Writs* case and extending to the signing of the Declaration of Independence.

John Adams's diary reveals much of the evolution of his own thoughts as events unfolded. In August 1761, he was ruminating about the nature of the British Constitution: "The English Constitution is founded, tis bottomed and grounded on the knowledge and good sense of the people. The very ground of our liberties, is the freedom of elections. Every man has in politicks as well as religion, a right to think and speak and act for himself." In early 1765, he stated that he considered the "settlement of America with reverence and wonder—as the opening of a grand scene and design in province, for the illumination of the ignorant and the emancipation of the slavish part of mankind all over the earth."

By 1764, the British government was looking for new sources of revenue to support the expenses of the French and Indian War, also known as the Seven Years' War, and to partially offset the ongoing expenses of its American empire. The first attempt was the Sugar Act, which imposed a duty on imported molasses—from which rum was made—and strengthened enforcement efforts against smuggling. Objections to the legislation were primarily economic, given that it substantially damaged colonial merchants and came during a post-war depression. Those considerations were the basis of its repeal in 1766. In Massachusetts, however, James Otis and Samuel Adams saw threats to liberty, including the beginning of calls for the colonies to unite to coordinate opposition.[32] Thus began a repeating pattern: Parliament passed a law to raise revenue, colonial opposition ensued, and then Parliament repealed the act.[33]

A second attempt to raise revenue was the Stamp Act in 1765, which was the first internal tax of the American colonies, and many historians mark its adoption as the point at which the colonists began to reexamine their views of their relationship with Great Britain. Indeed, Governor Bernard of Massachusetts at that time recognized that the controversy surrounding the Stamp Act disclosed the "wildly different" notions in the colonies and in Great Britain of the nature of their relationship.[34] That wide-ranging statute imposed a tax on virtually all documents and papers produced in the colonies, including newspapers, legal transactions, licenses to engage in business, commercial documents, and even playing cards. Stamps were printed in England and shipped to America, where local stamp masters were appointed to issue the stamps and collect the taxes. Without stamps, ports, courts, newspapers, and even taverns could not legally operate.

In Britain, it was held that sovereignty remained with the king and Parliament, including the power to tax.[35] From the colonials' point of view, if Parliament "can compel them to pay *one penny*, they may compel [the colonists] to pay the *last penny* they have."[36] It was said that it was not the tax itself but the "invasion of Americans' political rights" at stake.[37] The Stamp Act produced "massive colonial opposition" throughout the American colonies.[38] Led by Patrick Henry, the Virginia House of Delegates adopted the Virginia Resolves (published throughout the colonies), which in part asserted that Americans held the same rights as Englishmen and that the "principle of no taxation without representation was an essential part of the British Constitution;" only Virginia could tax Virginians.[39] There were riots throughout the colonies, with the "hated" stamp masters bearing the "full weight" of the opposition.[40] Stamp masters were forced to renounce their commissions, often done in front of a threatening mob, and driven out of the colony. Throughout the colonies, the Sons of Liberty were organizing, "which served as headquarters for the patriot leaders who set the mobs to work terrorizing stamp masters, burning the stamps, and mobbing all supporters of British 'tyranny.'"[41] In 1765, John Adams drafted the Braintree Instructions for the Massachusetts Assembly (the lower house of the colonial legislature), which was his first foray into politics. The instructions directed that Boston's representative to the Massachusetts General Court (the legislature) should oppose the Stamp Act, listing a variety of reasons, including the principle of no taxation without representation, and that judges and not juries should be the trier of fact when lawsuits to collect the taxes were brought. Eventually, forty towns in Massachusetts adopted those instructions.

The Massachusetts Assembly proposed a congress of all of the colonies—The Stamp Act Congress—which was held in New York in October 1765. Although only nine colonies sent delegates, the Congress asserted that individuals had certain natural rights, put forward the doctrine of no taxation without representation, and called for the repeal of the Stamp Act. Those views were subsequently adopted by every colony except Virginia, whose legislature had been prorogued by the royal governor.[42] Boycotts of British merchandise became widespread, creating pressure from the merchants on Britain to repeal the act. Committees of Correspondence formed to exchange views among the colonies; the Sons of Liberty's influence spread throughout the colonies.

Reflecting in his diary at the end of 1765, Adams observed that it had "been the most remarkable Year of my Life." He viewed the Stamp Act as an "enormous engine, fabricated by the British Parliament, for battering down all the rights and liberties of America." The colonial reaction had raised a spirit throughout the continent:

> In every colony, from Georgia to New Hampshire inclusively, the stamp distributors and inspectors have been compelled, by the unconquerable rage of the people, to renounce their offices.
>
> The People, even to the lowest ranks, have become more attentive to their liberties, more inquisitive about them, and more determined to defend them, than they were ever before known or had occasion to be. Innumerable have been the monuments of wit, humor, sense, learning, spirit, patriotism, and heroism, erected in the several Colonies and Provinces, in the course of this year. Our presses have groaned, our pulpits have thundered, our legislatures have resolved, our towns have voted. The Crown officers have everywhere trembled, and all their little tools and creatures, been afraid to speak and ashamed to be seen.[43]

One of the consequences of the Stamp Act was the closure of the courts based on the colonists' refusal to pay the tax. Adams's diary details his personal struggle as well as his professional role in seeking to combat the Stamp Act, including legal arguments before the royal governor seeking to open the courts without stamps on legal documents, consultations with leading members of the community, and preparations on what to say at a town hall meeting.[44] He wrote the first of his works on government, an essay entitled *A Dissertation on the Canon and Feudal Law*. That essay, published in the *Boston Gazette* beginning in August 1765, "struck an immediate accord."[45] Adams argued that "liberty must at all hazards be supported. We have a right to it, derived from our Maker. But if we have not, our fathers have earned and bought it for us at the expense of their ease, their estate, their pleasure, and their blood." He believed that British rights were not "grants of kings or parliaments" and many were "inherent and essential."[46]

Adams's thoughts in his diary on December 21, 1765, turned to the unthinkable:

> What are the consequences of the supposition that the courts are shut up? The King is the fountain of justice by the Constitution— And it is a maxim of the law, that the King never dies. Are not protection and allegiance reciprocal? And if we are out of the King's protection, are we not discharged from our allegiance. Are not all the ligaments of government dissolved? Is it not an abdication of the throne? In short where will such an horrid doctrine terminate? It would run us into treason![47]

The obverse of treason was independence, a word not spoken in public or written for publication by the colonists for many years. Identifying when independence firmly rooted in minds and hearts as the goal is elusive. Nonetheless, events and ideas pushed toward that end, although no recorded word advocating for it was uttered for many years.

Over the next decade, John Adams continued to record his thoughts in his diary as events unfolded: taxation without consent; riots; the purpose, structure, and grounds for government; the right to a jury trial; the importance of liberty, virtue, and happiness; town meetings; the Boston Massacre and Tea Party; the resolve of the people; evenings with the Sons of Liberty; the meaning of the words "British Constitution;" boycotts; reactions to acts of Parliament.

To recite just one event, Adams wrote in his diary that, on August 14, 1769, he dined with 350 Sons of Liberty at the Robinsons, under the "sign of the Liberty Tree," in Dorchester. There were two tables "in the open field by the barn, with between 300 and 400 plates," with a sail cloth for an awning, which came in handy when it rained. But he maintained that it was otherwise "a most agreeable day." After dinner, they drank toasts and sang the "Liberty Song," with the whole company joining in the chorus. Adams observed that such events were "cultivating the sensations of freedom" and that James Otis and Samuel Adams were "politick in promoting these festivals, for they tinge the minds of the people, they impregnate them with the sentiments of liberty. They render the people fond of their leaders in the cause, and averse and bitter against all opposers."

Resistance and building an alternative to British authority were not always so placid. There were riots over the years in many places, often organized by the Sons of Liberty or similar organizations. Lieutenant Governor Thomas Hutchinson's home was ransacked and burned in 1765 by a Boston mob protesting against the Stamp Act.[48] Coercive actions and threats were used against other Loyalists throughout the colonies, including those who violated nonimportation agreements or who sought to act as royal stamp collectors. John Adams, commenting on the responses across the colonies to the Stamp Act, observed: "So triumphant is the spirit of liberty, everywhere. Such an union was never before known in America."[49] Samuel Adams seemed to have ready access to a mob, calling them out on numerous occasions. His cousin, John Adams, was nowhere to be seen during such events. He represented the new order, not disorder, utilizing his legal background to shape and persuade others as his thoughts and events evolved. John Adams wrote about his cousin:

> [Samuel] Adams I believe has the most thorough understanding of liberty, and her resources, in the temper and character of the people, though not in the law and Constitution, as well as the most radical habit habitual, radical love of it, of any of them—as well as the most correct, genteel and artful pen. He is a man of refined policy, steadfast integrity, exquisite humanity, genteel erudition, obliging, engaging manners, real piety as well as professed piety, and a universal good character, unless it should be admitted that he is too attentive to the public and not enough so, to himself and his family.[50]

Parliament repealed the Stamp Act in 1766 but simultaneously passed the Declaratory Act, which proclaimed that Parliament had the right to legislate for the colonies "in all cases whatsoever." In 1767–68, Parliament again attempted to raise revenue with the Townsend Acts, which imposed duties on trade, created new customs enforcement offices, gave customs officials broad authority to enforce the taxes and punish smugglers through the use of writs of assistance, and denied the right to a jury trial in customs cases. The legislation directed that the salaries of judges and colonial governors be paid through the taxes raised, making them independent of colonial assemblies. Once again, colonial opposition was stiff, including economic boycotts of British goods, widespread protests, and civil disorder.[51] The Massachusetts Circular Letter, written by Samuel Adams and James Otis for the Massachusetts Assembly, argued that the Townsend Acts were unconstitutional due to the lack of colonial representation in Parliament, and they asked other colonies to join in resisting them. After the Assembly refused to rescind the letter, defying the order of the British secretary of state for the colonies to do so, Governor Francis Bernard dissolved it. In March 1770, most of the taxes were repealed, primarily to appease British merchants whose business had suffered, but Parliament retained a tax on tea.[52]

British authority in Boston was rapidly ebbing; in response to the disorder in Boston, four regiments of the British Army were sent to the town. On the night of March 5, 1770, a British squad under the command of Captain Preston opened fire on a Boston mob, killing five men. Were the actions in self-defense or murder? The next day, after being told that no other attorney would represent the soldiers, Adams agreed to do so, believing that it was his duty as a lawyer. At the subsequent trial of Preston, John Adams maintained that the evidence established that Preston did not order his men to fire, and a jury acquitted him. In a separate trial of the soldiers, Adams famously asserted that "facts are stubborn things" and recounted the extensive evidence of the mob's threats and violence directed at the soldiers. Six soldiers were acquitted, although two were found guilty of the lesser crime of manslaughter for which they were branded on their thumbs. Meanwhile, both before and after the trial, Adams's cousin was publishing and distributing propaganda that was so pervasive that, even today, the events are called the Boston Massacre.[53]

Samuel Adams organized an annual event to commemorate the Massacre, which was highlighted by an oration on each occasion. Remarkably, he asked his cousin John to give the 1773 oration, but John understandably declined. John Adams recorded that, even though the subject of the oration "was quite compatible" with the jury verdict and with the "absolute innocence of the soldiers," he believed that the public could not make such a distinction, thus exposing himself to "the lash of ignorant and malicious tongues on both sides of the question."[54] Adams wrote that his defense of Captain Preston and the soldiers had

> procured me anxiety, and obloquy enough. It was, however, one of the most gallant, generous, manly and disinterested actions of my whole life, and one of the best pieces of service I ever rendered my Country. Judgment of death against those soldiers would have been as foul a stain upon this Country as the executions of the Quakers or witches, anciently. As the evidence was, the verdict of the jury was exactly right. This however is no reason why the town should not call the action of that night a massacre, nor is it any argument in favor of the Governor or minister, who caused them to be sent here. But it is the strongest of proofs of the danger of standing armies.[55]

John Adams did, however, attend the March 5, 1773, commemoration and heard the oration of Doctor Benjamin Church on that date at a church "filled and crowded in every Pew, Seat, Alley, and Gallery, by an Audience of several Thousands of People of all Ages and Characters and of both Sexes."

John Adams, as a lawyer, would travel from town to town to represent clients in various courts. As an old man, he recounted in a letter to Benjamin Rush what he learned of the temper of the people in 1773 when he stopped for the night at a tavern at Shrewsbury, which is about forty miles from Boston. He wrote that he mentioned "this anecdote to show that the idea of independence was familiar even among the common people much earlier than some persons pretend." Adams was cold and wet and sat at

> a good fire in the bar room to dry my great coat and saddlebags; till a fire could be made in my chamber. There presently came in, one after another half a dozen or half a score substantial yeoman of the neighborhood, who, sitting down to the fire after lighting their pipes, began a lively conversation upon politicks. As I believed I was unknown to all of them, I sat in total silence to hear them. One said "The People of Boston are distracted." Another answered no wonder the people of Boston are distracted, oppression will make wise men mad. A third said, what would you say, if a fellow should come to your house and tell you he was come to take a list of your cattle that Parliament might tax you for them at so much a head? And how should you feel if he should go and break open your barn, to take down your oxen cows horses and sheep? What would I say? replied the first. I would knock him in the head. Well, said a fourth, if Parliament can take away Mr. Hancock's wharf and Mr. Row's wharf they can take away your barn and my house. After much more reasoning in this style, a fifth who had as yet been silent, broke out "Well it is high time for us to rebel. We must rebel, some time or others and we had better rebel, now than at any time to come. If we put it off for ten or twenty years, and let them go on as they have begun, they will get a strong party among us, and plague us a great deal more than they can now. As yet they have but a small party on their side."[56]

In 1773, Parliament passed the Tea Act, which granted the British East India Company a monopoly on tea sales in the colonies. Although the act made British tea less expensive, it established a small tax on the tea. The first ship carrying tea to arrive in Boston, the *Dartmouth*, had to unload the tea by December 17 to avoid seizure of the tea based on applicable statutes.[57] Boston patriots resolved to prevent the unloading, and the ship sat docked at Griffin's Wharf pending the outcome of events. The *Dartmouth*'s owner sought legal advice from John Adams and pleaded with Governor Hutchinson for help, who declined to intervene.[58] On December 16, at the Old South Meeting House, there was a town meeting attended by about six thousand people. After learning from the owner of the *Dartmouth* that the governor had refused to intervene, Samuel Adams gave what appears to have been a coded signal, saying that "this meeting can do nothing more to save the country."[59] Men, whose identities remain largely unknown to this day, started a "wild war whoop," broke away from the crowd, and boarded the *Dartmouth* and two other ships carrying tea, which were docked a short distance away. The intruders, disguised as Indians, systematically broke open 342 chests of tea and dumped the contents into the water. Forever known as the Boston Tea Party and observed by thousands, no eyewitnesses subsequently could be found.[60]

The Boston Tea Party, in the view of historian John C. Miller, was "the masterpiece of Sam Adams's efforts to create an unbridgeable gap between Great Britain and her American provinces."[61] Prior to the events, Samuel Adams had produced unity between Boston and the countryside through committees of correspondence and urgent express riders to the other towns; he created a sense of emergency that, if the tea were landed, unlimited taxes would follow.[62] John Adams, in his diary entry, described the tea's destruction as "the most magnificent movement of all. There is a dignity, a majesty, and sublimity, in this effort of the patriots that I greatly admire." He believed that the destruction of the tea was necessary: "To let it be landed would be giving up the principle of [no] taxation by Parliamentary authority, against which the continent [has] struggled for 10 years," and they would subject themselves to servitude. Looking forward, he thought that another event might find "dead carcasses" floating in the harbor and that the British were likely to punish Boston.[63]

Indeed, after news of the Boston Tea Party reached England in January 1774, Parliament imposed a series of Coercive Acts (called the "Intolerable Acts" by the colonists), closing the port of Boston, eliminating the Massachusetts Charter, and quartering troops in Boston. The port of Boston was to be closed until the colonists paid for the destroyed tea and restored order in the city. Under the Massachusetts Government Act, almost all governmental positions were to be appointed by the royal governor, Parliament, or the king. Town meetings in Massachusetts were limited to one a year unless called by the governor. The Administration of Justice Act allowed the governor to move trials of governmental officials outside of Massachusetts. The Quartering Act, which applied to all British colonies in North America, gave a governor authority to house soldiers in buildings if suitable quarters were not otherwise provided.

Another statute, the Quebec Act, enlarged the boundaries of the Province of Quebec to extend into much of what is now the Midwest, seemingly voiding colonial claims in that area, and guaranteeing the practice of Catholicism in Quebec. Although not directly related to the other legislation, it was seen by the colonists as one of the Intolerable Acts. On April 22, 1774, Prime Minister Lord North defended the legislation in the House of Commons, saying: "Whatever may be the consequences, we must risk something; if we do not, all is over."[64]

Any remaining bonds of affection toward the mother country in the colonies rapidly disappeared. The "Tyrannic Boston Port Bill," in Richard Henry Lee's words, was such a "shock" as to "universally move" Virginians to "astonishment, indignation, and concern." It was seen as "a most wicked system for destroying the liberty of America, and that it demanded a firm and determined union of all the Colonies to repel the common danger."[65]

The First Continental Congress was called in 1774 to coordinate opposition to the British measures, and it was held in Philadelphia beginning in September. The Massachusetts delegates who attended the Congress were Samuel and John Adams, Robert Treat Paine, and Thomas Cushing. John Adams left a detailed record of their leisurely travel to Philadelphia.[66] That pace was not without purpose; they met with many of the delegates and other important people along the way, developing friendships and measuring the depth of support for a coordinated response to the British measures. Each stop was accompanied by dining, touring, church services, and gathering information on a wide range of topics, including trade, science, medicine, and politics. There was a daily stream of conversations and meetings.

The four delegates had the use of "a Coach and four [horses] and four Servants." They boarded their coach on August 10, 1774, departed from

Boston, and rode to Watertown, accompanied by fifty or sixty gentlemen, where they dined and were offered entertainment. At about four in the afternoon, Adams wrote, the delegates "took our leave of them, amidst the kind wishes and fervent prayers of every man in the company for our health and success. This scene was truly affecting, beyond all description affecting."

On August 15, at Hartford, Silas Deane assured them of Connecticut's support for the resolutions of the Congress and that "the Congress is the grandest and most important assembly ever held in America, and that the all of America is intrusted to it and depends upon it." The next day, members of the Connecticut Committee of Correspondence "came to pay their Respects to Us, and to assure us that they thought, we had their all in our hands, and that they would abide by whatever should be determined on, even to a total stoppage of trade to Europe and the West Indies." As the Massachusetts delegation neared New Haven later that day, John Adams wrote, they were met by

> a great number of carriages and of horse men who had come out to meet us. The sherriff of the county and constable of the town and the justices of peace were in the train, as we were coming. We met others to the amount of I know not what number but a very great one. As we came into the town all the bells in town were set to ringing, and the people men, women and children, were crowding at the doors and windows as if it was to see a coronation. At nine o'clock the cannon were fired, about a dozen guns I think.
>
> These expressions of respect to us, are intended as demonstrations of the sympathy of this people with the Massachusetts Bay and its capital, and to shew their expectations from the Congress and their determination to carry into execution whatever shall be agreed on.
>
> No governor of a province, nor general of an army was ever treated with so much ceremony and assiduity, as we have been, throughout the whole Colony of Connecticut, hitherto, but especially all the way from Hartford to N. Haven, inclusively.

Still at New Haven on August 17, the delegates met with Roger Sherman, found him supportive, and were "very genteelly entertained, and spent the whole afternoon in politicks, the depths of politicks." At Stratford, on the eighteenth, they were informed that "the people here all say, Boston is suffering persecution, that now is the time for all the rest to be generous, and that Boston people must be supported."

The delegation arrived in the City of New York on August 20, which was a "Subject of much speculation" to John Adams. He recounted that they took a long walking tour of the city, including a fort, a prison, New York College, churches, markets, and a statue of King George III (which was soon to be melted down to make bullets for the colonial soldiers). "The Streets of this town are vastly more regular and elegant than those in Boston, and the houses are more grand as well as neat. They are almost all painted—brick buildings and all." They went to a coffee house and were introduced to various gentlemen and then were invited to Hull's Tavern, where the delegates supped "and had much conversation." On Sunday, the next day, John Adams attended services "at the old Presbyterian Society," hearing Dr. Rodgers urge the congregation to "'seek first the Kingdom of God and his righteousness and all other things shall be added unto you.'" Later that day, they met the delegates from New Hampshire.

Monday morning began with a coach ride to John Morin Scott's house on the Hudson River, where they had breakfast:

> We sat in a fine airy entry, till called into a front room to breakfast. A more elegant breakfast, I never saw—rich plate—a very large silver coffee pot, a very large silver tea pot—napkins of the very finest materials, and toast and bread and butter in great perfection. After breakfast, a plate of beautiful peaches, another of pears and another of plumbs and a muskmellen were placed on the table.

Then it was time for politics, where they heard that various parties in New York were less than united in support of Boston and the "cause of liberty."

By Tuesday, Adams had had enough of New York:

> With all the opulence and splendor of this city, there is very little good breeding to be found. We have been treated with an assiduous respect. But I have not seen one real gentleman, one well bred man since I came to town. At their entertainments there is no conversation that is agreeable. There is no modesty—No attention to one another. They talk very loud, very fast, and alltogether. If they ask you a question, before you can utter 3 words of your answer, they will break out upon you, again—and talk away.

Still in New York on August 25, the delegates "dined in the Exchange Chamber, at the invitation of the Committee of Correspondence, with more than 50 gentlemen, at the most splendid dinner I ever saw." Politics was also served in large portions both at the dinner and back at their lodgings.

On August 27, the delegation traveled to Princeton, New Jersey. After touring the college, the bell rang for prayers, and they went into the chapel. Adams remarked in his diary: "The scholars sing as badly as the Presbyterians at New York." The president of the college, John Witherspoon (subsequently a signer of the Declaration of Independence), Adams recorded, was "as high a Son of Liberty as any man in America." Witherspoon was on "the Committee of Correspondence, and was upon the Provincial Congress for appointing delegates from this Province to the general Congress." Witherspoon had sought to procure an instruction to the New Jersey delegates "that the tea should not be paid for." The next day the Massachusetts delegates gathered more information about delegates from other colonies.

Finally, on August 29, they crossed over the Delaware River into Pennsylvania. About five miles outside of Philadelphia, they were met by a "number of carriages and gentlemen," including delegates from several states, who welcomed them. The Massachusetts delegates took the opportunity to visit the City Tavern—the "most genteel" tavern in America—where they were introduced to more delegates and gentlemen, gathering more information about the upcoming Congress and about delegates from other colonies. Upon departing for their lodgings, Doctor Benjamin Rush joined them in the coach. Although it is said to be embellished and was written many years later, John Adams recalled that Rush and others met in a private apartment and offered information and advice. He wrote that "there appeared so much wisdom and good sense" in what was said that

> it made a deep impression on my mind, and it had an equal effect on all my colleagues: We were all suspected of having Independence in view. Now, said they, you must not utter the word Independence, nor give the least hint or insinuation of the idea, neither in Congress or any private conversation; if you do you are undone; for the idea of Independence is as unpopular in Pennsylvania and in all the middle and southern States as the Stamp Act itself. No man dares to speak of it. . . . You must not come forward with any bold measures; you must not pretend to take the lead. You know Virginia is the most populous State in the Union. They are very proud of their ancient Dominion, as they call it; they think they have a right to take the lead, and the southern States and middle States too, are too much disposed to yield it to them.[67]

Several more days of introductions, meetings, and dinners preceded the start of Congress, which convened on September 5, 1774. Congress settled into Carpenters' Hall. The very next day, as debate opened, Patrick Henry of Virginia declared: "The distinctions between Virginians, Pensylvanians, New Yorkers and New Englanders, are no more. I am not a Virginian, but an American. * * * I go upon the supposition, that government is at an end. All distinctions are thrown down. All America is all thrown into one mass."[68]

So there it was, at least for one important delegate—the transition from British to American was complete. The next evolution required was the intellectual and emotional one from being the subjects of Great Britain to gaining American independence. First, unity in Congress was achieved by graduated measures seeking redress and demonstrating resolve, as is noted in the Declaration of Independence.

On April 19, 1775, blood was spilled at Lexington and Concord when the British marched there seeking to seize military supplies that the colonists had collected and to arrest Samuel Adams and John Hancock;

the war began. As John Adams wrote, that day changed "the instruments of warfare from the pen to the sword."[69] The British then holed up in Boston and came under siege by colonial militia. Adams was at that time a delegate to the Second Continental Congress, meeting in Philadelphia beginning in May 1775. The members included many of the leading men in the colonies of that era: George Washington, Thomas Jefferson, Richard Henry Lee, Samuel Adams, John Hancock, Benjamin Franklin, and John Dickinson. John Adams, in Congress, nominated George Washington to be commander of the American forces, soon to be named the Continental Army. It took more than a year for the Congress to resolve to separate from Britain, with much spirited disagreement along the way. By November 1775, John Adams was openly advocating independence, but, in his words, "the child was not yet weaned."[70]

In early 1776, sentiment in the country continued to turn as events rushed forward. One singular influence was Thomas Paine's *Common Sense*, a widely read forty-seven-page pamphlet, which advocated independence: "Every thing that is right or natural pleads to separation." That "little pamphlet [became] a clarion call, rousing spirits within Congress and without as nothing else did."[71] The words and actions of the King of England, George III, were major factors: In late 1775, he declared the colonies in rebellion; he raised troops and strengthened the navy. Parliament passed the Prohibitory Act, which banned all commerce with the colonies, put the colonies outside the king's protection, declared all colonial ships and cargos forfeit, and allowed the impressment of sailors into the Royal Navy. The Royal Navy bombarded coastal towns. Battles were fought. At the time that Congress was debating independence, more than one hundred ships containing a large invasion force were assembling outside of New York, which was defended by the Continental Army under Washington. By the time Congress decided on Independence, the war was over a year old, which "made continued expressions of allegiance to the King absurd."[72] Frankly, as Jefferson put it near the end of his life, the Revolution was a "bold and doubtful election . . . for our country, between submission, or the sword."[73]

In the spring of 1776, various state delegations to Congress gained the authority to vote for independence. Finally, on June 7, 1776, Richard Henry Lee, for the Virginia delegation, moved in Congress that "these united colonies are and of right ought to be free and independent states." John Adams seconded the motion, and a fierce debate resulted over the next three days. A vote was postponed to allow delegates time to send for new instructions. Meanwhile, a committee was appointed to draft a declaration of independence, including Thomas Jefferson, John Adams, and Benjamin Franklin. Adams believed that he would have been a poor choice to do the draft because he had managed to alienate so many delegates with his "bluntness and impatience" regarding the slow movement toward the decision.[74] Adams recalled that he gave Jefferson several reasons why Jefferson should draft it: Jefferson was from Virginia in the south, Adams from Massachusetts in the north; because Adams "had been so obnoxious" in his "early and constant Zeal in promoting" independence, any draft by him would "undergo a more severe scrutiny and criticism" in Congress; and he thought Jefferson was a better writer.[75] Jefferson recalled the events differently, simply maintaining that the committee unanimously chose him to draft the document. According to the Massachusetts Historical Society, "exhaustive textual study and the discovery of further documents have greatly amplified both [Adams's] and Jefferson's accounts and corrected them in some respects, but the principal points on which they disagreed have not been and may never be resolved."[76]

Jefferson produced a rough draft, which has survived. As he later explained, his goal was "not to find out new principles, or new arguments;" instead, he sought "to place before mankind the common sense of the object." It was intended to be "an expression of the American mind, and to give to that expression the proper tone and spirit called for by the occasion."[77] The evolution of the draft before it was reported back to the full Congress is somewhat unclear[78] but it is known that Jefferson distributed the draft to both Franklin and John Adams because he believed "they were the two members of whose judgments and amendments I wished most to have the benefit."[79] Franklin offered some changes.

On July 1, 1776, the question was called for a vote and debate followed. John Dickinson of Pennsylvania, known as the "Pennsylvania Farmer," based on his writings seeking to obtain British rights for the colonists throughout the previous decade, gave an impassioned speech opposing independence.[80] John Adams responded, arguing in favor of independence as a thunderstorm roared outside of the hall. Years later, Thomas Jefferson recalled that Adams was so powerful in "thought & expression" that it "moved us from our seats." Adams was, Jefferson said, "our colossus on the floor."[81] A preliminary vote was taken, and only nine of the delegations voted in favor of independence. A motion was made to delay the final vote until the next day and Congress agreed.

Dickinson knew he was on the wrong side of history, but his vote would have prevented Pennsylvania from agreeing to independence. To his credit, he and another Pennsylvania delegate opposed to declaring independence absented themselves from Congress on July 2. The Pennsylvania delegation remained divided, with three members favoring independence and two opposed. But since each delegation had one vote, the one person majority within the delegation allowed Congress to unanimously agree to independence, with New York abstaining and South Carolina changing its vote to support independence. Delaware, which had previously abstained, also voted for independence.

Congress then considered Jefferson's draft, which was substantially edited. "Large sections were eviscerated."[82] In all, about a quarter of Jefferson's draft was rewritten or omitted. Later in life, Jefferson recalled that he suffered as the delegates edited the document. Franklin, who was sitting next to him, turned to Jefferson and related a story:

> I have made it a rule, said he, whenever in my power, to avoid becoming the draftsman of papers to be reviewed by a public body. I took my lesson from an incident which I will relate to you. When I was a journeyman printer, one of my companions, an apprentice Hatter, having served out his time, was about to open shop for himself. His first concern was to have a handsome signboard, with a proper inscription. He composed it in these words "John Thompson, Hatter, makes and sells hats for ready money," with a figure of a hat subjoined. But he thought he would submit it to his friends for their amendments. The first he showed it to thought the word "Hatter," tautologous, because followed by the words "makes hats" which shew he was a Hatter. It was struck out. The next observed that the word "makes" might as well be omitted,

> because his customers would not care who made the hats. If good & to their mind, they would buy, by whomsoever made. He struck it out. A third said he thought the words "for ready money," were useless as it was not the custom of the place to sell on credit. Every one who purchased expected to pay. They were parted with, and the inscription now stood "John Thomson sells hats." "Sells hats" says his next friend? Why nobody will expect you to give them away. What then is the use of that word? It was stricken out, and "hats" followed it, the rather, as there was one painted on the board. So his inscription was reduced ultimately to "John Thomson" with the figure of a hat subjoined.[83]

The final document—the Declaration of Independence—was formally adopted on July 4. The first public reading of the Declaration took place on July 8, 1776, in Philadelphia. Although there is disagreement over whether there were multiple signings, it appears that the official signing was on August 2, 1776. A story persists that, after signing his name so prominently that his signature became a synonym for a signature, John Hancock reportedly remarked: "There must be no pulling different ways . . . We must all hang together." To which Franklin is said to have replied: "Yes, we must, indeed, all hang together, or most assuredly we shall all hang separately."[84] There must be something to the story since Benjamin Rush, another signer of the Declaration, had a somewhat similar recollection in letter to John Adams in 1811:

> Do you recollect the pensive and awful silence which pervaded the house when we were called up, one after another, to the table of the President of Congress, to subscribe what was believed by many at that time to be our own death warrants? The silence & the gloom of the morning were interrupted I well recollect only for a moment by Col. Harrison of Virginia who said to Mr. Gerry at the table, "I shall have a great advantage over you Mr. Gerry when we are all hung for what we are now doing. From the size and weight of my body I shall die in a few minutes, but from the lightness of your body you will dance in the air an hour or two before you are dead."

> This Speech procured a transient smile, but it was soon succeeded by the Solemnity with which the whole business was conducted.[85]

"It was John Adams, more than anyone, who had made [independence] happen."[86] He was an early and stubborn advocate. In his correspondence to his wife on July 3, 1776, reflecting on the moment quoted in part above, Adams added:

> The Second Day of July 1776, will be the most memorable epocha, in the history of America. I am apt to believe that it will be celebrated, by succeeding generations, as the great anniversary Festival. It ought to be commemorated as the day of deliverance by solemn acts of devotion to God Almighty. It ought to be solemnized with pomp and parade, with shows, games, sports, guns, bells, bonfires and illuminations from one end of this continent to the other from this time forward forever more.
>
> You will think me transported with enthusiasm but I am not. -- I am well aware of the toil and blood and treasure, that it will cost us to maintain this declaration, and support and defend these States. -- Yet through all the gloom I can see the rays of ravishing light and glory. I can see that the end is more than worth all the means. And that posterity will triumph in that day's transaction, even although we should rue it, which I trust in God we shall not.[87]

Adams got the date wrong—July 2—but he was right about everything else.

In Philadelphia, after the delegates agreed to the text on July 4, other business was promptly addressed by Congress. Jefferson then went shopping.[88] By July 5, printed copies of the Declaration became available. On July 6, John Hancock, acting as president of the Second Continental Congress, sent copies of the Declaration to the States and to George Washington and other military leaders.[89] Also on July 6, the *Pennsylvania Evening Post* reprinted the entire document. On July 8, Philadelphia celebrated. At noon, the Declaration was read "aloud before an exuberant crowd." On the commons, there were thirteen cannon salutes, battalions parading, drums pounding, bells ringing into the night, bonfires roaring, houses illuminated by candles, and the king's arms removed from the State House and burned.[90]

Washington, at that time, was preparing to defend New York from imminent attack by an overwhelming British force. Upon receiving Hancock's letter and a copy of the Declaration, Washington ordered an assembly of his troops, stating in his order that the "declaration of Congress, showing the grounds & reasons of this measure, is to be read with an audible voice." Washington added that he hoped "this important event will serve as a fresh incentive to every officer, and soldier, to act with fidelity and courage, as knowing that now the peace and safety of his Country depends (under God) solely on the success of our arms," asserting that each soldier was "now in the service of a State, possessed of sufficient power to reward his merit, and advance him to the highest honors of a free Country."[91]

The troops assembled on the commons in New York[92] and responded to the reading with "three huzzas." Washington was "gratified by the 'hearty assent' of his men and their 'warmest approbation' of independence."[93] Washington could not predict the consequences of Congress's action but opined that it "behooves us to adopt such, as under the smiles of a Gracious & All kind Providence will be most likely to promote our happiness; I trust the late decisive part they have taken is calculated for that end, and will secure us that freedom and those privileges which have been and are refused us, contrary to the voice of nature and the British Constitution."[94]

After the Declaration was read, the "militiamen and civilians barreled down Broadway, destroying every relic of British influence in their path, including royal arms painted on tavern signs. At Bowling Green, at the foot of Broadway, they mobbed a gilded equestrian statue of George III, portrayed in Roman garb," and pulled George III down from his pedestal, decapitating him.[95] The severed head was paraded "around town to the lilting beat of fifes and drums."[96] The four thousand pounds of gilded lead was rushed off to Litchfield, Connecticut, where it was melted down to make 42,088 musket bullets. One wit predicted that the king's soldiers "'will probably have melted majesty fired at them.'"[97]

It took weeks or longer in some places to learn of the Declaration. The subsequent celebrations often focused on the text, given that the text was immediately important. The "most common method" of making the document known "was to read it before groups of people in a public and appropriately ceremonial manner."[98] The firing of thirteen salutes and thirteen toasts celebrating the union of the thirteen States was also common.[99] So too was the destruction of any signs of royal authority: "The King's arms or pictures of the King or the Crown on public buildings, coffeehouse and tavern signs, even in churches, were ripped down, trampled, torn, or otherwise broken to pieces, then consumed in great bonfires before crowds of people who responded with 'repeated huzzas.'"[100]

Savannah, Georgia, did not receive the Declaration until August 10, 1776. Similar to events elsewhere, it was read in the square outside the Assembly House "before a great concourse of people." The grenadier and light infantry companies "fired a general volley," followed by a procession to the Liberty Pole, with the grenadiers in front, the provost-marshall on horseback, with sword drawn; next came the secretary of the council and many others. At the Liberty Pole, the procession met the Georgia Battalion, which discharged cannons and "fired in platoons" after the Declaration had been read a second time. The celebrants then went to the battery, where the Declaration was read a third time, followed by a discharge of the battery's cannon. Dinner and toasts came next. That evening, the town was illuminated and there was a "very solemn funeral procession," accompanied by the drums and fifes of the militia; "George III was interred before the Court-House," with the interment committing George's "political existence to the ground, corruption for corruption, tyranny to the grave, and oppression to eternal infamy, in sure and certain hope that he will never obtain a resurrection to rule again over these United States of America."[101]

Reflecting on independence more than forty years after the Declaration, John Adams—always the lawyer—observed that, beginning with the first colonies, the relationship with Great Britain was "more like a treaty between independent sovereigns than like a charter or grant of privileges from a sovereign to his subjects."[102] "Our ancestors," he continued, had both the prospect and promise of independence in government, religion, commerce, and just about "everything else." So he posed the question, "Who, then, was the author, inventor, discoverer of independence?" Answering, he believed it was the first emigrants, and that Otis, Adams, Patrick Henry, Jefferson, and others "were only awakeners and revivers of the original principle of colonization."

Perhaps it could be said more plainly. A farmer and minuteman, Levi Preston of Danvers, was a veteran of that first battle on April 19, 1775, beginning at Lexington and Concord. Danvers was a small town north of Boston. When the minutemen learned of the battle, under the lead of Captain Gideon Foster, they marched or ran sixteen miles in four hours and struck the British's retreating column at West Cambridge. "Brave but incautious in flanking the red-coats, they were flanked themselves and badly pinched, leaving seven dead, two wounded, and one missing. Among those who escaped was Levi Preston, afterwards known as Captain Levi Preston."[103] He was interviewed many years later at the age of ninety-one and asked why he had fought. Preston submitted that it was not about stamps, a tea tax, or the influence of treatises on liberty. Instead, he maintained to his youthful interviewer: "Young man, what we meant in going for those Redcoats was this: we always had governed ourselves, and we always meant to."[104]

CHAPTER 2

George Washington: From an Inauspicious Prelude to an Emblem of Perseverance

America's story, highlighted often from events occurring on the Fourth of July, is a story of perseverance within the context of an expanding understanding of freedom. Capsulizing that long perseverance is the life of George Washington, whose own life saw many consequential July Fourths. Indeed, no other American can count so many. The first, July 4, 1754, was perhaps the nadir of our first president's life, more than two decades before the Revolution began. It was an inauspicious prologue. Others were as daunting. July 4, 1775, saw him taking command of the colonial forces surrounding the British troops holed up in Boston. On that day, the Continental Congress passed a resolution making those troops part of the new Continental Army. The next July 4 saw him in command of the Continental Army, preparing to defend New York City on the day that the Declaration of Independence was agreed to by the Continental Congress. Still more Fourth of Julys during the Revolution and during his presidency underline the enormous burden he bore as the United States struggled to survive. Washington led at every critical moment, up to and during the Revolution, during the framing of the Constitution, and as our first president. The many times that Washington served his country—admittedly including the times he sought that role—from age twenty-one to his death at sixty-seven—consumed the vast majority of his life; although weary at the end, he remained willing to serve. Washington's life is a story of learning from his mistakes—some grievous—but eventually finding success through persistence, dedication, and personal courage. It mirrors America's own story.

July 4, 1754, dawned as one of the worst days of George Washington's life. Near midnight of the day before, he had signed terms of surrender that included admitting he had assassinated a French officer on a diplomatic mission. This was after suffering a humiliating defeat at the hands of a combined French and Indian force. Washington had chosen the location and created Fort Necessity in what is now western Pennsylvania. The site was ill-chosen. His small force could have been annihilated after being surrounded. In the battle that followed on July 3, Washington's force did little to add credit to its commander's reputation. Now, on July 4, Washington led the remnants of his force back across the wilderness to Virginia after giving the French a major propaganda victory.

By the 1750s, the British colonies were well established along the Atlantic seaboard. But not far inland were the Allegheny Mountains. On the other side of that chain lay a vast wilderness and competing claims of the French and English to ownership. The French were penetrating the area and setting up a series of forts. Virginia, pursuant to British grants, claimed large amounts of that territory. The royal governor of Virginia, Robert Dinwiddie, obtained British permission to establish a series of forts in the Ohio Country and to send an envoy to the French to deliver an ultimatum demanding that they vacate the area.[1] Washington, upon learning of the directive, volunteered. Hence, at the age of twenty-one, Washington was sent to what is now the Pittsburgh area of western Pennsylvania to demand that the French leave. Accompanied by a guide and an interpreter, Washington made that difficult 250-mile journey in harsh winter conditions through what was almost completely uninhabited wilderness. Upon meeting with the French, they treated Washington with courtesy but politely declined to withdraw. The return to Virginia was marked by harrowing events, including being shot at by an Indian, falling into an ice-choked river, and spending the night on an island in the river in soaked clothes. Washington kept a detailed account of his extraordinary journey, which was published by the governor, entitled *The Journal of Major George Washington.*[2] That account was widely read in the colonies and in Europe, making Washington a sensation.

Just five days after his return to Virginia, Washington took on the task of recruiting and training a volunteer force to expel the French. Commissioned as a lieutenant colonel, Washington returned to the Ohio Country a few months later as second-in-command of a 160-man force, which was ill-equipped and poorly trained. The commander, Joshua Fry, was to lead another force and meet up with Washington, but he died en route. Other elements of the British forces included Native Americans, a small South Carolina contingent, and British regulars.

In May 1754, Washington's force surrounded and engaged a small party of French soldiers, killing ten of them and capturing twenty-one. The leader of the French force was Ensign Joseph Coulon de Villiers, Sieur de Jumonville, who bore a diplomatic message to the British, demanding that *they* evacuate the Ohio Country. The details of the skirmish are disputed.[3] It is also disputed how Jumonville was killed, but, by one account, after the French surrendered, he was attacked by Half King, an Indian member of Washington's force, who "split open [Jumonville's] head with a hatchet, then dipped his hands into the skull, rinsed them with the victim's brains, and scalped him."[4] The French claimed that, after being surrounded, Jumonville beseeched the English to cease firing, and, when they did, he was shot while reading his diplomatic message.[5] Washington argued that the French activities before the encounter belied their claim that the mission was diplomatic. Regardless, the two diplomats had been treated very differently. The skirmish, however it unfolded, served as the precipitating event for the French and Indian War, also known as the Seven Years' War.

Aware that a large French force was in the area and would soon be notified of the skirmish and Jumonville's death, Washington ordered his men to build Fort Necessity at Great Meadows. Washington described it in a letter to Governor Dinwiddie: "We have, with Nature's assistance made a good Intrenchment and by clearing the Bushes out of these Meadows prepared a charming field for an Encounter."[6] The recreated fort can be seen today.[7] It was a "crude, circular, palisade-style stockade" with trenches dug outside.[8] Biographer Ron Chernow describes it:

> An uncouth backwoods structure, covered with bark and animal skins, the fort was primarily defended by nine small cannon that

> spun on pivots. Because it could contain only sixty or seventy men, Washington had three-foot trenches dug around its perimeter to protect additional men and threw up earthen breastworks to bolster their position. Despite such precautions, Fort Necessity stood on low-lying grassland that was soft and boggy and would form stagnant ponds in the rain. It was also surrounded by woods and high ground that could protect marksmen within easy musket range of the fort. Significantly, the fort was open to the sky, affording no shelter from the elements.[9]

Washington's force was augmented by new arrivals, and he had about three hundred men, including a separate force commanded by Captain Mackay, a British regular, who declined to serve under Washington but had about one hundred men. The French force, according to intelligence reports, numbered eight hundred French soldiers and four hundred Indian allies. Importantly, it was commanded by Captain Louis Coulon de Villers, the older brother of Jumonville. On the morning of July 3, the French passed the location where Jumonville had been killed and observed the unburied bodies of their fellow countrymen.

The French advanced, surrounded Fort Necessity, and proceeded, along with their allies, to rain down fire "from every little rising, tree, stump, stone, and bush." Late in the afternoon, "the most tremendous rain that can be conceived" fell, flooding the trenches and turning the fort into a quagmire. The muskets became useless. Casualties amounted to one-third of Washington's total strength. The French lost three dead, and seventeen were wounded.[10]

Near nightfall, the French commander signaled a willingness to talk. By that point, half of Washington's men were drunk after raiding the rum supply. Washington had no choice. His interpreter, Jacob Van Braam, was picked to convey the terms of surrender, which he read from the French document to Washington. Chernow relates:

> As he shuffled between the two sides, Van Braam relayed an article of capitulation that the French assault had been in retaliation for the *assassination* of Jumonville—a provocative word indeed. When

Washington and Mackay signed the agreement around midnight, they imagined that the term used was the more neutral *death* or *loss* of Jumonville. Their inadvertent confession supplied the French with a major propaganda victory.[11]

The next day–July 4–the British and colonial forces withdrew; Washington wrote:

> Accordingly the next morning, with our drums beating and our colors flying, we began our March in good order, with our stores, &c. in convoy; but we were interrupted by the arrival of a reinforcement of 100 Indians among the French, who were hardly restrained from attacking us, and did us considerable damage by pilfering our baggage. We then proceeded, but soon found it necessary to leave our baggage and stores; the great scarcity of our provisions obliged us to use the utmost expedition, and having neither wagons nor horses to transport them. The enemy had deprived us of all our creatures; by killing, in the beginning of the engagement, our horses, cattle, and every living thing they could, even to the very dogs.[12]

In retreat, the baggage was ransacked by the French's Indian allies and Washington's force was harassed and taunted by Indians and suffered "wholesale desertions."[13]

The contest in western Pennsylvania was a spark that helped ignite the French and Indian War. The following year, Washington returned to the area as aide-de-camp to Major General Edward Braddock, who commanded a large force of British regulars and colonial recruits. The result was worse than the year before. On July 9, 1755, utilizing the protection of the forest and frontier tactics, a much smaller force of French and Indians leveled a punishing defeat, resulting in Braddock's death and the destruction of two-thirds of his army.[14] Of Braddock's eighty-six officers, sixty-three were killed or wounded. The engagement quickly turned into a rout, with British regulars fleeing the battlefield. Washington, however, gained a small measure of redemption as the British forces reeled. Pursuant to orders from Braddock, and with "exceptional pluck and coolness, young George Washington was soon riding all over the battlefield. . . . Because of his height, he presented a gigantic target on horseback, but again he displayed unblinking courage and a miraculous immunity in battle."[15]

Washington, shortly after the defeat, wrote to his brother:

> As I have heard since my arrival at this place, a circumstantial account of my death and dying speech, I take this early opportunity of contradicting the first and of assuring you that I have not, as yet, composed the latter. But by the all powerful dispensations of Providence, I have been protected beyond all human probability & expectation for I had 4 bullets through my coat, and two horses shot under me yet, although death was leveling my companions on every side of me, escaped unhurt. We have been most scandalously beaten by a trifling body of men.[16]

There is an enduring image of Washington on that battlefield, which was near the mouth of the Monongahela River:

> Washington's derring-do even fostered a lasting mystique among the Indians. A folk belief existed among some North American tribes that certain warriors enjoyed supernatural protection from death in battle, and this mythic structure was projected onto Washington. Fifteen years [after the battle] he encountered an Indian chief who distinctly recalled seeing him at the battle by the Monongahela and told how he had ordered his warriors, without success, to fire directly at him. The chief had concluded that some great spirit would guide him to momentous things in the future.[17]

Washington's presence is a consistent theme of those who met him, as was his "virtuosity with horses [which] excited comment throughout his life."[18] Shortly after Washington assumed command of the colonial forces surrounding Boston in 1775, a young doctor named James Thacher described seeing Washington:

> His Excellency was on horseback, in company with several military gentlemen. It was not difficult to distinguish him from all others; his personal appearance is truly noble and majestic, being tall and well proportioned. His dress is a blue coat with buff colored facings, a rich epaulette on each shoulder, buff under dress, and an elegant small sword; a black cockade in his hat.[19]

John Adams, not known for his easy praise of others, described Washington to his wife as modest, virtuous, amiable, generous, and brave.[20] After she met Washington a short time later in Cambridge, Abigail wrote to John: "I was struck with General Washington. You had prepared me to entertain a favorable opinion of him, but I thought the one half was not told me. Dignity with ease, and complacency, the gentleman and soldier look agreeably blended in him. Modesty marks every line and feature of his face."[21] David McCullough summarizes: Washington "carried himself like a soldier and sat a horse like a perfect Virginia gentleman. It was a look and bearing of a man accustomed to respect and being obeyed. He was not austere. There was no hint of arrogance."[22]

Washington served as a colonel in the Virginia militia during the French and Indian War and organized those forces from raw recruits. He resigned in 1758 and was elected to the Virginia House of Burgesses. In his letters and other actions leading up to the Revolution, he supported colonial rights and claims against British actions seen as impinging on those rights. Of particular note, on July 4, 1774, in a letter to Bryan Fairfax, he detailed his beliefs regarding the controversies with Great Britain in light of the British actions subsequent to the Boston Tea Party. He rejected additional petitions as useless and advocated for a nonimportation agreement, writing in part:

> Have we not addressed the Lords, and remonstrated to the Commons? And to what end? Did they deign to look at our petitions? Does it not appear, as clear as the sun in its meridian brightness, that there is a regular, systematic plan formed to fix the right and practice of taxation upon us? Does not the uniform conduct of Parliament for some years past confirm this? Do not

> all the debates, especially those just brought to us, in the House of Commons on the side of government, expressly declare that America must be taxed in aid of the British funds, and that she has no longer resources within herself? Is there any thing to be expected from petitioning after this? Is not the attack upon the liberty and property of the people of Boston, before restitution of the loss to the India Company was demanded, a plain and self-evident proof of what they are aiming at? Do not the subsequent bills (now I dare say acts), for depriving the Massachusetts Bay of its charter, and for transporting offenders into other colonies or to Great Britain for trial, where it is impossible from the nature of the thing that justice can be obtained, convince us that the administration is determined to stick at nothing to carry its point? Ought we not, then, to put our virtue and fortitude to the severest test?[23]

Washington was elected a delegate to the First and Second Continental Congresses. In June 1775, Washington was appointed by the Continental Congress to head the fledgling army surrounding the British Army at Boston. He arrived on July 2, 1775. On July 4, he made an address to the Massachusetts Provincial Congress, expressing his "highest ambition" to be "the happy instrument of vindicating" the rights of mankind and restoring "peace, liberty, and safety" to Massachusetts.[24] In that address, he responded to the Provincial Congress's warning not to expect regularity and discipline among the army surrounding Boston, politely saying that it was too soon to make an assessment of the state of the army. He was, in fact, appalled by it. There was no real army; no unified command structure, no order, no discipline, no money, no organized supplies.

Washington issued a list of orders on that July 4: sanitation rules, directing officers to "keep their men neat and clean," officer and staff appointments, and prohibiting the unnecessary firing of weapons.[25] Most significantly, he ordered that the assembled militias were "now the troops of the United Provinces of North America; and it is hoped that all distinctions of colonies will be laid aside; so that one and the same spirit may animate the whole, and the only contest be, who shall render, on this great and trying occasion, the most essential service to the great and common cause in which we are all engaged." On that same day, Congress incorporated those militias into the new Continental Army.[26] After the long seige of Boston, the British sailed away on March 27, 1776.

That next July Fourth saw him in New York, facing daunting odds while awaiting the British invasion. As he and his army prepared, Washington reflected back to the defeats by the French in western Pennsylvania more than twenty years before; in a letter on July 20, 1776, Washington recalled his "grateful remembrance of the escape we had at the Meadows and on the Banks of Monongahela. [T]he same Providence that protected us upon those occasions will, I hope, continue his mercies, and make us happy instruments in restoring peace & liberty to this once favored, but now distressed country."[27] The battle for New York, like the battle at Fort Necessity, was a resounding defeat for the Americans.

Throughout the American Revolution, when possible, Washington honored Independence Day with some ceremony. As detailed in Chapter One, after Washington received a copy of the Declaration in 1776, he ordered the Declaration read and the troops celebrated. On July 4, 1778, shortly after the inconclusive battle of Monmouth Courthouse, George Washington and the American Army celebrated the second anniversary on the banks of the Raritan River in present-day Johnson Park and New Brunswick with cannon fire, a musket salute, and a double allowance of rum for the troops. Washington ordered a *feu de joie*, that is, a rifle salute fired by the soldiers, with each soldier firing in succession along the ranks to make a continuous sound. The soldiers were also ordered to "adorn their hats with *green-boughs* and to make the best appearance possible."[28] He added that, at the conclusion of the firing of the cannons and muskets, "on a signal three cheers will be given, 'Perpetual and undisturbed independence to the United States of America.'"[29] (He also ordered that blank cartridges be fired, with the balls removed, to save ammunition.)

As the order dictated, at three o'clock in the afternoon on July 4, a cannon fired, signaling the troops to march. From four until five o'clock, as cannons fired, the eleven thousand soldiers marched across Landing Lane Bridge, forming two lines on the Brunswick side of the river. Thirteen cannons discharged and then a final cannon signal ordered the running fire to begin, followed by the cheers. "This celebration, so thunderous, was heard by the retreating British forces miles away at Sandy Hook."[30]

The next year was a more sober salute, given that the stock of rum was "too scanty to permit" distributing it to the soldiers.[31] Washington ordered the firing of thirteen cannons from West Point and granted a general pardon to all army prisoners under a sentence of death.[32] In 1780 and again in 1782, the men celebrated with rum.[33] But on July 4, 1781, the army was on the march to join up with French troops near Dobbs Ferry, New York, with Washington "extremely pleased with the regularity and order" in which the movement was performed.[34]

Washington led the Continental Army throughout the American Revolution, outlasting the British with the invaluable help of the French. Without him, history teaches, the war for Independence would not have been successful. He, of course, became our first president under the Constitution, serving two terms and setting the precedent—almost unmatched in history—of voluntarily relinquishing power twice: as commander during the Revolution and then as president. He learned from his early mistakes in western Pennsylvania but made numerous other mistakes during the Revolution. Nonetheless, "[t]he great teacher for Washington was experience"[35] and he persevered, and with him, the Continental Army, the Revolution, and the young nation. As General Henry Lee famously eulogized Washington, he was "First in war, first in peace, and first in the hearts of his countrymen."[36]

General Washington, when resigning his command, offered the young nation some advice, urging the nation to create a federal government that "will enable it to answer the ends of its institution. . . . For, according to the system of policy the States shall adopt at this moment, they will stand or fall." He maintained that it was yet to be decided whether the "Revolution must ultimately be considered a blessing or a curse: a blessing or a curse, not to the present age alone," but also for "the destiny of unborn millions."[37] President Washington, in declining to run for a third term, offered a broad range of reflections. He maintained that, in the discharge of trust given him as president, he had, "with good intentions, contributed towards the organization and administration of the government the best exertions of which a very fallible judgment was capable." He acknowledged the "debt of gratitude" that he owed "to my beloved country for the many honors it has conferred upon me; still more for the steadfast confidence with which it has supported me; and for the opportunities I have thence enjoyed of manifesting my inviolable attachment, by services faithful and persevering, though in usefulness unequal to my zeal." He proclaimed:

> The name of American, which belongs to you in your national capacity, must always exalt the just pride of patriotism more than any appellation derived from local discriminations. With slight shades of difference, you have the same religion, manners, habits, and political principles. You have in a common cause fought and triumphed together; the independence and liberty you possess are the work of joint counsels, and joint efforts of common dangers, sufferings, and successes.[38]

Washington's selfless purpose and how he sought to use power can be gleaned from some advice he gave to Joseph Reed. They met when Reed was a young Philadelphia lawyer when Washington was serving in the Continental Congress. After Washington's appointment as commander of the Continental troops, Reed agreed to accompany him as far as New York. Taken in by Washington's spell, Reed continued with the general to Boston, where he served as secretary and aide-de-camp to Washington.[39] He became an instrumental early appointment, and they remained close even after Reed returned to Philadelphia. Reed was eventually elected president of Pennsylvania's Supreme Executive Council, a position analogous to the modern office of governor. The Pennsylvania legislature gave Reed extraordinary powers during the Revolution to declare martial law and impose other emergency powers. Learning of this, on July 4, 1780, Washington offered Reed some advice based on "motives of friendship" and the public good. He observed that nothing could be "more delicate and critical than your situation," where Reed had "full discretionary power" and "great expectations in our Allies and in the People."

> In this dilemma there is a seeming danger and whatever side you take; it remains to choose that, which has least real danger, and will best promote the public weal. This in my opinion clearly is to exert the powers entrusted to you with a boldness & vigor suited to the emergency.
>
> In general I esteem it a good maxim, that the best way to preserve the confidence of the people durably, is to promote their true interest—there are particular exigencies when this maxim has peculiar force. When any great object is in view the popular mind is roused into expectation, and prepared to make sacrifices both of ease & property; if those to whom they confide the management of their affairs do not call them to make these sacrifices—and the object is not attained, or they are involved in the reproach of not having contributed as much as they ought to have done towards it—they will be mortified at the disappointment—they will feel the censure—& their resentment will rise against those who with sufficient authority have omitted to do what their interest and their honor required. Extensive powers not exercised as far as was necessary, have I believe scarcely ever failed to ruin the possessor—The legislature and the people in your case would be very glad to excuse themselves by condemning you. You would be assailed with blame from every quarter and your enemies would triumph.[40]

The power of that man over people, his presence among them, and their recognition of his dedication and importance to the cause of independence are illustrated in events near the end of the Revolution. By January 1782, military actions had essentially ended, and the Americans and British were engaged in a prolonged effort to reach an agreement. As was the case throughout the Revolution, the American Army was cold, underfed, and underpaid. Officers were near revolt by March 10, and there was a call for a mass meeting the next day "to air their grievances–a brazen affront to Washington's authority, and, to his mind, little short of an outright mutiny."[41] He banned the meeting but called his own meeting for March 15, although he was not expected to attend. Washington slipped into the meeting unannounced and addressed the assembled officers. He spoke as a friend and a fellow officer, "portraying himself as their friend and peer."[42] But the moving moment, recorded by history, was when he attempted to read a letter from a congressman. After tripping over a few sentences, he "pulled out his new spectacles, shocking his fellow officers," who had never seen him wearing glasses.[43] He observed: "Gentlemen, you will permit me to put on my spectacles, for, I have grown not only gray, but almost blind in the service of my country."[44] Washington's acknowledgment of the limitations of his own humanity and the infirmity he suffered as a result of his devotion to his country must have been completely unexpected and was clearly moving. Tears flowed from the officers and the threatened mutiny evaporated. One veteran later recalled, "I have ever considered that the United States are indebted for their republican form of government solely to the firm and determined republicanism of George Washington at this time."[45]

Unlike John Adams, who used his diary to record the important events of the era, to reflect on their importance, and to seek meaning in his own life, Washington's lifelong diary did none of this; his entries were not introspective nor did they comment on national events. He did not disclose his inner thoughts or beliefs. He did not speculate about the larger events of the day nor feel a need to create a historical record. For example, on May 18, 1769, he merely recorded in his diary that he dined at Mrs. Dawson's and then went to bed at 8 p.m. Yet, that was the day in which he and the principal men of the colony agreed to a nonimportation plan in response to the Townsend Acts,[46] a plan that he and George Mason conceived and developed.[47] Although his letters leading up to the Revolution sometimes included a detailed discussion of events and his views, his diary typically consisted of an incomplete sentence or two each day. Most were about the weather or farming. The diary grew to be his personal almanac. His longest period of time at Mount Vernon, which he inherited in 1761, was before his appointment as commander of the Continental Army in 1775. During that time, his diary entries were often about manuring, harvesting, and planting trees, corn, potatoes, wheat, flax, and grape vines. (He stopped growing tobacco in 1766.) He listed the construction of various plantation buildings, land transactions, and guests. Washington, on horseback, inspected his land holdings regularly, almost daily. Thus, on July 4, 1768, he recorded that he rode "to see my wheat at different places."[48] One particular activity was noted in many diary entries: He loved to fox hunt. In March 1768, he went fox hunting five times. On March 2, he recorded that he caught a fox with a bobbed tail and cut ears after a chase of seven hours, "in which most of the dogs were worsted." On March 16, he caught a fox after three hours and did so again on the twenty-ninth.[49]

Washington grew his land holdings to "upwards of 54,000 acres, including some 8,000 acres at Mount Vernon."[50] Slave labor worked those expanses and served to grow his wealth, an egregious blind spot shared with many Virginia planters and others. Absent from his descriptions of his laborers is the word "slave." For instance, he wrote of acquiring a stone mason as if he were purchasing a tool. In a letter dated July 2, 1766, he wrote to Joseph Thompson that he was sending him "a Negro (Tom) which I beg the favor of you to sell" in the Islands for whatever he could obtain, including molasses, rum, limes, tamarinds, and sweetmeats. Tom was good with a hoe but was a "Rogue & Runaway."[51] In a letter to Henry Lee in 1787, he said he did not wish to compete with him for the purchase of "tradesmen" that were for sale but that there was a particular "bricklayer" he was interested in, so long as that bricklayer's price "did not exceed one hundred or a few more pounds." He added that he would decline the purchase if the bricklayer's family was also part of the purchase or if the bricklayer "would reluctantly part" with his family: "his feeling I would not be the means of hurting in the latter case, nor at any rate be encumbered with the former."[52]

In his last will, drafted in July 1799, Washington inventoried his land holdings, amounting to 51,000 acres, and slaves, amounting to 277. Of that number of slaves, a substantial portion were dower slaves of his wife (which neither he nor Martha could free, being owned by the Curtis family heirs), but he directed that those he did own should be freed after his death and the death of Martha. He made special provisions for educating young slaves prior to their freedom and for Billy Lee, his long-time body servant, who was then incapacitated with knee problems.[53]

His life-long passion was Mount Vernon. During the Revolution, when he was away from it for almost the entire expanse of eight and a half years, his correspondence—in hundreds of letters—detailed explicit instructions to the overseer of his estates.[54] He returned to Mount Vernon on December 24, 1783, after resigning from the army and focused again on farming. On July 4, 1785, he was recording the weather in his diary: "Monday, 4th. Mercury at 76 in the morning–80 at noon and 82 at night. Tolerably pleasant in the afternoon, the wind being northwardly but warm afterwards."[55] He took a ride to check on his wheat harvest. No mention of it being Independence Day. Washington was traveling on July, 4, 1786, on business, but still recording the weather. His diary entries for April 1787 were all about the weather and farm activities; on the twenty-second, he was disappointed that only thirty thousand herring had been caught.[56]

His farm life was again interrupted beginning in 1787, when the Constitutional Convention was held in Philadelphia, with Washington serving as president. On the Fourth of July that year, Washington recorded that the convention had been adjourned to celebrate Independence and that he went to a wax museum, heard an oration on the anniversary, and then "dined with the State Society of the Cincinnati at Epplee's Tavern and drank tea at Mr. Powell's."[57] Washington wrote in a letter later that year that, although he had wished the proposed Constitution to be "more perfect," it was "the best that could be attained at this time," and, with the "political concerns of the Country . . . suspended by a thread," anarchy would have ensued without it.[58] The next year, on Independence Day, Washington recorded the weather and visiting his plantations, where he observed plowing, the cutting of rye, and other work. Later that day, James Madison arrived for a stay at Mount Vernon.[59]

In 1789, Washington was elected president, taking him away from his beloved Mount Vernon for eight more years. In New York, the temporary capital that July 4, he addressed the Society of Cincinnati, pledging his faithful efforts to promote prosperity and happiness.[60] In 1790, he celebrated Independence on July 5, since the Fourth was a Sunday. In one of his longer diary entries, he recounted how senators, house members, foreign dignitaries, military officers, and others "came with the compliments of the day to me." He attended an oration at Saint Paul's Chapel on how excellent the government was and how Americans had freed themselves from the attempts of Great Britain to enslave them. The one caution of the day, noted by Washington, was a report he received that the "traitor" Benedict Arnold had been seen in Detroit and that information had added to "conjecture that the British had some design on the Spanish settlements on the Mississippi and of course to surround the United States."[61] On that same day, he wrote a letter to the people of South Carolina in response to their congratulations on his election, summarizing the challenges of the Revolution and adding:

> The value of liberty was thus enhanced in our estimation by the difficulty of its attainment, and the worth of characters appreciated by the trial of adversity. The tempest of war having at length been succeeded by the sunshine of peace; our citizen-soldiers impressed an useful lesson of patriotism on mankind, by nobly returning with impaired constitutions and unsatisfied claims, after such long sufferings and severe disappointments, to their former occupations. Posterity as well as the present age will doubtless regard with admiration and gratitude the patience, perseverance, and valor, which achieved our revolution: they will cherish the remembrance of virtues which had but few parallels in former times, and which will add new luster to the most splendid page of history.
>
> If there be for me any peculiarly just subject of exaltation, and with an honest pride I avow the fact, it is in being the citizen of a country, whose inhabitants were so enlightened and disinterested as to sacrifice local prejudices and temporary systems for the sake of rendering secure and permanent that Independency, which had been the price of so much treasure and blood. Animated with the hope of transmitting to Posterity the spirit of a free constitution in its native purity; they have, since the conclusion of the war evinced the rectitude of their principles, as well as proved themselves by their practice worthy of their successes.[62]

Washington's duties on July 4 through his two terms were continuous but not always obvious in his diary. He spent 1791 in Frederick, Maryland, on July First and then in Lancaster, Pennsylvania, on the Fourth, hearing speeches and addressing the inhabitants.[63] But the next year had him thinking about his estate, giving directions on its management.[64] In 1793, after retiring from the presidency, he managed to be home for the Fourth and attended a celebration in nearby Alexandria.[65] In a letter that day, he expressed his relief at "bidding adieu to the walks of public life." He wrote: "At the age of 65, I am recommencing my Agricultural pursuits & rural amusements; which at all times have been the most pleasing occupation of my life, and most congenial with my temper, notwithstanding a small proportion of it has been spent in this way." He offered a rare reflection:

> It was my constant endeavor whilst I had the honor to administer the government of these United States, to preserve them in peace and friendship with all the world. Humanity, interest and policy all combined to dictate the measure; and I have reasons to believe that the gentleman who has succeeded to the Chair of State will pursue a similar policy; and if to stop the further effusion of human blood; the expenditure of national wealth; and the cries, & distresses of fatherless children & widows made so by the most destructive sword that has ever been drawn in modern times, are sufficient inducements for returning it to the scabbard, a general peace must surely be at hand. Be these things however as they may, as my glass is nearly run, I shall endeavor in the shade of my vine & fig tree to view things in the "calm lights of mild philosophy."[66]

But America was still not done with Washington. On the next Fourth of July,[67] Washington was writing to James McHenry, the secretary of war, in response to his possible appointment to marshal an army to address a possible French invasion. He wrote:

> Under circumstances like these, accompanied by an actual Invasion of our territorial rights, it would be difficult for me, at any time, to remain an idle spectator under the plea of age or retirement. With sorrow, it is true, I should quit the shades of my peaceful abode; and the ease & happiness I now enjoy, to encounter anew the turmoils of war; to which, possibly, my strength and powers might

> be found incompetent. These, however, should not be stumbling blocks in my own way.[68]

Washington detailed his concerns, including whether public opinion would support his returning to public life as commander and the structure of the army then in the process of creation. After more correspondence, President Adams appointed him "Lieutenant General and Commander in Chief of all the Armies raised, or to be raised, for the Service of the U.S."[69] Washington journeyed to Philadelphia in November, where he and Alexander Hamilton worked on plans for the new army. He left to return home on December 14, 1798, exactly one year to the day before his death.[70]

Finally, on the last Independence Day of his life, July 4, 1799, Washington was home at Mount Vernon. His diary entry for the date recorded: "Morning heavy. Mer. at 74 and Wind So. Et. Clouds in every qr. & sprinklings of Rain. Mer. 80 at Night. Went up to Alexa. and dined with a number of the Citizens there in celebration of the anniversary of the declaration of American Independe. at Kemps Tavern."[71] That was to be his last Independence Day. On December 12, 1799, and again on the next day, Washington wrote in his diary:

> 12. Morning Cloudy—Wind at No. Et. & Mer. 33. A large circle round the Moon last Night. About 1 oclock it began to snow—soon after to Hail and then turned to a settled cold Rain. Mer. 28 at Night.
>
> 13. Morning Snowing & abt. 3 Inches deep. Wind at No. Et. & Mer. at 30. Contg. Snowing till 1 Oclock and abt. 4 it became perfectly clear. Wind in the same place but not hard. Mer. 28 at Night.[72]

Those were his last entries. On December 12, despite the day's severe weather, Washington made a five-hour inspection of his farms on horseback, becoming wet and chilled. On the thirteenth, in spite of a sore throat, he went out in the late afternoon to the front lawn to mark some trees for cutting. During the night, he awoke with an inflammation of the throat and labored breathing. He convinced Martha Washington to wait until morning to seek help. Throughout the day of December 14, Washington received various ineffective treatments from attending physicians. Toward evening, he remarked: "I feel myself going" and that he wished to "go off quietly. I cannot last long." Ron Chernow observes: "With his stoic toughness, somber gallantry, and clear conscience, the patient was reconciled to his own mortality."[73] George Washington quietly passed away in his bed at Mount Vernon that evening.

There is one more Fourth of July associated with Washington. On July 4, 1976, Washington was posthumously promoted to the rank General of the Armies by a joint congressional resolution. The resolution stated that Washington's seniority had rank and precedence over all other grades of the Armed Forces, making him the highest-ranking United States officer of all time.

CHAPTER 3

The Last of the Revolutionary Giants

Fifty years to the date of the Declaration of Independence—July 4, 1826—Thomas Jefferson and John Adams died. They were the last of the giants, as Lincoln called the Founders. The two former presidents had had a long and complicated relationship but, in their fading years, began a correspondence that healed old wounds. Both men knew the end was coming and, by early 1826, both were struggling to hold on to reach the fiftieth anniversary.

The two men had met in Philadelphia during the Second Continental Congress and, as detailed in other chapters, collaborated in drafting the Declaration of Independence, with Jefferson being the primary draftsman and Adams the main protagonist for independence.[1] Each played a crucial role in Europe as a diplomat during the Revolution. While in Europe, the two men became very close. Both went on to serve their country at the highest levels for decades. As Jefferson later observed, the two men

> were fellow laborers in the same cause, struggling for what is most valuable to man, his right of self-government. Laboring always at the same oar, with some wave ever ahead threatening to overwhelm us & yet passing harmless under our bark we knew not how, we rode through the storm with heart & hand, and made a happy port. Still we did not expect to be without rubs and difficulties; and we have had them.[2]

After the Constitution was adopted, Adams became George Washington's vice president for two terms, eventually succeeding him as president. The vice president had no duties other than to preside over the Senate, and Adams's eight years in that role were unremarkable. Jefferson served as secretary of state in the first Washington administration until 1793. He came in second to Adams in the election of 1796 and, based on the provisions of the Constitution at that time, became vice president. In that office, Jefferson spent a good deal of his time "tending–quietly–to the construction and nurture of the Republican opposition to Adams' Federalist government."[3] Jefferson's efforts, according to Jon Meacham, were always designed to "do what it took, within reason, to arrange the world as [Jefferson] wanted it to be."[4] Those efforts included financially supporting James Callender, who published defamatory anti-Adams attacks that characterized Adams as seeking to destroy democracy and the very social fabric of the Republic.[5] Jefferson, the Southern aristocratic slaveholder, successfully portrayed himself as a man of the people—a Republican who asserted that "a little rebellion now and then is a good thing." At the same time, Adams was labeled as an aspiring monarchist.[6]

After Adams's defeat in the presidential election of 1800 to Jefferson, he learned the nature of Jefferson's activities. Adams did not even attend the inauguration on March 4, 1801, leaving by public stagecoach to return to his farm in Quincy, Massachusetts, early that day. His political career and public life ended, and he lived there for the rest of his life.

Years passed without a word between the two men. Jefferson's second term ended in March 1809, and he retired to his plantation in Charlottesville, Virginia.[7] Benjamin Rush, a Philadelphia doctor and signer of the Declaration, was a long-time friend of both men. He believed it was time for the former presidents to renew their friendship. Rush wrote Adams a letter on October 17, 1809, in which he claimed he was repeating his dream about reading a history book:[8]

> In the month of November 1809 Mr. Adams addressed a short letter to his old friend Mr. Jefferson in which he congratulated him upon his escape to the shades of retirement and domestic happiness, and concluded it with assurances of his regard and good wishes for his welfare. This letter did great honor to Mr. Adams. It discovered a magnanimity known only to great minds. Mr. Jefferson replied

> to this letter, and reciprocated expressions of regard and esteem. These letters were followed by a correspondence of several years, in which they mutually reviewed the scenes of business in which they had been engaged, and candidly acknowledged to each other all the errors of opinion & conduct into which they had fallen during the time they filled the same stations in the Service of their country. Many precious aphorisms, the result of observation, experience, & profound reflection it is said are contained in these letters. It is to be hoped, the world will be favored with a sight of them, when they can neither injure nor displease any persons or families whose ancestor's follies or crimes were mentioned in them. These gentlemen sunk into the grave nearly at the same time, full of years, and rich in the gratitude and praises of their country (for they outlived the heterogeneous parties that were opposed to them) and to their numerous merits and honors posterity has added, that they were rival friends.

Adams responded in a letter that the dream was not history but "it may be prophecy"[9]—and, remarkably, it was closely parallel to later events. Nonetheless, more than two years passed without any correspondence between Adams and Jefferson. In December 1811, Rush again wrote Adams, seeking to rekindle the relationship. Rush wrote that he had had a letter from Jefferson in which Jefferson reported on a visit by some neighbors to Adams. During that visit, Adams had acknowledged that he "always loved Jefferson, and still love him." Jefferson stated that that was all he needed "to revive towards [Adams] all the affections of the most cordial moments of our lives." He asserted that he had defended Adams when assailed by others, with the exception of Adams's political opinions, but that his affection for Adams was "unchanged." Rush, writing to Adams, urged him to "receive the olive branch which has thus been offered to you by the hand of a man who still loves you."[10]

On Christmas Day, Adams responded to Rush that he had nothing to say to Jefferson except to "wish him an easy journey to Heaven when he goes." Nonetheless, he added: "Time and chance, however, or possibly design may produce e'er long a letter between us."[11] Only a few days later, on New Year's Day 1812, Adams relented, writing Jefferson a short letter wishing him "many happy New Years."[12] Jefferson replied with a long letter, observing that Adams's letter "calls up recollections very dear to my mind."[13] Doctor Rush, upon learning of the exchange of letters, wrote to Adams that he rejoiced in the correspondence and observed that he considered Adams and Jefferson "the North and South Poles of the American Revolution. Some talked, some wrote—and some fought to promote & establish it, but you and Mr. Jefferson *thought* for us all."[14]

Thus began a long series of correspondence—158 letters—between the two former presidents, ending only with their deaths. In that era, certainly more so than in modern times, how a person closed a letter was telling. It is called the complementary close or the valediction. In his first letter, Adams merely concluded with "your Friend and Servant."[15] Jefferson, in reply, encouraged Adams to write again, closing:

> I should have the pleasure of knowing that, in the race of life, you do not keep, in its physical decline, the same distance ahead of me which you have done in political honors & achievements. No circumstances have lessened the interest I feel in these particulars respecting yourself; none have suspended for one moment my sincere esteem for you; and I now salute you with unchanged affections and respect.[16]

At first, Adams was concluding with "kind regards,"[17] but soon was writing "with great esteem and regard your friend and servant."[18] Within a year, Jefferson signed off that, despite their differing views on government, he would not let such differences "affect the sentiments of sincere friendship and respect, consecrated to you by so long a course of time, and which I now repeat sincere assurances."[19]

By 1816, Adams wrote as Jefferson's "old friend,"[20] while Jefferson was assuring Adams "of my constant attachment and consideration."[21] In 1819, Adams signed that he was "my dear Sir your invariable friend,"[22] to which Jefferson responded: "I am and shall always be affectionately and respectfully yours."[23] The volume of letters and their length continued to decline, but the expressions of affection grew. The next year, Jefferson ended: "I am sure that I really know many, many, things, and none more surely than that I love you with all my heart, and pray for the continuance of your life until you shall be tired of it yourself."[24] In 1821, Adams's letter concluded that the "friendship which I feel for you, ardent and sincere as it is, would be over clouded by constant fears of its termination."[25]

Finally, as the end neared in 1825, Adams wrote:

> I wish your health may continue to the last much better than mine. The little strength of mind and the considerable strength of body that I once possessed appear to be all gone—but while I breathe I shall be your friend. We shall meet again so wishes and so believes your friend—but if we are disappointed we shall never know it.[26]

One evening, in June 1820, while visiting relatives, Adams read aloud a letter from Jefferson. He was asked how he could be on such good terms with Jefferson after all that Jefferson had done. Adams replied, according to Josiah Quincy's diary:

> I do not believe that Mr. Jefferson ever hated me. On the contrary, I believe he always liked *me:* but he detested [Alexander] Hamilton and my whole administration. Then he wished to be President of the United States, and I stood in his way. So he did everything he could to pull me down. But if I quarrel with him for that, I might quarrel with every man I have had anything to do with in my life. This is human nature. . . . I forgive my enemies and hope they may find mercy in Heaven. Mr. Jefferson and I have grown old and retired from public life. So we are upon our ancient terms of good will.[27]

David McCullough characterizes the large volume of letters that traveled on the roads between Quincy and Monticello as "one of the most extraordinary correspondences in American history—indeed in the English language."[28] Remarkably, given the distance and modes of transportation at the time, letters were being delivered in seven or eight days, which astounded Adams.[29] The topics of the letters ranged widely, notes McCullough, including everyday events such as walking, books, memories, politics, education, relations with the British and French, "and always, and repeatedly, the American Revolution."[30] More specifically, the men recalled the decision to seek Independence, the circumstances surrounding that decision, and their fellow signers, numerous times. In his first letter to Adams, on January 12, 1812, Jefferson noted that there were only seven signers still alive—"fellow laborers" he called them, with only Jefferson on his side of the Potomac River.[31] Doctor Rush, one of the signers and the man responsible for reuniting the two former presidents, died in 1813, prompting Jefferson to write to Adams that a better man could not have left them, "more benevolent, more learned, of finer genius, or more honest."[32] Adams replied that he also lamented the loss of Rush, adding: "I know of no character living or dead who has done more real good in America."[33]

They debated whether a document that surfaced—the Mecklenburg County Declaration of Independence—which allegedly predated the Declaration written by Jefferson by a year, was, in fact, genuine. After receiving Jefferson's letter maintaining that it was "spurious," and detailing why it was a fabrication[34] (as it was subsequently proven to be),[35] Adams agreed, referring to Jefferson as "the undoubted acknowledged draftsman of the Declaration of Independence" and that the Mecklenburg document, if had been real, would have created such a sensation at the time that it would have "flown through the universe like a wildfire."[36] They mused over the question of who could write the history of the American Revolution, with Adams detailing how the documents, debates, and deliberations of Congress from 1774 to1783 were then still secret "and lost forever."[37] Jefferson replied that no one could write it "except merely it's external facts." He noted that all of Congress's proceedings had been behind closed doors and no member took notes. As an aside, he added, that it had become known that letters were being exchanged between the two presidents: "would you believe that a printer has had the effrontery to propose to me the letting him publish [the letters]? These people think they have a right to everything however secret or sacred."[38]

The two Founders ruminated on the question regarding when the Revolution had begun (and Adams's views on this are also discussed in

Chapter One), with Adams maintaining his view distinguishing between the war and the Revolution, that is, the Revolution "was in the minds of the people and this was effected from 1760 to 1775, in the course of fifteen years before a drop of blood was drawn at Lexington."[39] He later opined that it "began as early as the first plantation of the Country. Independence of church and parliament was a fixed principle of our predecessors in 1620."[40]

They were optimistic about America, although Jefferson was consistently more so. Jefferson, again in his first letter: "We shall go on, puzzled and prospering, beyond example in the history of man," multiplying and prospering "until we exhibit an association [that is] powerful, wise, and happy, beyond what has been seen by man."[41] Adams, always more cautious, foresaw that the "prospect of the future" depended on the Union and how it was preserved.[42] It remained for him "an object of as much anxiety as ever Independence was."[43] On July 5, 1813, he wrote: "My Friend! You and I have passed our lives in serious times."[44] It should be noted that the United States was at war with Great Britain from 1812 to 1815 and that there was substantial internal dissension and even talk of secession by the New England states. Many other storms—or waves, to use one of their favorite expressions—arose over the course of time that the two giants corresponded. In 1819, the slavery question came to the fore with the debate over whether Missouri should be admitted as a slave state, prompting Adams to hope that the controversy "will follow other waves under the ship and do no harm."[45] He nonetheless saw slavery as a "black cloud" hanging over the country and conceded he had none of the "genius of Franklin to invent a rod to draw from the cloud [. . .] its thunder and lightning."[46] Jefferson, although noting that he and Adams differed once the Constitution was established, saw common ground:

> We act[ed] in perfect harmony thro' a long and perilous contest for our liberty and independence. A constitution has been acquired which, tho neither of us think perfect, yet both consider as competent to render our fellow-citizens the happiest and the securest on whom the sun has ever shone. If we do not think

> exactly alike as to its imperfections, it matters little to our country which, after devoting to it long lives of disinterested labor, we have delivered over to our successors in life, who will be able to take care of it, and of themselves.[47]

Both saw the United States as an example to other nations, even the Europeans, who seemed continually at war. Jefferson wrote:

> We are destined to be a barrier against the returns of ignorance and barbarism. Old Europe will have to lean on our shoulders, and to hobble along by our side, under the monkish trammels of priests & kings, as she can. What a Colossus shall we be when the Southern continent comes up to our mark! What a stand will it secure as a ralliance for the reason & freedom of the globe! I like the dreams of the future better than the history of the past. So good night! I will dream on, always fancying that Mrs. Adams and yourself are by my side marking the progress and the obliquities of ages and countries.[48]

He maintained that he "shall not die without hope that light and liberty are on steady advance." He asserted that the "flames kindled on the 4th of July 1776 have spread over too much of the globe to be extinguished by the feeble engines of despotism. On the contrary, they will consume these engines and all who work them."[49] Adams, for his part, looked at the "golden days when Virginia and Massachusetts lived and acted together like a band of brothers" and hoped for the return of such a world.[50]

The two Founders wrote often about their declining health and occasionally debated the question whether they would want to be young again.[51] Jefferson was all for it, although acknowledging the present, still "steer[ing] my bark with hope in the head, leaving fear astern."[52] Upon further reflection, he would limit his return to between twenty-five and sixty, perhaps younger, but not older than sixty. He noted that Benjamin Franklin, "at age of 80, thought the residuum of his life, not worth that price." He, however, was happy with what was around him, yet "ripe for leaving all, this year, this day, this hour."[53] To Jefferson in 1825, in one of his last letters to him, Adams discussed the end that was coming:

> I ought not to have neglected so long to write you an account of the delightful visit I received from Mr. and Mrs. Cooledge, Mrs. C—— deserves all the high praises I have constantly heard concerning her. She entertained me with accounts of your sentiments of human life, which accorded so perfectly with mine that it gave me great delight—In one point however I could not agree—She said, she had heard you say that you would like to go over life again, in this I could not agree. I had rather go forward and meet whatever is to come—I have met in this life, with great trials—I have had a Father, and lost him—I have had a Mother and lost her—I have had a Wife and lost her—I have had Children and lost them—I have had honorable and worthy Friends and lost them—and instead of suffering these griefs again I had rather go forward and meet my destiny—[54]

Early 1826, leading up to the fiftieth anniversary of the Declaration of Independence, saw only three of the signers still alive. Along with eighty-three-year-old Thomas Jefferson and ninety-year-old John Adams was eighty-eight-year-old Charles Carroll of Maryland, who would live until 1832. Invitations to attend July Fourth events "poured into Quincy and Charlottesville," but Adams and Jefferson declined them all as they "grew steadily more feeble."[55] In his last letter to Adams, dated March 25, 1826, Jefferson requested that Adams permit a visit from his grandson, Thomas Jefferson Randolph, stating:

> Like other young people, he wishes to be able, in the winter nights of old age, to recount to those around him what he has heard and learnt of the Heroic age preceding his birth, and which of the Argonauts particularly he was in time to have seen. It was the lot of our early years to witness nothing but the dull monotony of Colonial subservience, and of our riper ones to breast the labors and perils of working out of it. Theirs are the Halcyon calms

> succeeding the storm which our Argosy had so stoutly weathered. Gratify his ambition then by receiving his best bow, and my solicitude for your health by enabling him to bring me a favorable account of it. Mine is but indifferent, but not so my friendship and respect for you.[56]

On June 24, Jefferson wrote a letter to the mayor of Washington, declining an invitation to the Fourth of July celebration in that city. The letter, soon reprinted throughout the country, noted that Jefferson would have been delighted to join the celebrations regarding "the bold and doubtful election we were to make for our country, between submission or the sword; and to have enjoyed with them the consolatory fact, that our fellow citizens, after half a century of experience and prosperity, continue to approve the choice we made." He added:

> May it be to the world, what I believe it will be, (to some parts sooner, to others later, but finally to all,) the signal of arousing men to burst the chains under which monkish ignorance and superstition had persuaded them to bind themselves, and to assume the blessings and security of self-government. That form which we have substituted, restores the free right to the unbounded exercise of reason and freedom of opinion. All eyes are opened, or opening, to the rights of man. The general spread of the light of science has already laid open to every view the palpable truth, that the mass of mankind has not been born with saddles on their backs, nor a favored few booted and spurred, ready to ride them legitimately, by the grace of God. These are grounds of hope for others. For ourselves, let the annual return of this day forever refresh our recollections of these rights, and an undiminished devotion to them.[57]

On June 30, a small delegation from the town of Quincy called on Adams and asked him to propose a toast that they would read aloud at the celebration on the Fourth. Adams replied: "I will give you," he said, "Independence forever!" Asked if he would add anything, he said: "Not a word."[58] By the Fourth, as the end neared, when awakened and told it was the Fourth, Adams answered clearly that it was a "great day. It is a *good* day."[59] As the hours passed, with cannons firing in the distance and then after a midday thunderstorm struck, "Adams lay peacefully, his mind clear, by all signs." Late in the afternoon, he stirred and spoke clearly: "Thomas Jefferson survives."[60] At 6:20 p.m., Adams was dead.

Jefferson had not. He had been in and out of consciousness since the night of July 2, attended by a doctor and his daughter Martha. During the evening of July 3, he awoke and uttered either "This is the Fourth" or "This is the Fourth of July." Told that it would be soon, he slept again. Two hours later, he awoke again and declined further medication. He asked again if it was the Fourth, and Nicolas Trist, who was by his bedside, "could not bring himself to disappoint the old man, and lied by nodding that yes, it was indeed the Fourth. 'Ah,' Jefferson said. 'Just as I wished.'"[61] Early in the morning on the Fourth, Jefferson called for his servants, saying his last, unrecorded words. He died at ten minutes before one o'clock in the afternoon.[62]

The two deaths were as intertwined as the lives of the two great men, prompting many observations and eulogies, interpreting the deaths as "proof that the United States had a special place in [God's] plans and affections."[63] Adams had had the satisfaction of seeing his son, John Quincy Adams, elected president in 1824. Learning of the two deaths, John Quincy Adams wrote that it was "among the remarkable incidents" of the fiftieth Fourth of July "that it retained its power over the minds of both the men, to whom it was so momentous, and occupied the last of their thoughts upon Earth. We cannot perhaps without presumption, attribute special incidents of mortality to special purposes of Providence."[64]

Daniel Webster was the greatest orator of the era. His joint eulogy for Adams and Jefferson before a large audience at Faneuil Hall in Boston on August 2, 1826, captured the meaning of the timing of the deaths to Americans of the era. He spoke in the eloquent language of the times in the hall where so much had happened during the colonial era.[65] Webster maintained that, if either of those men had died on Independence Day, it would have been "an immense void in our American society" because each had been so intimately "blended with the history of the country, and especially" with the Revolution. He believed that the nation would have "felt that one great link, connecting us with former times, was broken" and that "the presence of the Revolution itself, and of the act of independence "had become greatly removed." But, he believed, the "concurrence" of their deaths was "striking and extraordinary," and proof that the country was an object cared for by Providence. He continued that, although the two great men were no more, "the concurrence of their death on the anniversary of Independence has naturally awakened stronger emotions."

> To their country they yet live, and live forever. They live in all that perpetuates the remembrance of men on earth; in the recorded proofs of their own great actions, in the offspring of their intellect, in the deep-engraved lines of public gratitude, and in the respect and homage of mankind. They live in their example; and they live, emphatically, and will live, in the influence which their lives and efforts, their principles and opinions, now exercise, and will continue to exercise, on the affairs of men, not only in their own country but throughout the civilized world. . . .
>
> Their work doth not perish with them. The tree which they assisted to plant will flourish, although they water it and protect it no longer; for it has struck its roots deep, it has sent them to the very center; no storm . . . can overturn it; its branches spread wide; they stretch their protecting arms broader and broader, and its top is destined to reach the heavens. We are not deceived. There is no delusion here. No age will come in which the American Revolution will appear less than it is, one of the greatest events in human history. No age will come in which it shall cease to be seen and felt, on either continent, that a mighty step, a great advance, not only in American affairs, but in human affairs, was made on the 4th of July, 1776. And no age will come, we trust, so ignorant or so unjust as not to see and acknowledge the efficient agency of those we now honor in producing that momentous event. . . .
>
> And now, fellow-citizens, let us not retire from this occasion without a deep and solemn conviction of the duties which have

developed upon us. This lovely land, this glorious liberty, these benign institutions, the dear purchase of our fathers, are ours; ours to enjoy, ours to preserve, ours to transmit. Generations past and generations to come hold us responsible for this sacred trust. Our fathers, from behind, admonish us, with their anxious paternal voices; posterity calls out to us, from the bosom of the future; the world turns hither its solicitous eyes; all, conjure us to act wisely, and faithfully, in the relation which we sustain. . . .

It cannot be denied, but by those who would dispute against the sun, that with America, and in America, a new era commences in human affairs. This era is distinguished by free representative governments, by entire religious liberty, by improved systems of national intercourse, by a newly awakened and unconquerable spirit of free inquiry, and by a diffusion of knowledge through the community, such as has been before altogether unknown and unheard of. America, America, our country, fellow-citizens, our own dear and native land, is inseparably connected, fast bound up, in fortune and by fate, with these great interests. If they fall, we fall with them; if they stand, it will be because we have maintained them.

PART II

The Evolution of the Promises of Freedom and Equality

This part examines the enduring aspect of the Declaration of Independence, which offered the view that all men were created equal and had fundamental rights to life, liberty, and the pursuit of happiness. Chapter Four sets forth the Declaration's words and the basic evolution of the meaning of those words. Chapter Five examines the views of one agitator for freedom, Frederick Douglass, and his powerful indictment of slavery prior to the Civil War. Chapter Six looks at the costs of freedom highlighted by two Fourth of Julys during the Civil War—Vicksburg and Gettysburg. Missing from the Declaration were women, and their long road to change is discussed in Chapter Seven, highlighted by their protest at the Nation's Centennial celebration on July 4, 1876. There are others who have come within the jurisdiction of the United States, including Puerto Rico and the Philippines. The promises of the Declaration, also long delayed, were finally extended to each, formally decreed on two different July Fourths.

CHAPTER 4

The Promises of Freedom and Equality

> *We hold these Truths to be self-evident, that all Men are created equal, that they are endowed by their Creator with certain unalienable Rights, that among these are Life, Liberty, and the Pursuit of Happiness—That to secure these Rights, Governments are instituted among Men, deriving their just Powers from the Consent of the Governed, that whenever any Form of Government becomes destructive of these Ends, it is the Right of the People to alter or to abolish it, and to institute new Government, laying its Foundation on such Principles, and organizing its Powers in such Form, as to them shall seem most likely to effect their Safety and Happiness.*

So promises the Declaration, authored primarily by Thomas Jefferson. Jefferson's rough draft of the Declaration of Independence had one notable edit by Benjamin Franklin. Jefferson wrote: "We hold these truths to be sacred & undeniable," but Franklin suggested it be changed to its final form, that the truths are "self-evident."[1] The remainder of the document, discussed in the first chapter, was a compilation of the reasons for separating from Great Britain. Once that separation had occurred, that facet of the Declaration is interesting only for a historical understanding of the basis for the Revolution. The language examined here is the aspect of the Declaration that has continued importance. It is, on its face, a promise of fundamental rights—the core reason the United States exists. It is the reason we celebrate the

Fourth of July every year: All individuals are created equal, all have inalienable rights, including life, liberty, and the pursuit of happiness, and the government must be structured to ensure the conditions to further those inalienable rights. Yet, that modern interpretation was belied by the circumstances in the United States at the time of the Declaration, and that view was rejected by its author. African Americans and women were not considered within the scope of the Declaration's promises.

Jefferson's draft contained what, at first blush, appears to be a condemnation of the British monarch for promoting slavery in America:

> [The King] has waged cruel war against human nature itself, violating its most sacred rights of life & liberty in the persons of a distant people who never offended him, captivating & carrying them into slavery in another hemisphere, or to incur miserable death in their transportation thither. This piratical warfare, the opprobrium of *infidel* powers, is the warfare of the CHRISTIAN king of Great Britain. Determined to keep open a market where MEN should be bought & sold, he has prostituted his negative for suppressing every legislative attempt to prohibit or to restrain this execrable commerce: and that this assemblage of horrors might want no fact of distinguished die, he is now exciting those very people to rise in arms among us, and to purchase that liberty of which *he* has deprived them, & murdering the people upon whom *he* also obtruded them; thus paying off former crimes committed against the *liberties* of one people, with crimes which he urges them to commit against the *lives* of another.[2]

This remarkable language came from the pen of a man who, over his lifetime, owned more than six hundred slaves and at any one time had about two hundred.[3] His slaves included Sally Hemings, with whom Jefferson had five children, all of which Jefferson held as slaves.[4] Jefferson never acknowledged Sally or the children.[5] "What suited Jefferson was the code of denial that defined life in the slave-holding states. It was his plantation, his world, and he would live as he wished."[6] How was it possible, wrote British essayist Samuel Johnson at the start of the war, "that we hear the loudest yelps for liberty among the drivers of Negroes?"[7] The loyalist former governor of Massachusetts, Thomas Hutchinson, echoed those sentiments in his response to the Declaration: "I could wish to ask the Delegates of Maryland, Virginia, and the Carolinas, how their constituents justify the depriving more than an hundred thousand Africans of their rights to liberty, and the pursuit of happiness, and in some degree to their lives, if these rights are so absolutely unalienable."[8]

Jefferson's proposed language requires a closer look. First, what is clear, as David McCullough has observed, is that "slavery and the slave trade were hardly the fault of George III, however ardently Jefferson wished to fix the blame on the distant monarch."[9] The exact reasons why that section was removed from Jefferson's draft, like all the other changes, is shrouded in secrecy—there was no official record of the debates surrounding the Declaration. Nonetheless, it has been argued that the removal of the slave trade language from Jefferson's draft was fueled by political and economic expediencies. Southern plantations (including George Washington's) were important components of the colonial economy, exploiting slave labor to produce tobacco, cotton, and other cash crops for export. New England shipping was extensively involved in the "lucrative slave trade."[10] In an apparent contradiction, Virginia, through legislation, had attempted to slow the import of slaves by imposing tariffs on the trade; those legislative efforts had been repeatedly vetoed by royal governors. However, the motivation for the legislation was highly cynical. The richer landowners had plenty of slaves and did not want their value diluted by competition from imported slaves. Those attempts to limit the trade were opposed by others, including poorer landowners and by other Southern colonies.[11]

Jefferson was also making another claim in his draft, that is, that the king was enlisting slaves to rebel against their American masters, join the British, and receive their freedom in return. That claim was based on the proclamation of Royal Governor of Virginia, John Murray, Lord Dunmore, which he issued on November 7, 1775; it urged slaves to join the British and fight against their masters in return for freedom. Hence, Jefferson's draft sought to "denounce the novel 'atrocity' of freeing slaves."[12] This "twisted language and logic" did not survive.[13] In

Congress, all of Jefferson's proposed language was omitted, and the final document simply asserted that the king had "excited domestic insurrection amongst us."

What remains is the obvious contradiction between the majestic promise of the Declaration of equality, inalienable rights, and liberty with the institution of slavery. Jefferson, it has been argued, perceived no contradiction:

> It is erroneous to say that Jefferson denied either equality or self-rule to the blacks as a matter of right. But he thought they had, what all men have, the right to self-rule *as a people*. Deportation was necessary so they could exercise that right. . . . His deportation scheme was meant to assure for blacks the same rights Americans were asserting. But the blacks had first to have a *separate* station, for that to become an *equal* one.[14]

Whether that argument correctly summarizes Jefferson's actual views is debatable. Nonetheless, that viewpoint was essentially formalized in the *Dred Scott* decision of the United States Supreme Court in 1857.[15] In that decision, despite the "general words" of the Declaration of Independence that "would seem to embrace the whole human family," the Court found that "the enslaved African race were not intended to be included, and formed no part of the people who framed and adopted this declaration." The Court asserted in *Dred Scott* that the Framers "perfectly understood the meaning of the language they used, and how it would be understood by others; and they knew that it would not in any part of the civilized world be supposed to embrace the Negro race, which, by common consent, had been excluded from civilized Governments and the family of nations, and doomed to slavery."

Historian Pauline Maier has traced the evolution of the Declaration's promises after its proclamation. She maintains that the modern reading of the Declaration began in the 1790s and became "increasingly common after the 1820s."[16] Maier details that the document could not be used to strike down laws or practices that violated its principles but that it was useful to seize the moral high ground in public debate.[17] She observed:

> The inconsistency between American principle and practice was recognized in the Northern states, which, one after another, ended their slave systems in the first decades after Independence, whether in the courts or the legislatures, immediately or over time. New York's gradual-emancipation act took effect appropriately on July 4, 1799, New Jersey's on the same day five years later. The cause of emancipation also commanded substantial support in those Southern states that held the greatest concentration of slaves as long as it included plans to "colonize" free blacks elsewhere, such as in the West Indies or Africa. So as late as 1831–32, the Virginia legislature seriously debated an emancipation proposal submitted by Thomas Jefferson Randolph that would have freed slaves born after July 4, 1840. By then, however, reasons of security were as much a consideration as ideological consistency: Virginia was reeling under the impact of Nat Turner's slave uprising—which had been originally planned to begin on July 4, 1831.[18]

The debate denying or affirming the equality of men was made throughout the pre-Civil War era and increasingly tied to the extension of slavery to new states,[19] which was the occasion for the *Dred Scott* decision. In contrast to that decision's views were those of Abraham Lincoln, at first a little-known lawyer and former one-term congressman from Illinois. By the 1850s, Lincoln had begun finding inspiration in the Declaration's promises; he was "reworking the ideas from speech to speech, pushing their logic, and eventually arriving at a simple statement of profound eloquence."[20] Lincoln developed his views while opposing the views of Stephen Douglas—primarily within the framework of the famous Lincoln-Douglas senate debates in the late 1850s.[21]

Douglas rejected the view that the Declaration affirmed the equality of man; instead, he claimed that its sole purpose was to justify independence from Great Britain.[22] Lincoln replied that, if that were so, the document would have "no practical use now—mere rubbish—old wadding left to rot on the battle-field after the victory was won."[23] Lincoln stated at one point: "If the Negro is a *man*, why then my ancient faith teaches me that 'all men are created equal'; and that there can be no moral right in connection with one man's making a slave of another."[24] In the wake of the *Dred Scott* opinion, he detailed his views on the Declaration:

> I think the authors of that notable instrument intended to include *all* men, but they did not intend to declare all men equal *in all respects*. They did not mean to say all were equal in color, size, intellect, moral developments, or social capacity. They defined with tolerable distinctness in what respects they did consider all men created equal—equal with "certain inalienable rights, among which are life, liberty, and the pursuit of happiness." This they said, and this they meant. They did not mean to assert the obvious untruth that all were then actually enjoying that equality, nor yet that they were about to confer it immediately upon them. In fact, they had no power to confer such a boon. They meant simply to declare the right, so that enforcement of it might follow as fast as circumstances should permit.
>
> They meant to set up a standard maxim for free society, which should be familiar to all, and revered by all; constantly looked to, constantly labored for, and even though never perfectly attained, constantly approximated, and thereby constantly spreading and deepening its influence and augmenting the happiness and value of life to all people of all colors everywhere. The assertion that "all men are created equal" was of no practical use in effecting our separation from Great Britain; and it was placed in the Declaration not for that, but for future use. Its authors meant it to be—as, thank God, it is now proving itself—a stumbling-block to all those who in after times might seek to turn a free people back into the hateful paths of despotism. They knew the proneness of prosperity to breed tyrants, and they meant when such should reappear in this fair land and commence their vocation, they should find left for them at least one hard nut to crack.[25]

Lincoln "devoted intense thought to his chosen theme for nearly a decade,"[26] ultimately perfecting it in his famous address at Gettysburg, dedicating that national cemetery for those who died in that great battle that ended on July 4, 1863: "Four score and seven years ago our fathers brought forth on this continent, a new nation, conceived in Liberty, and dedicated to the proposition that all men are created equal. Now we are engaged in a great civil war, testing whether that nation, or any nation so conceived and so dedicated, can long endure." Lincoln's remarks served to "recontract" our society on the basis of the promises contained in the Declaration of Independence,[27] using the Declaration as he had many times before as the basis for his views.

Although the reshaping of the meaning of the Declaration "was not an individual but a collective act that drew on the thoughts of many people,"[28] much of the credit goes to Abraham Lincoln, who invigorated the language of the Declaration to be what we think it to be—an equality-affirming principle, applying it to all individuals, specifying basic indisputable rights. It was, in his view and actions, "a living document for an established society, a set of goals to be realized over time."[29]

Women were also absent from the Declaration of Independence, and their struggle for legal equality—or at least the legal right to vote—took them well into the twentieth century. Their absence from the Declaration was little noticed at the time, with the exception of a few voices. Abigail Adams, on March 31, 1776, wrote her husband, John, that he and the delegates should "remember the ladies," stating:

> I long to hear that you have declared an independency—and by the way in the new code of laws which I suppose it will be necessary for you to make I desire you would remember the ladies, and be more generous and favorable to them than your ancestors. Do not put such unlimited power into the hands of the husbands. Remember all men would be tyrants if they could. If particular care and attention is not paid to the ladies we are determined to foment a rebellion, and will not hold ourselves bound by any laws in which we have no voice, or representation.
>
> That your sex are naturally tyrannical is a truth so thoroughly established as to admit of no dispute, but such of you as wish to be happy willingly give up the harsh title of master for the more tender and endearing one of friend. Why then, not put it out of the power of the vicious and the lawless to use us with cruelty and indignity with impunity. Men of sense in all ages abhor those customs which

> treat us only as the vassals of your sex. Regard us then as beings placed by providence under your protection and in imitation of the Supreme Being make use of that power only for our happiness.[30]

Her husband responded:

> As to Declarations of Independency, be patient. . . . As to your extraordinary code of laws, I cannot but laugh. We have been told that our struggle has loosened the bands of government every where. That children and apprentices were disobedient—that schools and colleges were grown turbulent—that Indians slighted their guardians and Negroes grew insolent to their masters. But your letter was the first intimation that another Tribe more numerous and powerful than all the rest were grown discontented.—This is rather too coarse a compliment but you are so saucy, I won't blot it out.
>
> Depend upon it. We know better than to repeal our masculine systems. Although they are in full force, you know they are little more than theory. We dare not exert our power in its full latitude. We are obliged to go fair, and softly, and in practice you know we are the subjects. We have only the name of masters, and rather than give up this, which would completely subject us to the despotism of the petticoat, I hope General Washington, and all our brave heroes would fight.[31]

Abigail was not amused, replying:

> I cannot say that I think you very generous to the ladies, for whilst you are proclaiming peace and good will to men, emancipating all nations, you insist upon retaining an absolute power over wives. But you must remember that arbitrary power is like most other things which are very hard, very liable to be broken—and notwithstanding all your wise laws and maxims we have it in our power not only to free ourselves but to subdue our masters, and without violence throw both your natural and legal authority at our feet.[32]

John Adams, perhaps prompted by his wife's letters, made more serious remarks in a letter a short time later to James Sullivan on limitations on the voting franchise in a representative government. At the time of the Declaration, the voting franchise was typically restricted to a subclass of white men, not all white men, and a common requirement was that they be property holders. Adams's views expressed in the letter are decidedly discordant with modern views:

> It is certain in theory that the only moral foundation of government is the consent of the people. But to what an extent shall we carry this principle? Shall we say, that every individual of the community, old and young, male and female, as well as rich and poor, must consent, expressly to every act of legislation? No, you will say. This is impossible. How then does the right arise in the majority to govern the minority, against their will? Whence arises the right of the men to govern women, without their consent? Whence the right of the old to bind the young, without theirs.
>
> But why exclude Women? You will say, because their delicacy renders them unfit for practice and experience, in the great business of life, and the hardy enterprises of war, as well as the arduous cares of state. Besides, their attention is so much engaged with the necessary nurture of their children, that nature has made them fittest for domestic cares. And children have not judgment or will of their own.

Adams continued in that letter that those reasons also applied to men who had no property. Such men were "also too little acquainted with public affairs to form a right judgment, and too dependent upon other men to have a will of their own." Such men, he wrote, "talk and vote as they are directed by some man of property, who has attached their minds to his interest." Supporting that view, he affirmed that "the balance of power in a society accompanies the balance of property in land." His solution, however, was to expand the ability to acquire land in "small quantities so that the multitude may be possessed of landed estates. If the multitude is possessed of the balance of real estate, the multitude will have the balance of power, and in that case the multitude will take care of the liberty, virtue, and interest of the multitude in all acts of government." In contrast, if all men could vote, then that "same reasoning" would apply to women and children:

> For generally speaking, women and children, have as good judgment, and as independent minds as those men who are wholly destitute of property: these last being to all intents and purposes as much dependent upon others, who will please to feed, clothe, and employ them, as women are upon their husbands, or children on their parents.[33]

Hannah Lee Corbin was Virginia's earliest known proponent of voting rights for women. She was the oldest daughter of Hannah Ludwell Lee and Thomas Lee, a prominent member of the House of Burgesses and later acting governor of the colony. Several of her brothers were important leaders during the Revolution, including Richard Henry Lee. In June 1776, Richard Henry introduced in the Continental Congress the motion to seek independence from Great Britain. By the time of the Revolution, Hannah was a widow who managed her own large plantations, which she had inherited from her husband upon his death. (Hannah remained unmarried but lived with Richard Lingan Hall, with whom she had children. Under the terms of her husband's will, she would have lost her lands if she had remarried.) Apparently, Hannah wrote Richard Henry a letter in 1778, objecting to the lack of voting rights for women. Richard, in response, wrote that the "doctrine of representation is a large subject" but he was "certain that it ought to be extended [as] far as wisdom and policy can allow." He wrote that neither of those considerations would prevent widows having property from voting, "notwithstanding it has never been the practice either here or in England." He speculated why they had not been allowed to vote: "Perhaps 'twas thought rather out of character for women to press into those tumultuous assemblies of men where the business of choosing representative[s] is conducted." He added that it "might also have been considered as not so necessary" since representatives were themselves subject to any tax imposed on property. "This then is the widow's security as well as the never married women who have lands in their own right, for both of whom I have the greatest respect, and would at any time give my consent to establish their right of voting, although I am persuaded that it would not give them greater security, nor alter the mode of taxation you complain of."[34]

Women, who clearly did not fare well with the Framers, also did not fare much better in the Supreme Court than did Dred Scott. In *Minor v. Happerssett*,[35] after the adoption of the Fourteenth Amendment (which guaranteed all citizens "the privileges or immunities of citizens of the United States"), it was contended that the constitution of the State of Missouri violated that provision because it barred women from voting. In a unanimous opinion, the Supreme Court held that "the Constitution of the United States does not confer the right of suffrage upon any one, and that the constitutions and laws of the several States which commit that important trust to men alone are not necessarily void." Although the Court determined that women are citizens, it concluded that voting was not one of the privileges and immunities protected by the amendment. It reasoned that states had always had the power to determine who was eligible to vote within each state and that all of them had, both at the time of the Revolution and thereafter, limited that right in numerous ways. The almost universal exclusion was women from the franchise. Indeed, although New Jersey initially permitted women to vote, in 1807 the state withdrew the franchise. The Court in *Minor* summarized: "For nearly ninety years the people have acted upon the idea that the Constitution, when it conferred citizenship, did not necessarily confer the right of suffrage. If uniform practice long continued can settle the construction of so important an instrument as the Constitution of the United States confessedly is, most certainly it has been done here."

The promise contained in the Declaration—life, liberty, and the pursuit of happiness—has been neither a simple slogan nor holy scripture but, instead, an evolving ideal. Time does work changes. It should be recalled that the right to alter the government to better effectuate the purpose of government is itself a promise of the Declaration, embodied in the Constitution as the amendment process. Jefferson, writing in 1790, observed that "the ground of liberty is to be gained by inches, that we must be contented to secure what we can get from time to time, and eternally press forward for what is yet to get."[36] Lincoln perceived the Declaration's equality principle as "the electric cord that links the hearts of patriotic and liberty-loving men together, that will link those patriotic hearts as long as the love of freedom exists in the minds of men throughout the world."[37] The Declaration for him was a "beacon" to guide the Founders' children and their children's children to "take courage to renew the battle which their fathers began."[38] For Lincoln, "all the governed" must have "an equal voice in the government."[39] Moreover, he believed, all must have an equal opportunity.

After being elected president, Lincoln spoke at Independence Hall in Philadelphia on February 22, 1861 (the birthday of George Washington). He noted that he was "filled with deep emotion at finding myself standing here in the place where were collected together the wisdom, the patriotism, the devotion to principle, from which sprang the institutions under which we live." He observed:

> I have never had a feeling politically that did not spring from the sentiments embodied in the Declaration of Independence. . . . I have often inquired of myself, what great principle or idea it was that kept this Confederacy so long together. It was not the mere matter of the separation of the colonies from the mother land; but something in that Declaration giving liberty, not alone to the people of this country, but hope to the world for all future time. It was that which gave promise that in due time the weights should be lifted from the shoulders of all men, and that all should have an equal chance. This is the sentiment embodied in that Declaration of Independence.[40]

In his address to a special session of Congress on July 4, 1861, he explained: "On the side of the Union, it is a struggle for maintaining in the world, that form, and substance of government, whose leading object is, to elevate the condition of men—to lift artificial weights from all shoulders—to clear the paths of laudable pursuit for all—to afford all, an unfettered start, and a fair chance, in the race of life."[41]

CHAPTER 5

Frederick Douglass: Agitating for Freedom

Frederick Douglass, in 1838, obtained his own independence—his physical freedom but not his legal freedom—when he escaped from slavery in Maryland and crossed the border to the free state of Pennsylvania.[1] He had spent the first twenty years of his life as a slave, beginning with a plantation on the Eastern Shore of Maryland and then in Baltimore for several years, only to return to plantation slavery again, but this time subject to worse conditions, including deprivation of food, whippings, and other gross mistreatment. Eventually, he was sent back to Baltimore, where, as a slave, he learned a trade—caulking ships—with all the income from that work going to his master. Douglass recounted this part of his life in the 1845 book *Narrative of the Life of Frederick Douglass: An American Slave.*

Douglass wrote that, as a young boy on the plantation, he "was seldom whipped by his old master" but suffered from hunger and cold. He "was kept almost naked—no shoes, no stockings, no jacket, no trousers, nothing on but a course tow linen shirt, reaching only to my knees." When informed at age seven or eight that he was being sent to Baltimore, he was overjoyed and spent much of the next "three days in the creek, washing off the plantation scurf, and preparing myself for my departure." He was given a pair of trousers, apparently for the first time in his life.[2] In Baltimore, his new master was Hugh Auld, along with his wife, Sofia Auld. Douglass was charged with the care of their young son. In his autobiography, Douglass writes of being greeted with "the most kindly emotions" by Sofia Auld, who promptly started to teach him to read. Mr. Auld soon learned of this and had her stop; otherwise, he asserted, Douglass would be unfit to be a slave.[3]

What happened next is truly remarkable, indicating the depth of the inner strength that Douglass demonstrated. He recounted that Mr. Auld's "words sank deep into my heart" and served as a "special revelation" about the white man's power to enslave a black man. Douglass "set out with high hope, and a fixed purpose, at whatever cost of trouble, to learn how to read." Over the next seven years, Douglass learned to read and to write, using "various stratagems." This included "making friends of all the little white boys" that he met. He converted many of them into teachers. When he was sent on an errand, he finished it quickly and then read the book he had surreptitiously carried with him. He took bread with him and traded it for lessons from the "poor white children." He read books on slavery and emancipation. To learn to write, he copied letters and challenged white boys to contests as to who could write better. When left alone in the house, he used the Auld's son's lesson books, copying what that boy had written.[4] Later in life, Douglass employed, as few have so well, those skills he worked so hard to obtain.

His city life ended for a time in 1832, when Douglass was returned to plantation living on the Eastern Shore and to the meanest of masters, Thomas Auld, the brother of Hugh. Two years of dehumanization of the worst kind passed at Thomas Auld's and other slave drivers' hands. Douglass wrote that he experienced "the bitterest dregs of slavery" during that time.[5] Douglass was assigned to a less brutal master in 1834 and later returned to Baltimore and the Hugh Auld household, where he learned a trade, although he was still a slave. From there, he made his escape in 1838. Douglass recounts in his *Narrative* that he had been frequently asked how it felt to reach a free state. He recalled:

> I have never been able to answer the question with any satisfaction to myself. It was the moment of the highest excitement I ever experienced. I suppose I felt as one may imagine the unarmed mariner to feel when he is rescued by a friendly-man-of war from the pursuit of a pirate. In writing a dear friend, immediately after my arrival in New York, I said I felt like one who had escaped a den of hungry lions.[6]

Douglass briefly stayed in New York and then, with his new wife, moved to New Bedford, Massachusetts. He became involved in the antislavery movement and began to speak at events. His *Narrative* became a bestseller, and he became famous. Over the next five decades, he used his writing and oratorical skills to agitate for freedom. His famous address, delivered on July 5, 1852 (because the Fourth was a Sunday), was in front of the ladies of the Rochester Anti-Slavery Sewing Society. The speech came to be known as "What to the Slave Is the Fourth of July?"[7]

He began his address by stating that the Fourth of July was "the birthday of your National Independence, and of your political freedom." Pointedly, he did not say "our" independence and "our" political freedom. He nonetheless paid tribute to the Declaration of Independence and to the Founders. Regarding the Declaration, he observed that it was the "corner-stone of the national superstructure" and that "the principles contained in that instrument are saving principles. Stand by those principles, be true to them on all occasions, in all places, against all foes, and at whatever cost." As for the Founders, he asserted:

> The signers of the Declaration of Independence were brave men. They were great men too—great enough to give fame to a great age. It does not often happen to a nation to raise, at one time, such a number of truly great men. The point from which I am compelled to view them is not, certainly the most favorable; and yet I cannot contemplate their great deeds with less than admiration. They were statesmen, patriots and heroes, and for the good they did, and the principles they contended for, I will unite with you to honor their memory.

The Founders, Douglass continued, believed "nothing was 'settled' that was not right. With them, justice, liberty and humanity were 'final;' not slavery and oppression."[8]

Turning to the present, Douglass challenged his audience:

> Fellow-citizens, pardon me, allow me to ask, why am I called upon to speak here today? What have I, or those I represent, to do with

> your national independence? Are the great principles of political freedom and of natural justice, embodied in that Declaration of Independence, extended to us? and am I, therefore, called upon to bring our humble offering to the national altar, and to confess the benefits and express devout gratitude for the blessings resulting from your independence to us?
>
> I am not included within the pale of this glorious anniversary! Your high independence only reveals the immeasurable distance between us. The blessings in which you, this day, rejoice, are not enjoyed in common. The rich inheritance of justice, liberty, prosperity and independence, bequeathed by your fathers, is shared by you, not by me. The sunlight that brought life and healing to you, has brought stripes and death to me. This Fourth of July is yours, not mine. You may rejoice, I must mourn. To drag a man in fetters into the grand illuminated temple of liberty, and call upon him to join you in joyous anthems, were inhuman mockery and sacrilegious irony. Do you mean, citizens, to mock me, by asking me to speak today?

Rather than "tumultuous joy" on the Fourth of July, Douglass said he heard

> the mournful wail of millions! whose chains, heavy and grievous yesterday, are, today, rendered more intolerable by the jubilee shouts that reach them. I shall see, this day, and its popular characteristics, from the slave's point of view. Standing, there, identified with the American bondman, making his wrongs mine, I do not hesitate to declare, with all my soul, that the character and conduct of this nation never looked blacker to me than on this 4th of July! Whether we turn to the declarations of the past, or to the professions of the present, the conduct of the nation seems equally hideous and revolting. America is false to the past, false to the present, and solemnly binds herself to be false to the future. Standing with God and the crushed and bleeding slave on this occasion, I will, in the name of humanity which is outraged, in the

> name of liberty which is fettered, in the name of the constitution and the Bible, which are disregarded and trampled upon, dare to call in question and to denounce, with all the emphasis I can command, everything that serves to perpetuate slavery–the great sin and shame of America!

He rejected as insulting the view that he had to argue that a Negro was a man and entitled to liberty. He further rejected any need to establish the immorality of slavery:

> What, am I to argue that it is wrong to make men brutes, to rob them of their liberty, to work them without wages, to keep them ignorant of their relations to their fellow men, to beat them with sticks, to flay their flesh with the lash, to load their limbs with irons, to hunt them with dogs, to sell them at auction, to sunder their families, to knock out their teeth, to burn their flesh, to starve them into obedience and submission to their masters? Must I argue that a system thus marked with blood, and stained with pollution, is wrong? No I will not.

Douglass proclaimed that "convincing argument" was not needed. Instead, he maintained that "it is not light that is needed, but fire; it is not the gentle shower, but thunder." He believed that the "conscience of the nation must be roused" and the "hypocrisy of the nation" exposed, and "its crimes against God and man must be proclaimed and denounced." So he asked: "What, to the American slave, is your 4th of July?" In answer, he observed that it was

> a day that reveals to him, more than all other days in the year, the gross injustice and cruelty to which lie is the constant victim. To him, your celebration is a sham; your boasted liberty, an unholy license; your national greatness, swelling vanity; your sounds of rejoicing are empty and heartless; your denunciations of tyrants, brass fronted impudence; your shouts of liberty and equality, hollow mockery; your prayers and hymns, your sermons and

> thanksgivings, with all your religious parade, and solemnity, are, to him, mere bombast, fraud, deception, impiety, and hypocrisy—a thin veil to cover up crimes which would disgrace a nation of savages. There is not a nation on the earth guilty of practices, more shocking and bloody, than are the people of these United States, at this very hour.

Douglass detailed the horrors of the internal slave trade, into which he was born. For him, it was "a terrible reality. When a child, my soul was often pierced with a sense of its horrors." He had lived at Fell's Point in Baltimore, where he "watched from the wharves, the slave ships in the Basin, anchored from the shore, with their cargoes of human flesh, waiting for favorable winds to waft them down the Chesapeake." He detailed:

> Here you will see men and women, reared like swine, for the market. You know what is a swine-drover? I will show you a man-drover. They inhabit all our Southern States. They perambulate the country, and crowd the highways of the nation, with droves of human stock. You will see one of these human flesh jobbers, armed with pistol, whip and bowie-knife, driving a company of a hundred men, women, and children, from the Potomac to the slave market at New Orleans. These wretched people are to be sold singly, or in lots, to suit purchasers. They are food for the cotton-field, and the deadly sugar-mill. Mark the sad procession, as it moves wearily along, and the inhuman wretch who drives them. Hear his savage yells and his blood-chilling oaths, as he hurries on his affrighted captives! There, see the old man, with locks thinned and gray. Cast one glance, if you please, upon that young mother, whose shoulders are bare to the scorching sun, her briny tears falling on the brow of the babe in her arms. See, too, that girl of thirteen, weeping, yes! weeping, as she thinks of the mother from whom she has been torn! The drove moves tardily. Heat and sorrow have nearly consumed their strength; suddenly you hear a quick snap, like the discharge of a rifle; the fetters clank, and the chain rattles simultaneously; your ears are saluted with a scream, that seems to have torn its way

> to the centre of your soul! The crack you heard, was the sound of the slave-whip; the scream you heard, was from the woman you saw with the babe. Her speed had faltered under the weight of her child and her chains! that gash on her shoulder tells her to move on. Follow this drove to New Orleans. Attend the auction; see men examined like horses; see the forms of women rudely and brutally exposed to the shocking gaze of American slave-buyers. See this drove sold and separated for ever; and never forget the deep, sad sobs that arose from that scattered multitude. Tell me citizens, WHERE, under the sun, you can witness a spectacle more fiendish and shocking. Yet this is but a glance at the American slave-trade, as it exists, at this moment, in the ruling part of the United States.

Douglass criticized the manner in which Christianity was practiced in light of the wickedness of slavery, asserting in detail that the churches (with some exceptions) took the side of the oppressors, teaching that slavery was "ordained of God." This "horrible blasphemy" was "a religion for oppressors, tyrants, man-stealers, and thugs." Looking more broadly, he saw flagrant inconsistency:

> You boast of your love of liberty, your superior civilization, and your pure christianity, while the whole political power of the nation . . . is solemnly pledged to support and perpetuate the enslavement of three millions of your countrymen. . . . You profess to believe "that, of one blood, God made all nations of men to dwell on the face of all the earth," and hath commanded all men, everywhere to love one another; yet you notoriously hate, (and glory in your hatred,) all men whose skins are not colored like your own. You declare, before the world, and are understood by the world to declare, that you "hold these truths to be self evident, that all men are created equal; and are endowed by their Creator with certain, inalienable rights; and that, among these are, life, liberty, and the pursuit of happiness;" and yet, you hold securely, in a bondage, which according to your own Thomas Jefferson, "is worse

> than ages of that which your fathers rose in rebellion to oppose," a seventh part of the inhabitants of your country.

Douglass concluded with an expression of hope because he could see "forces in operation, which must inevitably, work the downfall of slavery." He drew "encouragement from 'the Declaration of Independence,' the great principles it contains, and the genius of American Institutions." His spirit was "cheered by the obvious tendencies of the age," which included the expansion of knowledge, the increased influence of nations on each other, new ideas, and intelligence "penetrating the darkest corners of the globe." He believed the hour would come when the tyranny of slavery would end.

During the Civil War, Douglass was a frequent critic of President Lincoln. Douglass was disappointed in Lincoln's conciliatory approach to the South at the beginning of Lincoln's Administration.[9] In 1862, Douglass still maintained that view, stating at a July Fourth address that year in Himrod, New York, that regardless of Lincoln's intentions, his actions had been "calculated in a marked and decided way to shield and protect slavery."[10] He urged instead: "Recognize the fact, for it is the great fact, and never more palpable than at the present moment, that the only choice left to this nation, is abolition or destruction. You must abolish slavery or abandon the union."[11]

There was an important change in that address. Douglass said: "Our country is now on fire. . . . The claims of our fathers upon our memory, admiration and gratitude, are founded in the fact that they wisely, and bravely, and successfully met the crisis of their day. And if the men of this generation would deserve well of posterity they must like their fathers, discharge the duties and responsibilities of their age." He referred to "the birth of our national Independence."[12] In 1852, it was *your* national independence and of *your* political freedom; in 1862, it was *our* country and *our* fathers, *our* national independence. He added in 1862: "We are only continuing the tremendous struggle, which *your* fathers, and *my* fathers began eighty-six years ago."[13] In that 1862 speech, Douglass detailed the many ways in which he believed that slaves could be freed, including by a presidential proclamation.

In September 1862, President Lincoln issued his preliminary Emancipation Proclamation, declaring that all slaves of rebel owners would be freed as of January 1, 1863. News of that proclamation saw Douglass shout for joy.[14] The final proclamation was issued on January 1, 1863, promoting Douglass to observe that January 1 and July 4 would be the twin birthdays of liberty.[15] Douglass soon forged a personal relationship with Lincoln, meeting with him and providing advice on a range of topics.[16] They first met at the White House in July 1863.[17] At one point, Douglass noted that "Abraham Lincoln may be slow . . . but Abraham Lincoln is not the man to reconsider, retract and contradict words and purposes solemnly proclaimed over his official signature. . . . If he has taught us to confide in nothing else, he has taught us to confide in his word."[18] Eventually, after another meeting, Douglass observed that Lincoln was a "remarkable man" while Lincoln offered that Douglass was "one of the most meritorious men in America."[19]

It took a long, bloody Civil War, with some 750,000 dead, to free African Americans from slavery, which was constitutionally established by the Thirteenth Amendment's ratification in 1865. Douglas knew that the work of obtaining equality had just begun. When the Thirteenth Amendment banning slavery became part of the Constitution, Douglass remarked that unless freed blacks received voting rights, "we should have slavery back again, in spirit if not in form."[20] The next two amendments granted citizenship to all former slaves and gave black men the right to vote.

Frederick Douglass had a long life with many achievements. Among his many activities, Douglass wrote two autobiographies in addition to his *Narrative* and published newspapers both before and after the Civil War; in Rochester, New York, he called his newspaper *The North Star*, which was so named because slaves followed the North Star in the night sky to freedom. During the Civil War, he served as a recruiter of African Americans to serve in the Union Army, including the all-Black 54th Massachusetts Infantry Regiment, where two of his sons served.[21] After the war, he fought for full civil rights for freedmen. Douglass served as secretary of the Santo Domingo Commission, U.S. Marshal in the District of Columbia, and U.S. minister and consul general to the Republic of Haiti.

Just weeks after his famous July 4, 1852 speech, Douglass spoke at the convention of the Western Anti-Slavery Society in Salem, Ohio. In that address, on August 23, 1852, Douglass urged the attendees: "The work is to be done by exposing the damning deeds of Slavery, the abominations of the church, in short by agitation. Agitate, agitate. This is the grand instrumentality, and without this you Free Soilers will come to nothing."[22]

Less than a month before his death in 1895, when a young Black man asked him what advice Douglass would give to him just starting out in the world, Douglass replied: "Agitate! Agitate! Agitate!"[23] His life was a testament to his own advice.

CHAPTER 6

Two Important Union Victories: Contrasting Words of Dissent and Affirmation

Two critical Civil War campaigns came to an end on July 4, 1863. One was a long Union campaign in the Mississippi Valley to capture Vicksburg. The other, a gamble by the Confederates to invade the North, ended at Gettysburg. Both were decisive Union victories, signaling to those who had vision, the promise of an ultimate Northern triumph, however distant. On the same date, the governor of New York was attacking Lincoln administration policies as violations of fundamental rights, calling the war a failure, and saying that promises of victory were hollow, all adding fuel to the draft riots in New York City a few days later. Lincoln, in contrast, captured the importance of the moment in contemporaneous statements and in his famous address at Gettysburg later that fall.

By July 1863, the American Civil War had been raging for more than two years, with almost two more to go before the South succumbed. In the east, Union armies had made little headway, except for the capture of some coastal areas. In the west, the trend was better for the Union. Large portions of Tennessee, Louisiana, and Arkansas had been lost by the Confederacy, and most of the Mississippi River was under Union control. The Confederacy was shrinking in the west but one fundamental link remained across the Mississippi River to Texas, Arkansas, and Louisiana—Vicksburg. Confederate President Jefferson Davis viewed Vicksburg as the "nailhead that holds the South's two halves together." President Abraham Lincoln remarked that "Vicksburg is the key" to victory and that "the war can never be brought to a close until that key is in our pocket."

Vicksburg, Mississippi, is located on a bend of the Mississippi River and sits on a high bluff from which Confederate guns controlled the river. The northern approach to the city featured extensive, almost impassable swampy areas, bordered by the high ground controlled by the Confederates. The dry ground was to the south of the city. By the fall of 1862, only Richmond, the Confederate capital, was more fortified.[1]

Union General Ulysses S. Grant was given the responsibility[2] to take Vicksburg, and the campaign took much effort, with numerous failed attempts to secure a viable approach to the city.[3] It began in late 1862 with a plan to assault Vicksburg from the north, with General William Tecumseh Sherman leading one prong, sent by boats, and Grant another, to proceed by land. Grant's supply base at Holly Springs was captured, forcing him to return to Memphis and canceling his thrust toward Vicksburg. Sherman, unaware of this, was repulsed at Chickasaw Bluffs on December 29, 1862, suffering disproportionate losses. Grant then began a series of fruitless efforts to circumvent Vicksburg to launch an attack from the south. A canal was dug in an attempt to divert the Mississippi around Vicksburg; another was dug to Lake Providence, seeking to reach the Red River, which enters the Mississippi south of Vicksburg. A levee was breached at Yahoo Pass, some three hundred miles north of Vicksburg, in an attempt to gain access to a series of interconnected rivers, ending at the Yahoo River, north of Vicksburg. Yet another effort sought to reach the upper Yahoo River through Steele's Bayou. All of these projects failed and it was a "miserable time for Grant," who was widely criticized in the press and scoffed at as "stuck in the mud of northern Mississippi."[4]

Finally, in April 1863, Grant developed a plan in solitude—viewed at the time as highly risky by Sherman and Rear Admiral David Dixon Porter, who commanded the Mississippi Squadron of gunboats—to attack Vicksburg from the south.[5] Sherman said that he had less confidence in the plan "than any similar undertaking of the war, but it [was] his duty to cooperate with zeal."[6] The plan depended on naval cooperation, and, despite his misgivings, Porter also gave Grant his full support. On the night of April 16, Porter ran seven ironclads, a wooden gunboat, one tug, three transports, and nineteen barges past the Confederate batteries at Vicksburg.[7] One by one, the boats floated silently downstream. Grant observed the events from the shore, cigar in his mouth. For an hour and a half, the Rebel batteries discharged 525 times, but registered only sixty-eight hits. One steamer went down in flames and another transport was slightly damaged.[8] Only fourteen men were wounded. On April 22, packed with vital supplies, six more steamers and twelve barges were sent past Vicksburg's batteries. Grant counted five hundred shots as he watched.[9] Several were sunk, but Grant then had the naval force he needed to cross the river downstream.[10]

Once the boats cleared Vicksburg, Grant marched his army on the Louisiana side of the river through very difficult conditions. Water was everywhere, with bayous and heavy rain along with mud and muck. The next part of Grant's "unorthodox strategy" has been hailed as brilliant and historic.[11] It had many interlocking parts and required deception and diversionary tactics to disperse the Rebel forces to defeat them piecemeal.

To reach the eastern shore, Grant's troops had to be transported by boat past the Rebel batteries at Grand Junction. After reaching the eastern shore of the Mississippi, Grant later wrote in his memoirs that he "felt a degree of relief scarcely ever equaled since." Although Vicksburg had not been taken nor its defenders demoralized, he observed that the army was finally "on dry ground on the same side of the river with the enemy. All of the campaigns, labors, hardships and exposures from the month of December previous to this time that had been made and endured, were for the accomplishment of this one object."[12]

Grant's army drove north—not to Vicksburg but toward Jackson, the capital of Mississippi. Grant had no base to fall back on, having cut the army loose from its communications. In a striking series of battles, Union victories at Port Gibson, Raymond, Jackson, Champion's Hill, and Big Black River ultimately forced the Confederates to withdraw into Vicksburg. So quick was the Union Army's entrance into Jackson that Grant and Sherman walked into a factory where the "looms were still at work weaving tent-cloth marked 'C.S.A.' and their presence hardly noticed until Grant suggested that the work might stop, as he wished to set fire to the factory."[13] Overall, the "swiftness and unexpectedness of the Union movements had dislocated the mental balance of the Confederate command."[14] Military theorist and historian B.H. Liddell Hart characterized Grant's "high risk" plan for its "very audacity," perplexing and paralyzing the Confederate forces.[15] Another military historian, Christopher R. Gabel, has written of the campaign on the eastern shore of the Mississippi:

> The artful manner in which Grant identified objectives, weighed options, and structured effective courses of action continues to instruct officers today. Perhaps the greatest lesson to be gleaned from such a study is the way in which Grant adapted to developments, swiftly altering his plans to accommodate the contingencies of war and exploit the weaknesses of his adversaries. For Grant there was no boundary between "plan" and "execute," and he rarely allowed his plans to drive his actions when circumstances in the field called for other solutions.[16]

The Confederates at Vicksburg, commanded by Lieutenant General John Pemberton, were surrounded. Grant attempted two assaults on the city in the next few days but then settled into a forty-six-day siege. "On 28 June, Pemberton received a mysterious letter signed 'Many Soldiers' stating that the army had reached the limits of endurance. 'If you can't feed us, you had better surrender us.' Pemberton knew that a general Union assault was coming, and he feared that his army was incapable of mounting a defense."[17]

At 10 a.m. on July 3, white flags appeared on a portion of the Confederate works. Firing ceased, and two rebel officers crossed the Union lines bearing a white flag and carrying a letter to Grant from Pemberton. Rejecting Pemberton's written proposal that commissioners be appointed to discuss terms of surrender, Grant replied that the surrender must be unconditional. He nonetheless agreed to meet between the lines at three in the afternoon. The conference did not yield a surrender, but Grant agreed to submit his final terms by ten o'clock that evening. That night, Grant relented somewhat and agreed to parole the rebels, meaning that they were to be freed based on each man's written promise not to return to the fight. The horse officers were allowed a sidearm, clothing, and a horse. After Pemberton sought somewhat more lenient terms, Grant rejected them and threatened a full assault. Pemberton reluctantly accepted Grant's terms the next day, July 4,[18] surrendering his 31,600-man army.[19] Grant later wrote:

> I have no doubt that Pemberton commenced his correspondence on the 3d for the twofold purpose; first, to avoid an assault, which he knew would be successful, and second, to prevent the capture taking place on the great national holiday, the anniversary of the Declaration of American Independence. Holding out for better terms, as he did, he defeated his aim in the latter particular. At the 4th, at the appointed hour, the garrison of Vicksburg marched out of their works, and formed line in front, stacked arms, and marched back in good order. Our whole army present witnessed this scene without cheering.[20]

Sherman, learning of the negotiations, wired Grant, saying: "If you are in Vicksburg. Glory, hallelujah! the best fourth of July since 1776."[21]

Union control of the entire length of the Mississippi became complete with the capture of Port Hudson five days later. The South had been split in two. With the fall of Vicksburg, Lincoln said, "The Father of Waters again goes unvexed to the sea."[22] Grant later recalled:

> During the siege there had been a good deal of friendly sparring between the soldiers of the two armies, on picket and where the lines were close together. All rebels were known as "Johnnies"; all Union troops as "Yanks." Often "Johnny" would call, "Well, Yank, when are you coming into town?" The reply was sometimes: "We propose to celebrate the 4th of July there." Sometimes it would be: "We always treat our prisoners with kindness and do not want to hurt them"; or, "We are holding you as prisoners of war while you are feeding yourselves." The garrison, from the commanding general down, undoubtedly expected an assault on the 4th. They knew

> from the temper of their men it would be successful when made, and that would be a greater humiliation than to surrender. Besides it would be attended with severe loss to them.
>
> The Vicksburg paper, which we received regularly through the courtesy of the rebel pickets, said prior to the 4th, in speaking of the "Yankee" boast that they would take dinner in Vicksburg that day, that the best recipe for cooking rabbit was, "First ketch your rabbit." The paper at this time, and for some time previous, was printed on the plain side of wall paper. The last was issued on the 4th and announced that we had "caught our rabbit."[23]

The importance of the victory cannot be overstated. Liddell Hart called it "the great turning point of the war" due to the Confederacy's loss of hope of regaining access to the men, food, and supplies from the states west of the Mississippi.[24] The South had lost an entire army of thirty thousand men, sixty thousand small arms, and 260 cannon; Confederate military operations had been severed in two; and the South's internal transportation system was seriously crippled. In contrast, the North had gained complete control of the Mississippi, allowing it to move troops and Union trade from the Midwest. An entire arena of conflict had been substantially shut down, allowing the Union to increasingly focus its military strength toward the Confederate center of power in the east.[25] Grant, in his memoirs, succinctly stated: "The fate of the Confederacy was sealed when Vicksburg fell. Much hard fighting was to be done afterward and many precious lives were to be sacrificed but the morale was with the supporters of the Union ever after."[26]

In the east, Confederate General Robert E. Lee's army began an invasion of the North, with plans to strike southern Pennsylvania, perhaps including Harrisburg and Philadelphia, with the hope that it would force Grant to move to help defend Washington, thus breaking the Vicksburg siege. By mid-June, the Confederates were across the Potomac, being pursued by the Army of the Potomac under General Joseph Hooker. On June 28, Hooker was replaced by General George G. Meade. The Union army was unsure of Lee's destination, and Lee did not know where the Union Army was, due to the absence of his cavalry force under General

Jeb Stuart, who was too far ahead of the advancing Rebel forces to maintain contact.

On July 1, the opposing armies began to concentrate at Gettysburg, and for three days, the greatest battle on American soil was fought. It was a close contest, with numerous instances when the final result might have been different. The names of the locations where combat occurred within the battlefield are more famous than the individual *battles* fought during the Vicksburg campaign: Culp's Hill, Cemetery Hill, Big Round Top, Little Round Top, Devil's Den, the Wheat Field, and the Peach Orchard. The final and deciding episode, on July 3, was the ill-considered frontal assault of federal lines on Cemetery Ridge, known as Pickett's Charge. General George E. Pickett was one of three Confederate generals who led their commands, totaling 12,500 men, across about a mile of open ground. General James Longstreet urged Lee not to order the assault: "It is my opinion that no fifteen thousand men ever arrayed for battle can take that position."

William Faulkner, in his 1948 novel *Intruder In The Dust*, wrote about the portent that afternoon held for the Southern cause, the moment before the Confederate attack:

> For every Southern boy fourteen years old, not once but whenever he wants it, there is the instant when it's still not yet two o'clock on that July afternoon in 1863, the brigades are in position behind the rail fence, the guns are laid and ready in the woods and the furled flags are already loosened to break out and Pickett himself with his long oiled ringlets and his hat in one hand probably and his sword in the other looking up the hill waiting for Longstreet to give the word and it's all in the balance, it hasn't happened yet, it hasn't even begun yet, it not only hasn't begun yet but there is still time for it not to begin against that position and those circumstances.

But it did. The Union artillery swept the field as the Rebels marched in line; the final yards saw volley after volley mowing down Rebel soldiers. One Union officer recalled that a "moan went up from the field" as the Rebel lines were "enveloped in a dense cloud of dust."[27] Some elements of the Rebel ranks reached the ridge in a place called the Angle, now called the high water mark of the Confederacy. Close quarter combat ensued but then the Confederate advance turned into a retreat. Watching the survivors return, Lee acknowledged that it had been his fault for ordering the charge despite strong advice otherwise. When Lee told Pickett to rally his division to defend against a possible Union counter-attack, Pickett allegedly replied, "General, I have no division."

After three days, the Confederates had suffered twenty-eight thousand casualties compared to the Union's twenty-three thousand. A combined total of seven thousand died, and forty-four thousand were wounded at Gettysburg. Lee had lost almost a third of his army. Throughout most of the Fourth of July, the armies watched each other. A Union lieutenant observed that it was a "somber and terrible national anniversary, with indescribable horrors of the field, as yet hardly mitigated by the work of mercy, before the eye in every direction. The army did not know the extent of the victory; the nation did not realize as yet what had been done."[28] A tremendous rainstorm marked the evening as Lee began his retreat to Virginia. A seventeen-mile wagon train of wounded Confederates snaked ahead of him. Left behind were the dead and dying, along with more than twenty-two thousand wounded (in a town of only about two thousand). "A fearful odor of decay lay over the field."[29] The multitude of tasks for the living was overwhelming: burying the thousands of dead, caring for the wounded, and collecting "an immense harvest of weapons," including thirty-seven thousand muskets, many of them still loaded.[30]

Lincoln announced victory at Gettysburg by telegram on the morning of July 4, which was sent throughout the North.[31] The secretary of the navy, Gideon Welles, received a dispatch from Admiral Porter that same day, informing him of the surrender at Vicksburg. Welles immediately went to see the president and informed him of the news. Welles wrote in his diary that Lincoln beamed with joy. "[H]e caught my hand, and, throwing his arm around me, exclaimed: 'What can we do for the Secretary of the Navy for this glorious intelligence? He is always giving us good news. I cannot, in words, tell you my joy over this result. It is great, Mr. Welles, it is great!'" This, Lincoln said, "will inspire me."[32]

Celebrations occurred throughout the North.[33] In Washington, Welles recounted in his diary that there was "a degree of enthusiasm not excelled during the war." A band played and speeches were made. Welles wrote: "The rejoicing in regard to Vicksburg is immense. Admiral Porter's brief dispatch to me was promptly transmitted over the whole country, and led, everywhere, to spontaneous gatherings, firing of guns, ringing of bells, and general gratification and gladness. The price of gold, to use the perverted method of speech, fell ten or fifteen cents and the whole country is joyous."[34]

In Washington, before a large crowd on July 7, Lincoln offered remarks on the importance of the date:

> I do most sincerely thank Almighty God for the occasion on which you have called. How long ago is it—eighty odd years—since on the Fourth of July for the first time in the history of the world a nation by its representatives, assembled and declared as a self-evident truth that "all men are created equal." That was the birthday of the United States of America. Since then the Fourth of July has had several peculiar recognitions. The two most distinguished men in the framing and support of the Declaration were Thomas Jefferson and John Adams—the one having penned it and the other sustained it the most forcibly in debate—the only two of the fifty-five who sustained it being elected President of the United States. Precisely fifty years after they put their hands to the paper it pleased Almighty God to take both from the stage of action. This was indeed an extraordinary and remarkable event in our history. Another President [James Monroe], five years after, was called from this stage of existence on the same day and month of the year; and now, on this last Fourth of July just passed, when we have a gigantic Rebellion, at the bottom of which is an effort to overthrow the principle that all men are created equal, we have the surrender of a most powerful position and army on that very day, and not only so, but in a succession of battles in Pennsylvania, near to us, through three days, so rapidly fought that they might be called one great battle on the 1st, 2d, and 3d of the month of July; and on the 4th

> the cohorts of those who opposed the declaration that all men are created equal, "turned tail" and ran.[35]

The celebrations continued in Washington that night and throughout the next day. Vicksburg would not celebrate the Fourth of July again for eighty-one years.

Horatio Seymour, a Peace Democrat, was governor of New York on July 4, 1863. During the war, he was a severe critic of Lincoln's leadership. On that day, in an incendiary speech, he attacked the administration for violating Americans' basic rights. Perhaps he did not know of the events in Mississippi and Pennsylvania when he spoke. Seymour said that he did not expect victories but saw those contests as "carrying down to bloody graves so many of our fellow-countrymen, so many of our friends." He asserted that the administration was "hostile to our rights and liberties," and that it was "trampling" our rights. Bordering on sedition in the views of many at the time, Seymour continued:

> Is it not revolution which you are thus creating when you say that our persons may be rightfully seized, our property confiscated, our homes entered? Are you not exposing yourselves, your own interests, to as great a peril as that with which you threaten us? Remember this, that the bloody, and treasonable, and revolutionary doctrine of public necessity can be proclaimed by a mob as well as by a government.

Seymour maintained that the war was between two small parties composed of fanatics and that they had brought the country "to the very brink of national ruin." He concluded that the Republicans should "ask yourselves whether, in giving way to your passions and to your prejudices, you will not endanger your own safety and your own homes?"[36]

The Draft Act of 1863 required all men between the ages of twenty and forty-five to register and, if drafted, serve for three years. Individuals who had been drafted could avoid military service by paying another to fight in his stead or by paying $300 as a "commutation fee." Hence, it was perceived as a rich man's bill. On July 11, the names of the first draftees were drawn in New York City. The next day, those names appeared in the newspapers, along with long lists of casualties at Gettysburg.[37]

With the draft drawings due to resume on Monday, July 13, thousands of people mobbed the Draft Office at Third Avenue and Forty-Seventh Street. When one of the building's windows was broken, the crowd surged into the building, smashed the election wheel, and set the building on fire. Later, the mobs began to loot, rob, and attack the offices of pro-war newspapers such as the *New York Times* and the *New York Tribune*. Horrifically, some of the rioters burned the Colored Orphan Asylum and assaulted and lynched local African Americans. Hundreds were injured and 105 killed.[38]

Governor Seymour, who opposed federal conscription as a violation of states' rights, spoke outside of City Hall to the rioters on July 14. Addressing the rioters as "my friends," he said he had sent his "Adjutant-General to Washington to confer with the authorities there, and to have this draft suspended and stopped."[39] The speech was widely viewed as tantamount to treason: "The serious matter was his intimation that the draft justified the riot, and that if the rioters would cease from their violence the draft should be stopped."[40] Gideon Welles, the secretary of the navy, wrote in his diary that he believed that Seymour "encouraged" the rioters and was chiefly responsible for the "outrage."[41] That belief was shared by many others. Union troops, fresh from the battle at Gettysburg, were sent to the city to restore order and the riots ended on July 16. The draft was not suspended.

In comparison, President Lincoln, on July 15, the day after Seymour's calling the rioters friends, issued a proclamation of Thanksgiving. The two victories, Lincoln stated,

> furnish reasonable grounds for augmented confidence that the Union of these States will be maintained, their constitution preserved, and their peace and prosperity permanently restored. But these victories have been accorded not without sacrifices of life, limb, health and liberty incurred by brave, loyal and patriotic citizens. Domestic affliction in every part of the country follows in the train of these fearful bereavements.

The contrast could not have been more stark. Lincoln asked the citizens to observe "a day for National Thanksgiving, Praise and Prayer" on August 6, and he invited

> the People of the United States to assemble on that occasion in their customary places of worship, and in the forms approved by their own consciences, render the homage due to the Divine Majesty, for the wonderful things he has done in the Nation's behalf, and invoke the influence of His Holy Spirit to subdue the anger, which has produced, and so long sustained a needless and cruel rebellion, to change the hearts of the insurgents, to guide the counsels of the Government with wisdom adequate to so great a national emergency, and to visit with tender care and consolation throughout the length and breadth of our land all those who, through the vicissitudes of marches, voyages, battles and sieges, have been brought to suffer in mind, body or estate, and finally to lead the whole nation, through the paths of repentance and submission to the Divine Will, back to the perfect enjoyment of Union and fraternal peace.[42]

The cemetery at Gettysburg was dedicated on November 19, 1863. More than nine thousand people attended. The story is a familiar one: Lincoln was asked to come as an afterthought. The featured speaker, Edward Everett, was a renowned orator and spoke for almost two hours. Lincoln, who had been asked to say a "few appropriate remarks," rose and spoke 269 words—the now-famous Gettysburg Address. Its power was not apparent to the assembled crowd, although contemporary accounts differ; however, Lincoln was disappointed by his performance.[43] The next day, however, Everett wrote to Lincoln that he wished he "could flatter myself that I came as near the central idea of the occasion, in two hours, as you did in two minutes."[44] Once again recalling the Declaration of Independence, and this time perfecting his vision of its meaning, Lincoln in full stated:

> Four score and seven years ago our fathers brought forth on this continent, a new nation, conceived in Liberty, and dedicated to the

> proposition that all men are created equal. Now we are engaged in a great civil war, testing whether that nation, or any nation so conceived and so dedicated, can long endure. We are met on a great battle-field of that war. We have come to dedicate a portion of that field, as a final resting place for those who here gave their lives that that nation might live. It is altogether fitting and proper that we should do this.
>
> But, in a larger sense, we can not dedicate – we can not consecrate – we can not hallow – this ground. The brave men, living and dead, who struggled here, have consecrated it, far above our poor power to add or detract. The world will little note, nor long remember what we say here, but it can never forget what they did here. It is for us the living, rather, to be dedicated here to the unfinished work which they who fought here have thus far so nobly advanced. It is rather for us to be here dedicated to the great task remaining before us – that from these honored dead we take increased devotion to that cause for which they gave the last full measure of devotion – that we here highly resolve that these dead shall not have died in vain – that this nation, under God, shall have a new birth of freedom – and that government of the people, by the people, for the people, shall not perish from the earth.

Vicksburg and Gettysburg represented the turning of the tide, but much suffering lay ahead. The cost of the war in lives: between 620,000 and 750,000 soldiers dead and an unknown number of civilian deaths. Three million slaves were freed. Seymour became the Democratic Party nominee for president in the 1868 presidential election. He lost the election to Grant, the Republican Party nominee; the electoral count was 214–80.

CHAPTER 7

The Centennial and Suffrage

The year 1876 marked the Centennial of the Declaration of Independence. Leading up to that year, Congress authorized funds for a grand celebration in Philadelphia, the birthplace of the Declaration and the site of the first celebrations. The planning evolved into the first World's Fair in the United States, which was held from May 10 to November 10, 1876. Nearly ten million visitors attended the exposition (out of a population of forty-six million in the United States), and numerous countries participated in it. It was a large undertaking, with more than two hundred buildings constructed for the fair and numerous exhibits, including the right arm and torch of the soon-to-be-assembled Statue of Liberty, bicycles, cannons, agricultural devices, and mining equipment, befitting the official title of the fair, the International Exhibition of Arts, Manufactures, and Products of the Soil and Mine.[1] Other attractions included inventions such as the telephone, typewriter, sewing machine, Heinz Ketchup, and Hires Root Beer.[2]

July 4, 1876, was the obvious cornerstone for the celebrations, and numerous officials and other notables were invited to attend the events for that date. As one contemporary account enthused:

> That Philadelphia is the Mecca of every patriotic American heart which turns as surely as the needle to the pole to the birth-place of American Independence, even a century after it was declared, the unparalleled influx of visitors into the city on the days preceding July 3d and 4th of this Centennial year was a striking proof. It was estimated that not less than 150,000 strangers swelled the population of the city from July 1st to 4th inclusive, and the

> hospitality of Philadelphia was put to a severe test, but was worthy of the Centennial event.[3]

July 3, in "trying heat," featured a parade by five thousand veterans of the Grand Army of the Republic, the old Civil War soldiers, with "tattered old battle-flags." The crowds "packed the sidewalks in one dense mass," giving "vent to their enthusiasm in hearty cheers" and "tearful eyes."[4] Events continued throughout the day, including a midnight torchlight parade watched by at least three hundred thousand spectators. Along the route, houses and stores were decorated with "flags, transparencies and illuminations." Drums beat, trumpets sounded, rockets and guns were fired. At midnight, when the procession reached Independence Hall, a new Liberty Bell was presented by a patriotic citizen, which rang out "the same tones which 100 years ago proclaimed liberty throughout the land."[5]

The next day, Independence Day, brought forth crowds from early in the day. A large military parade began the festivities. The main events of the day were at Independence Square, and they began at 10 a.m. Independence Square, then as it does today, adjoins Independence Hall, the site where the Continental Congress agreed to the Declaration of Independence. "There were probably 50,000 people on that historic ground; even the trees were filled with men and boys who were determined to see what was going on." But only those with tickets could be inside the reserved area for the events. Inside that area were reserved seats facing a wooden platform. "The platform sloped gently down toward the front so that at the rail, where the speaker's stand occupied the centre, it was only a few feet from the ground. Seats for 4,000 were provided upon it for invited guests, and it is needless to say that every one was filled."[6]

Dignitaries and distinguished guests present on the platform included General Joseph R. Hawley, president of the Centennial Commission; Generals William Tecumseh Sherman and Phil Sheridan; Senator and President Pro Tempore Thomas W. Ferry of Michigan, who represented President Grant; and many governors and foreign dignitaries, including Dora Pedro, emperor of Brazil. The official summary recalled that the ceremonies consisted of orations, odes, hymns, and songs.

But that does not tell the whole story.

The women's suffrage movement began to take shape at a convention held in Seneca Falls, New York, in 1848; the convention is now known as the Seneca Falls Convention. The convention produced a document, the Declaration of Sentiments, also known as the Declaration of Rights and Sentiments, signed by some of the three hundred attendees. The principal author of the Declaration was Elizabeth Cady Stanton, who modeled it upon the Declaration of Independence. The document stated in part:

> We hold these truths to be self-evident: that all men and women are created equal; that they are endowed by their Creator with certain inalienable rights; that among these are life, liberty, and the pursuit of happiness; that to secure these rights governments are instituted, deriving their just powers powers from the consent of the governed. . . . The history of mankind is a history of repeated injuries and usurpation on the part of man toward woman, having in direct object the establishment of an absolute tyranny over her. To prove this, let facts be submitted to a candid world.

The Declaration of Sentiments contained a list of those injuries and usurpations, including denial of the right to vote, submission to laws in which she has no voice, denial of a separate legal existence upon marriage, and denial to a married woman of "all right in property, even to the wages she earns. . . . In the covenant of marriage, she is compelled to promise obedience to her husband, he becoming, to all intents and purposes, her master, the law giving him power to deprive her of her liberty, and to administer chastisement." Man has fashioned the laws of divorce and guardianship of children to favor him, and he "has monopolized nearly all the profitable employments, and from those she is permitted to follow, she receives but a scanty remuneration." He has denied access to colleges to obtain an education, allowed her only a subordinate position in the church and state, and created a different code of morals for men and women.[7]

Leading up to the Civil War and through its course, the abolitionist and woman suffrage movements were more or less closely aligned. For example, Frederick Douglass, a close friend of Elizabeth Cady Stanton and Susan B. Anthony, had supported the women's cause since the Seneca Falls Convention in 1848.[8] The two women were crucial advocates of women's rights: they "dominated news coverage, interacted with powerful men, chose the movement's strategies, and crafted the arguments with which the women's cause became identified."[9] Stanton and Anthony, during the war, thought that black freedom would force the country to also address women's rights at the same time.[10] At the conclusion of the war, however, cracks set in, and the two movements diverged, with substantial fractures within the women's movement.[11] The fundamental reason for the divergence and fractures was based on a premise articulated by Wendell Phillips, a long-time influential abolitionist and ally of women's suffrage. He proclaimed that it was "the Negro's Hour"—meaning black men—and that women would have to wait.[12] That phrase capsulized the split that would persist throughout the Reconstruction Era as the country debated amendments to the Constitution, and variations of that phrase were repeated by many to justify deferring rights to women.[13] Meeting with Stanton and Anthony in New York in 1866, Phillips opined that women's suffrage had no chance in that generation, but that black men's suffrage could be achieved. He urged them to help in that effort. Stanton later called the meeting "very demoralizing."[14]

The Thirteenth Amendment, adopted in 1865, abolished slavery and was supported by the women's movement. But the next two caused deep divisions. The Fourteenth Amendment, adopted in 1868, gave citizenship to the former slaves in Section 1 and promised all citizens the "privileges and immunities" of the United States, along with equal protection and due process rights. What proved controversial was Section 2, which introduced the word "male" into the Constitution. That section provided that if any state "denied to any of the male inhabitants of such State" the right to vote for those twenty-one years of age or older, then the representation of that state would be reduced. The Fifteenth Amendment, adopted in 1870, established that the right "to vote shall not be denied or abridged . . . on account of race, color, or previous condition of servitude." Missing from that list was the word "sex," which would have established the right of women to vote.

Illustrative of the split were speeches by some of the important figures of the era. In May 1867, Sojourner Truth addressed a convention of the American Equal Rights Association, responding to the view that black men must first be given the vote.[15] Truth, describing herself as one of the few black female speakers in the country, observed: "I come from another field—the country of the slave." Noting that slavery had only been partly destroyed, she declared:

> I want it root and branch destroyed. Then we will all be free indeed. I feel that if I have to answer for the deeds done in my body just as much as a man, I have a right to have just as much as a man. There is a great stir about colored men getting their rights, but not a word about the colored women; and if colored men get their rights, and not colored women theirs, you see the colored men will be masters over the women, and it will be just as bad as it was before. So I am for keeping the thing going while things are stirring; because if we wait till it is still, it will take a great while to get it going again. . . .
>
> I want women to have their rights. In the courts women have no right, no voice; nobody speaks for them. I wish woman to have her voice there among the pettifoggers. If it is not a fit place for women, it is unfit for men to be there. I am above eighty years old; it is about time for me to be going. I have been forty years a slave and forty years free, and would be here forty years more to have equal rights for all. I suppose I am kept here because something remains for me to do; break the chain. I have done a great deal of work; as much as a man, but did not get so much pay. I used to work in the field and bind grain, keeping up with the cradler; but men doing no more, got twice as much pay. . . . We do as much, we eat as much, we want as much. I suppose I am about the only colored woman that goes about to speak for the rights of the colored women. I want to keep the thing stirring, now that the ice is cracked.[16]

Two years later, at another American Equal Rights Association convention, Frederick Douglass spoke:

> I must say that I do not see how any one can pretend that there is the same urgency in giving the ballot to woman as to the Negro. With us, the matter is a question of life and death, at least, in fifteen States of the Union. When women, because they are women, are hunted down through the cities of New York and New Orleans; when they are dragged from their houses and hung upon lampposts; when their children are torn from their arms, and their brains dashed out upon the pavement; when they are objects of insult and outrage at every turn; when they are in danger of having their homes burnt down over their heads; when their children are not allowed to enter schools; then they will have an urgency to obtain the ballot equal to our own.
>
> **A Voice:** Is that not all true about black women?
>
> **Mr. DOUGLASS:** Yes, yes, yes; it is true of the black woman, but not because she is a woman, but because she is black. Howe at the conclusion of her great speech delivered at the convention in Boston last year, said: "I am willing that the Negro shall get the ballot before me." Woman! why, she has 10,000 modes of grappling with her difficulties. I believe that all the virtue of the world can take care of all the evil. I believe that all the intelligence can take care of all the ignorance. I am in favor of woman's suffrage in order that we shall have all the virtue and vice confronted.[17]

There were also voices in the middle. Shortly after Douglass spoke, Lucy Stone had her turn. Stone, from Massachusetts, was an early and important advocate for black and women's rights and later acknowledged in other forums that "women must wait for the Negro."[18] Nonetheless, at the 1867 convention, she replied to previous speakers:

> Mrs. Stanton will, of course, advocate the precedence for her sex, and Mr. Douglass will strive for the first position for his, and both are perhaps right. If it be true that the government derives its

> authority from the consent of the governed, we are safe in trusting that principle to the uttermost. . . . The gentleman who addressed you claimed that the Negroes had the first right to the suffrage, and drew a picture which only his great word-power can do. . . . But woman suffrage is more imperative than his own; and I want to remind the audience that when he says what the Ku-Kluxes did all over the South, the Ku-Kluxes here in the North in the shape of men, take away the children from the mother, and separate them as completely as if done on the block of the auctioneer. Over in New Jersey they have a law which says that any father—he might be the most brutal man that ever existed—any father, it says, whether he be under age or not, may by his last will and testament dispose of the custody of his child, born or to be born, and that such disposition shall be good against all persons, and that the mother may not recover her child; and that law modified in form exists over every State in the Union except in Kansas. Woman has an ocean of wrongs too deep for any plummet, and the Negro, too, has an ocean of wrongs that can not be fathomed. There are two great oceans; in the one is the black man, and in the other is the woman. But I thank God for that [Fifteenth] Amendment, and hope that it will be adopted in every State.
>
> I will be thankful in my soul if anybody can get out of the terrible pit. But I believe that the safety of the government would be more promoted by the admission of woman as an element of restoration and harmony than the Negro. I believe that the influence of woman will save the country before every other power.[19]

Anthony and Stanton, "ever on the watch-tower for legislation affecting women," had been at the forefront of the attempts to secure rights for women as the amendments were being drafted and debated, sounding the alarm that the amendments would disenfranchise "citizens on the ground of sex."[20] The struggle to exclude the word "male" in the Fourteenth Amendment and then the attempt to include "sex" in the list of attributes for which the franchise could not be restricted in the Fifteenth Amendment both failed. The advocates for black male rights had succeeded. Susan B. Anthony, at a Senate Judiciary Hearing in January 1872, summarized the situation:

> When the [Fourteenth] Amendment was first proposed in Congress, we rushed to you with petitions, praying you not to insert the word "male" in the second clause. Our best woman-suffrage men, on the floor of Congress, said to us the insertion of the word there puts up no new barrier against woman; therefore do not embarrass us, but wait until the Negro question is settled. So the [Fourteenth] Amendment, with the word "male," was adopted. Then, when the [Fifteenth] Amendment was presented without the word "sex," we again petitioned and protested, and again our friends declared to us that the absence of that word was no hindrance to us, and again they begged us to wait until they had finished the work of the war. "After we have freed the Negro, and given him a vote, we will take up your case." But have they done as they promised?[21]

Since the obvious answer was "no," another forum was sought. Numerous women in the early 1870s sought to vote and did so, arguing that the Fourteenth Amendment's Privileges and Immunities Clause protected that right.[22] One of those women, Anthony, voted in the federal election on November 5, 1872; she was then indicted for voting without right to do so. The trial made national headlines, generating publicity for the issue.[23] The *History of Woman's Suffrage*, in a passage likely written by Anthony herself, not surprisingly had little good to say about the presiding judge:

> On the bench sat Judge Hunt, a small-brained, pale-faced, prim looking man, enveloped in a faultless suit of black broadcloth, and a snowy white necktie. This was the first criminal case he had been called on to try since his appointment, and with remarkable forethought, he had penned his decision before hearing it.[24]

After it was established that Anthony did, in fact, vote, the judge instructed the jury to return a verdict of guilty. (This was a blatant violation of her fundamental right to a jury trial, protected by the Constitution.) The judge stated to that all-white male jury:

> The question, gentlemen of the jury . . . is wholly a question or questions of law, and I have decided as a question of law, in the first place, that under the XIV Amendment, which Miss Anthony claims protects her, she was not protected in a right to vote. And I have decided also that her belief and the advice which she took do not protect her in the act which she committed. If I am right in this, the result must be a verdict on your part of guilty, and I therefore direct that you find a verdict of guilty.[25]

Speaking after the verdict, Anthony said to the judge that, by ordering the verdict of guilty, he had

> trampled underfoot every vital principle of our government. My natural rights, my civil rights, my political rights, are all alike ignored. Robbed of the fundamental privilege of citizenship, I am degraded from the status of a citizen to that of a subject; and not only myself individually, but all of my sex, are, by your honor's verdict, doomed to political subjection under this so-called Republican government.

The judge repeatedly interrupted her, directing her to stop talking. But she persisted for some time: "Your denial of my citizen's right to vote is the denial of my right of consent as one of the governed, the denial of my right of representation as one of the taxed, the denial of my right to a trial by a jury of my peers as an offender against law, therefore, the denial of my sacred rights to life, liberty, property." After again being admonished to be quiet, Anthony added that, even if the case had been decided by the jury, they were not her peers:

> for not one of those men was my peer; but, native or foreign, white or black, rich or poor, educated or ignorant, awake or asleep, sober or drunk, each and every man of them was my political superior; hence, in no sense, my peer. Even, under such circumstances, a

> commoner of England, tried before a jury of lords, would have far less cause to complain than should I, a woman, tried before a jury of men. . . . Precisely as no disfranchised person is entitled to sit upon a jury, and no woman is entitled to the franchise, so, none but a regularly admitted lawyer is allowed to practice in the courts, and no woman can gain admission to the bar—hence, jury, judge, counsel, must all be of the superior class.

After the judge asserted that she had been "tried according to the established forms of law," Anthony responded that the trial had been "by forms of law all made by men, interpreted by men, administered by men, in favor of men, and against women."[26] The court fined her one hundred dollars, which was never paid. (Two years later, as detailed in Chapter Four, the Supreme Court in the *Minor* case held that the Privileges and Immunities Clause of the Constitution did not include a woman's right to vote.)

Amid the failures and frustrations surrounding the efforts to be included in the post-Civil War Constitutional amendments, Susan B. Anthony, Stanton, and others formed the National Woman Suffrage Association (NWSA) in 1869. In early 1876, the NWSA decided to protest at the upcoming Centennial in Philadelphia. In May 1876, Matilda Gage, chair of the executive committee of the NWSA, went to Philadelphia to secure a location for their Centennial headquarters. She located rooms, terms were agreed upon, and a lease was drafted. But Gage had negotiated with a married woman, and that woman could not complete the transaction because, under Pennsylvania law at the time, a husband's signature on the lease was required.[27] The woman's husband denied his consent and tore up the lease. Alternative quarters were ultimately obtained, but only Susan B. Anthony, who was unmarried, could legally sign the lease; she alone assumed responsibility for the rooms.[28] Thereafter, the NWSA widely distributed an open letter announcing the Fourth of July protest, indicating that it would issue a "declaration of rights for women" on that date.[29]

Anthony, on behalf of the NWSA, requested of General Hawley fifty seats at the Independence Day celebrations. Hawley replied that "'only officials were invited'—that his own wife had no place—that merely representatives and officers of the government had seats assigned to them."[30] Undaunted, Anthony obtained a reporter's ticket, representing her brother's newspaper at the event. Four other NWSA members also obtained tickets.[31] Stanton, as president of the association, wrote General Hawley, requesting the opportunity to present the protest and bill of rights at the close of the reading of the Declaration of Independence. She did not ask to read the NWSA declaration but simply to present it to him so it "may become an historical part of the proceedings." Hawley again refused, although he acknowledged it seemed "a very slight request," maintaining that the program had been published and arrangements for the day were already set.[32] Senator Ferry, representing President Grant at the ceremonies, refused a similar request.

"Though refused by their own countrymen a place and part in the Centennial celebration, the women who had taken this presentation in hand were not to be conquered."[33] The five women with tickets resolved to present the document at the conclusion of the reading of the Declaration of Independence. On the Fourth of July, the five made their way to their seats. The ceremonies commenced. A poet read his specially composed "National Ode" to the assembly. Richard Henry Lee of Virginia (whose grandfather had made the motion for separation from Great Britain one hundred years earlier in the Continental Congress) then read the original Declaration of Independence aloud. At that point, the five women, headed by Anthony, walked onto the platform and handed *their* Declaration to Senator Ferry. "Mr. Ferry's face paled, as bowing low, with no word, he received the declaration, which thus became part of the day's proceedings; the ladies turned, scattering printed copies, as they deliberately walked down the platform." Men asked for copies as General Hawley called out: "Order, order!"[34]

The women then walked to the front of Independence Hall, where Susan B. Anthony read the Women's Declaration aloud. Afterwards she invited everyone to the NWSA convention at the nearby Unitarian Church. At the convention, Stanton read the document to the audience. One participant, deeply moved by the reading, wrote: "Thrill after thrill went through my veins, and the whole scene formed a picture that will yet be the subject of artists' pencils and poets' pens."[35] Stanton, in a letter a few days later, reflected back to the Seneca Falls convention:

> Could we have foreseen, when we called that convention, the ridicule, persecution, and misrepresentation that the demand for woman's political, religious and social equality would involve; the long weary years of waiting and hoping without success; I fear we should not have had the courage and conscience to begin such a protracted struggle, nor the faith and hope to continue the work.[36]

The Declaration of Rights of Women, by the NWSA in 1876, was not the same Declaration of Sentiments from the Seneca convention. The 1876 Declaration, in part, asserted:

> Our faith is firm and unwavering in the broad principles of human rights proclaimed in 1776, not only as abstract truths, but as the corner stones of a republic. Yet we cannot forget, even in this glad hour, that while all men of every race, and clime, and condition, have been invested with the full rights of citizenship under our hospitable flag, all women still suffer the degradation of disenfranchisement.
>
> The history of our country the past hundred years has been a series of assumptions and usurpations of power over woman, in direct opposition to the principles of just government, acknowledged by the United States as its foundation, which are:
>
> *First* – The natural rights of each individual.
> *Second* – The equality of these rights.
> *Third* – That rights not delegated are retained by the individual.
> *Fourth* – That no person can exercise the rights of others without delegated authority.
> *Fifth* – That the non-use of rights does not destroy them.

The Declaration was accompanied by "articles of impeachment" of the male rulers. The charges supporting impeachment included denying women the right to vote, denying married women rights against their husbands, denying the right of a jury of their peers because women could not sit on juries, taxing women without representation, and subjecting women to different codes of conduct, legal rules, and morals than were men.

It would be forty-four more years before women gained the right to vote. Over the course of that time, the movement engaged in a "pause-less" effort, including 480 campaigns to persuade state legislatures to insert suffrage into state constitutions, forty-seven campaigns to obtain state constitutional conventions, 277 campaigns at state party conventions, thirty at presidential party conventions, and nineteen consecutive campaigns directed at Congress.[37] The amendment that ultimately came to be the Nineteenth Amendment was drafted by Susan B. Anthony in 1875.[38] It was introduced in the Senate in 1878, but that proposal sat in a committee until 1887, when it was rejected by the full Senate in a 16–34 vote. Several more attempts to pass the amendment failed in subsequent years, including five different attempts in Congress in 1918 and 1919. The successful suffrage amendment finally passed the House of Representatives on May 21, 1919, followed by the Senate on June 4, 1919. It was then submitted to the states for ratification. After obtaining the requisite thirty-six states, the Nineteenth Amendment's adoption was certified on August 26, 1920,[39] that year being the one-hundredth anniversary of the birth of Susan B. Anthony.

Susan B. Anthony did not live to see it, having died in 1906. She had dedicated her life to the effort:

> She not only helped create the first women's movement in this country, she led it, brilliantly, for more than fifty years. Indeed, it was her tireless dedication to the Cause—the drive for the most crucial political right of all, the vote—and her astounding skill at organization that not only changed laws and attitudes, but also helped introduce the entire realm of equal rights to a very reluctant nation.[40]

The right to vote, Anthony maintained throughout her life, was the necessary precondition to any progress for women to obtain their rights. Everything a woman has, she insisted, "is on an insecure basis till woman holds in her own hand the ballot—that little piece of paper which can make or unmake laws and legislators, which compels respectful consideration from the representatives."[41] She explained in an 1888 speech:

> What is this little thing we are asking for? It seems so little; it is yet everything. . . . What does your right to vote in this country, men and brethren, say to you? What does that right say to every possible man, native and foreign, black and white, rich and poor, educated and ignorant, drunk and sober, to every possible man outside of State prison, the idiot and the lunatic asylums? What does it everywhere under the shadow of the American flag say to every man? It says, "Your judgment is sound, your opinion is worthy to be counted." That is it. And now, on the other hand, what does it say to every possible woman, native and foreign, black and white, rich and poor, educated and ignorant, virtuous and vicious, to every possible woman under the shadow of our flag? It says, "Your judgment is not sound, your opinion is not worthy to be counted."[42]

Anthony knew that not every evil would be eliminated by possession of the franchise, but she maintained that it would put women "in a position to say what remedies shall be adopted."[43] Toward the end of her life, Anthony remained confident that suffrage would be achieved but that she would not live to see it.[44] Some years earlier, Anthony had created her own epitaph, remarking at a family reunion: "When it is a funeral, remember that I want there should be no tears. Pass on, and go on with the work."[45]

In her last public address, just days before her death, Anthony urged on the members of the women's convention of 1906 to carry on and, "with such women consecrating their lives, failure is impossible."[46]

James Otis

Samuel Adams

Franklin, John Adams, and Jefferson drafting the Declaration of Independence

Signing of the Declaration of Independence: Trumbull version

George Washington

Celebrating the first Fourth

Henry David Thoreau

Frederick Douglass in 1864

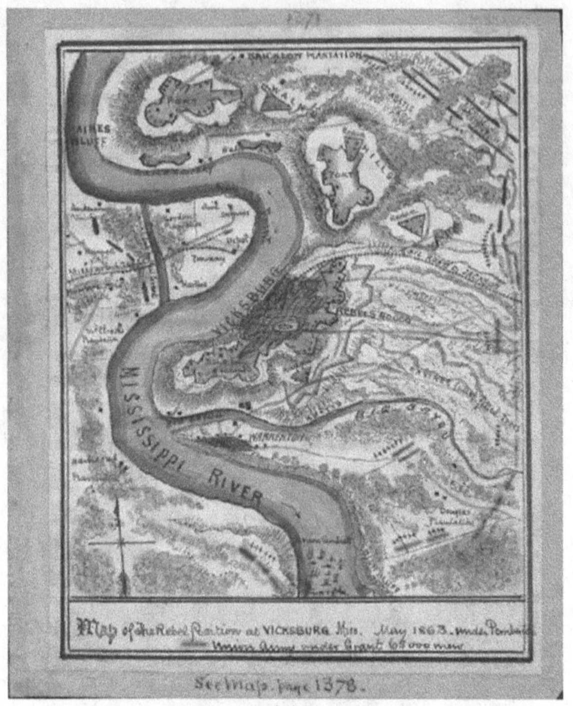

Map of Vicksburg

Generals Grant and Pemberton at Vicksburg

Ulysses S. Grant at Cold Harbor

Abraham Lincoln by Matthew Brady

Governor Seymour Cartoon

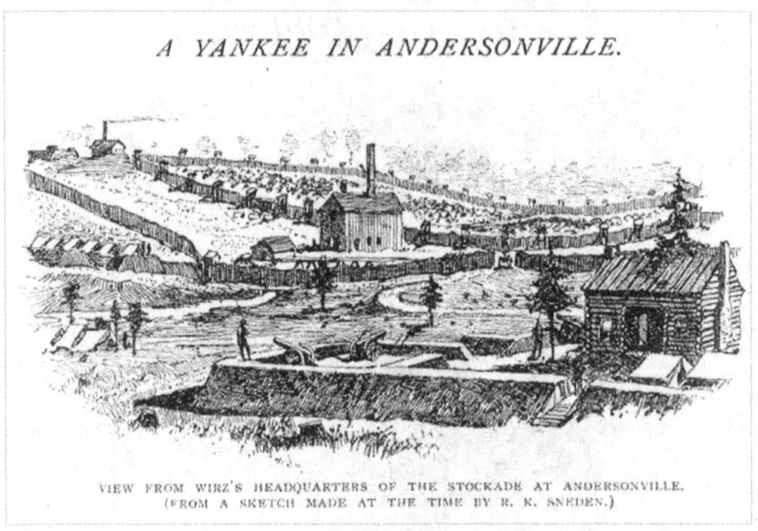

Sneden Sketch of Andersonville

Banner held by suffragette

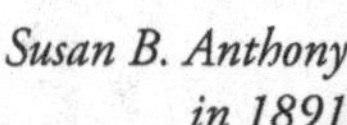

Susan B. Anthony in 1891

Lee reading the Declaration at the Centennial

Theodore Roosevelt

Lou Gehrig

President Roxas taking his oath of office

1976 protest poster

TRADITIONAL FOURTH OF JULY CELEBRATIONS

Copyright

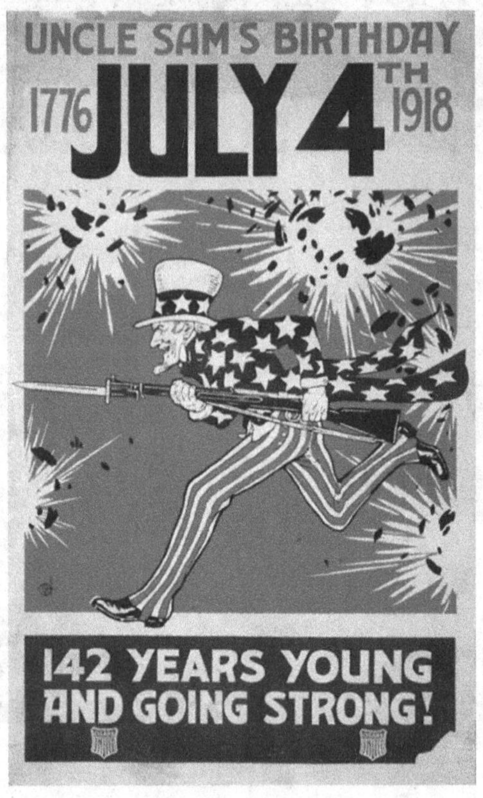
UNCLE SAM'S BIRTHDAY
1776 JULY 4TH 1918
142 YEARS YOUNG
AND GOING STRONG!

WITH CARTOON SUPPLEMENT: ALTON BROOKS PARKER.
PRICE TEN CENTS.
Puck
July 4th 1904

HMS Jersey

CHAPTER 8

Island Expansions: A Mixed Legacy

The United States, having continuously expanded across the North American continent since its earliest days, saw the official close of the last frontier in 1890. Although there were anti-imperialists, the predominant sentiment of the country remained expansive in nature. This was also an era of aggressive colonial expansion by European powers, such as Great Britain, France, and late-comer Germany. So too was Japan in East Asia. In 1898, the United States occupied five island groups, primarily as a consequence of the Spanish-American war. Ultimately, each had a different fate. Hawaii eventually became a state, Cuba's independence was recognized before the invasion occurred, Guam became and remains a U.S. territory, Puerto Rico eventually became a commonwealth, and the Philippines, after a long occupation as a territory, became independent.

American settlers overthrew the Hawaiian monarchy in 1893 and sought annexation. The Cleveland Administration refused, and the Republic of Hawaii, declared on July 4, 1894, was instead recognized. On July 7, 1898, after William McKinley became president, Hawaii was annexed, in part as a base to project power into the Pacific and in part to forestall a possible Japanese annexation.[1] McKinley said at the time: "We need Hawaii just as much and a good deal more than we did California."[2] Hawaii eventually became a state on July 4, 1960. For Hawaii, the Fourth of July date was intentionally chosen at least twice to mark the change in status. As the United States expanded to other islands, the Fourth of July date was sometimes consciously chosen to signify an important milestone, but the date was also significant for events that coincided with that day.

By the last decade of the nineteenth century, the Spanish Empire neared its final stages of collapse. The nation that had ruled large portions of the new world, initiated by Christopher Columbus's bold venture in 1492, was a shadow of its former self, as was its empire. Still, it possessed the Philippines, Cuba, Puerto Rico, Guam, and a few other overseas possessions. Cuba had been ruled by the Spanish since 1511. By the latter half of the nineteenth century, the Cubans had arisen numerous times in revolt, and by the mid-1890s, conditions produced another revolt.[3] Spanish attempts at suppressing that rebellion were brutal.[4] Complex negotiations regarding Cuba between the United States and Spain during the McKinley Administration failed to produce an agreement. Spain was willing to make large concessions to avoid war but refused the American demand requiring Spanish withdrawal from Cuba and recognition of the island's independence. Other events, including the destruction of the battleship USS *Maine* in Havana Harbor on February 15, 1898, with the death of 262 on board, moved the countries toward war. After the United States recognized Cuban independence on April 19, 1898, Spain broke off diplomatic relations and Congress then declared war.

Historians differ on how much influence various individuals had on the decision of the United States to go to war and the motivation for that decision. Characterizations of the reasons—and the relative weight assigned to them—included imperialism, outrage regarding the Spanish actions, sympathy for the oppressed Cubans, protection of Americans in Cuba, and protection of approaches to the proposed Central American canal and other American interests in the area. A naval strategist who had significant influence on others, Captain Alfred Thayer Mahan, argued that future national security and greatness depended upon a large navy supported by bases throughout the world. He asserted that "Americans must now begin to look outward" based on the growth of the country and "public sentiment." He wrote that the position of the United States "between the two Old Worlds and the two great oceans" supported that claim, which was going to be strengthened by the creation of a canal joining the Atlantic and Pacific, along with the "growth of the European colonies in the Pacific, by the advancing civilization of Japan, and by the rapid peopling of our Pacific."[5]

Among those influenced were Theodore Roosevelt and Senator Henry Cabot Lodge, who were early and loud voices for intervention in Cuba.[6] Roosevelt was serving as assistant secretary of the navy in 1897 and was an ardent convert to Mahan's theories on the importance of naval power. He played a leading role in preparing the navy for war, including putting the navy on a war footing before hostilities commenced.[7] Senator Lodge was a leading voice in favor of expansion; three years before the war, in a speech on the Senate floor, Lodge called for the United States to possess Hawaii, Cuba, Puerto Rico, and a canal across the Panamanian isthmus.[8] Those three men—Mahan, Roosevelt, and Lodge—knew the purpose of naval forces: "projecting power into the world for purposes of trade and wealth and national prestige around the globe."[9]

Cuban patriots in New York and Miami used those locations as staging areas for the insurrection. They spread stories of Spanish atrocities, raised funds, outfitted ships with supplies, and otherwise used them as bases to oppose the Spanish authorities in Cuba. They found invaluable assistance from two New York newspapers, William Randolph Hearst's *New York Journal* and Joseph Pulitzer's *New York World*.[10] Hearst, in particular, published sensational (and often fictional) accounts of barbaric Spanish actions in Cuba. He sent artist Frederic Remington to Cuba to report on the situation; when Remington observed that there was no trouble in Cuba and he wished to return, Hearst famously responded: "Please remain. You furnish the pictures and I'll furnish the war."[11] The Spanish, in fact, were waging a cruel war, as were the rebels. The Spanish systematically emptied whole towns, "reconcentrating" the inhabitants to "squalid makeshift camps," where 10% of the population died of hunger and disease.[12]

William McKinley was elected president in 1896. Some writers view him as not much more than an observer of events regarding the war with Spain, with others, such as Hearst and Roosevelt, the central characters, if not the ultimate decision-makers. In contrast, Robert W. Merry, in his biography of McKinley, portrays McKinley as a central moving force. Merry says this of McKinley: "He was cautious, methodical, a master of incrementalism. Such traits contributed to the McKinley mystery. He never moved in a straight line, seldom declared where he wanted to take the country, somehow moved people and events in the shadows."[13] After his election, McKinley sought to avoid war with Spain, but he sympathized with the rebels. Merry details how McKinley's administration engaged in extensive negotiations with Spain to resolve the Cuban situation and conducted a detailed naval inquiry to investigate the cause of the *Maine* disaster despite sensational claims of Spanish culpability and calls for revenge. Only after concluding that Spain was unwilling to accept Cuban independence did he move toward war. The decision was admittedly influenced by a fevered atmosphere in Washington and in the country, enhanced by the naval commission report that the *Maine* had been destroyed by an external explosive. (The validity of that conclusion has been questioned by subsequent inquiries.) Nonetheless, Merry maintains that McKinley neither sought the war nor was he dragged unwillingly into it; instead, he took measured steps that he understood would render war "increasingly inevitable."[14]

The war was short; it was described by John Hay, who had been Abraham Lincoln's secretary and later secretary of state under McKinley, as a "splendid little war."[15] That was, of course, the American point of view. The Spanish view certainly differed, given that the country lost Cuba, Puerto Rico, Guam, and the Philippines in the war, along with thousands of soldiers and sailors.

Although Cuba was the cause of the war, Spain was the enemy, and the United States believed that the Spanish fleet in the Philippines and the city of Manila were necessary targets.[16] The United States Navy, on May 1, 1898, destroyed a Spanish fleet in Manila Bay. The sea battle was one-sided. The American force, under Commodore George Dewey, destroyed the Spanish fleet in seven hours, with only eight wounded Americans.[17] The rest of the war also did not go well for Spain. An invasion force was assembled at Tampa, Florida, which included the Rough Riders, with Theodore Roosevelt second-in-command as a lieutenant colonel. (He had resigned his position as assistant secretary of the navy and, with Colonel Leonard Wood, formed the volunteer army unit known as the Rough Riders.) The U.S. Army preparations for the invasion of Cuba were characterized by inefficient organization and poor planning. Finally, on June 14, 1898, under the command of Major General William Shafter, a force of seventeen thousand men in thirty-two transports steamed south toward Cuba.[18] Unopposed landings began on June 22. There were several battles and skirmishes in the following days, including Roosevelt's famous charge leading the Rough Riders up San Juan Hill (although it was actually nearby Kettle Hill). On July 3, an American naval force destroyed an obsolete Spanish fleet under the command of Admiral Pascual Cervera in Santiago Bay. The next day, Rear Admiral William Sampson sent his famous message: "The Fleet under my command offers the nation as a Fourth of July present, the whole of Cervera's Fleet." Thereafter, a large Spanish land force surrendered at Santiago on July 17, ending the fighting in Cuba. Meanwhile, Puerto Rico and Guam were taken with virtually no fighting. On August 13, Manila fell to the Americans.

On July 26, Spain made peace overtures, and on August 12, the United States and Spain signed a preliminary peace treaty in Washington, D.C. Negotiators met in Paris to draw up a definitive agreement. Spain recognized the independence of Cuba[19] and ceded Puerto Rico and Guam[20] to the United States. The Spanish sold the Philippines to the United States for twenty million dollars. The Treaty of Paris was signed on December 10, 1898, and came into effect on April 11, 1899, when the documents of ratification were exchanged.

Puerto Rico has had a few notable dates since the end of the Spanish-American War that coincided with the Fourth of July. July Fourth is a holiday, celebrated as Independence Day, given that Puerto Rico remains a part of the United States. It became a territory as a result of the treaty with Spain,[21] and, after temporary military governing measures, its governmental structure has been largely determined by acts of Congress. "In the ensuing hundred-plus years, the United States and Puerto Rico have forged a unique political relationship, built on the island's evolution into a constitutional democracy exercising local self-rule."[22] Over time, Congress put in place incremental measures of autonomy.[23] The most significant changes began on July 3, 1950, when Congress enacted Public Law 600, "in the nature of a compact" with Puerto Rico and subject to approval by the voters of Puerto Rico. It was signed by President Harry S. Truman that same day. Puerto Rico accepted the compact, and on July 3, 1952, Congress approved, with minor amendments, a constitution drafted and adopted by the Puerto Rican people. Pursuant to that constitution, Puerto Rico became a commonwealth (called a Free Associated State in Spanish). "The Commonwealth's power, the [Puerto Rico] Constitution proclaims, 'emanates from the people and shall be exercised in accordance with their will, within the terms of the compact agreed upon between the people of Puerto Rico and the United States.'"[24] Under the compact, the federal government relinquished its control over Puerto Rico's local affairs, granting it "a measure of autonomy comparable to that possessed by the States."[25] "Puerto Rico, like a State, is an autonomous political entity, sovereign over matters not ruled by the [federal] Constitution."[26]

On July 3, 1952, Truman signed the constitution giving Puerto Rico self-rule. Thus, July 4, 1952, was the first full day for Puerto Rico to be a commonwealth. In Truman's proclamation, he remarked that the

> people of the United States and the people of Puerto Rico are about to enter into a relationship based on mutual consent and esteem. The Constitution of the Commonwealth of Puerto Rico and the procedures by which it has come into being are matters of which every American can be justly proud. They are in accordance with principles we proclaim as the right of free peoples everywhere.

Puerto Rico's relationship with the United States has always been subject to significant debate and occasional violence.[27] The legal status controversy still remains as to whether Puerto Rico should remain a commonwealth, become a state, or become an independent country. Since the United States occupied it, there have been votes on the question but no definitive resolution.

Filipinos were engaged in a rebellion against Spain when the Spanish-American War began. The insurgency's leader, Emilio Aguinaldo, who had been exiled, was brought to the Philippines by the Americans. Dewey met with him on May 19 and formed an informal alliance.[28] Aguinaldo's junta proclaimed that the Americans were not there "from mercenary motives" but were "our redeemers."[29] Aguinaldo declared independence, asserting: "Under the protection of the Powerful and Humanitarian Nation, the United States of America, we do hereby proclaim and declare solemnly in the name by authority of the people of the Philippine Islands, that they are and have the right to be free and independent."[30] Despite Aguinaldo's urging, Dewey did not recognize that independence. Nor did the United States government.

The rebels successfully attacked Spanish positions and soon surrounded Manila. The American Navy controlled the bay. After negotiations with the Americans and a token resistance to save honor, the Spanish governor-general surrendered Manila to the Americans on August 13, excluding the rebels.[31] Aguinaldo sought joint occupation of the city, which the Americans refused, even as the Filipino rebel forces continued to surround the city. A standoff began, with the United States occupying Manila, surrounded by insurgents.

Meanwhile, only after Dewey destroyed the Spanish fleet at Manila did the United States begin to consider what to do with the Philippines. Within the army, there was a difference of opinion over what the mission was and how to accomplish it. Major General Wesley Merritt, the army's second-highest-ranking officer, saw the goal as subduing the entire archipelago, and he argued for a large number of well-trained regular troops. General Nelson Miles, the commanding officer of the Army, merely sought to garrison the harbor at Manila so that Dewey's fleet could be relieved. McKinley, in a letter, ambiguously asserted that the mission was to control the bay, but also to become "an arm of occupation to the Philippines for the twofold purpose of completing the reduction of Spanish power in that quarter and of giving order and security to the islands while in the possession of the United States."[32]

As late as September 1898, McKinley still did not know what he wanted to do with the Philippines or at least did not articulate his goals.[33] He believed that the islands could not be returned to Spain because it was unfit to rule.[34] McKinley consulted with military officials who offered several considerations: it would be difficult to hold Manila as a naval base without holding the entire island of Luzon, and that would be difficult without holding nearby islands if other powers took possession of them; the islands had thirty separate and antagonistic ethnic groups; the Spanish had largely ignored development of the islands; natives had had no place in the Spanish colonial government, which was characterized by arbitrary decision making; the rebel leadership was unprepared to lead the country and a power vacuum would emerge; and the United States would benefit by exploiting natural resources if the country could be stabilized and infrastructure upgraded.[35] McKinley finally decided that the United States had to take all of the Philippines and bought the archipelago from a reluctant Spain. In effect, the Filipinos had exchanged one occupier for another.

On December 21, McKinley declared sovereignty over the country and directed that military authority be extended over the whole of the Philippines. He maintained that the United States came as "friends" and were there to protect Filipinos.[36] After a months-long standoff at Manila, conflict arose on February 4, 1899, and a new war began, sometimes called the Philippines Insurrection or the American-Philippines War. The war flared for several years, at first featuring large Filipino forces arrayed against American forces, which were typically smaller in number but with vastly better weapons and training. Over time, and with the defeat and the shattering of the larger Filipino units, the conflict evolved, with the insurgents fading into the mountains and jungles and engaging in smaller-scale assaults on isolated American positions.[37] Weather and sickness caused many American casualties. Both sides resorted to atrocities.[38] Americans learned "water cure,"[39] which was the predecessor of the waterboarding of the twenty-first-century War on Terror. As time moved forward, the United States extended its reach throughout the archipelago. In March 1901, Aguinaldo was captured. He was brought to Manila, and, on April 19, 1901, "he took the oath of allegiance to the American government and called upon his followers to lay down their arms."[40] Nonetheless, some resistance continued, along with massacres and reprisals.

Meanwhile, President McKinley began efforts to improve the lives of Filipinos while defending his decision to exercise sovereignty over the country. He maintained in a speech in Boston on February 15, 1899, that the United States had no real choice, given that the archipelago would have been left in anarchy or carved up by other international powers. He maintained that the welfare of the Filipinos "is our aim."[41] McKinley appointed a commission to investigate and to make recommendations. The commission recommended a transitional approach to governance, moving from military occupation to civilian governance as conditions permitted in various sections of the country.[42] Thereafter, a second commission, headed by William Howard Taft, was given civil power over the country. Taft became governor-general on July 4, 1901,[43] and the office of military governor was terminated on July 4, 1902.[44] As conditions improved in sections of the country, civilian control superseded military control. Starting with smaller governmental units, the native population began filling governmental positions. (In 1914, more than one in four governmental positions were held by mainlanders; by 1921, it was less than one in twenty.[45]) Some saw the policy as arrogant and patronizing, but McKinley believed a methodical approach merely reflected the realities of the situation.[46] Taft saw his tenure in the Philippines as "the most gratifying period in his long public career."[47] (This was from the only man to serve as president and later as Chief Justice of the Supreme Court.).

Taft engaged in a policy of reconciliation and took many steps to reach out to the Filipinos, including gestures to show social equality.[48] Taft willingly embraced native culture, learning the national dance, called the rigodon, and the Spanish language. The commission engaged in public works construction—schools, roads, hospitals, public buildings—and improved health care and sanitation, to mention some of its work. It revised legal and tax codes.[49] The commission held open hearings and traveled throughout the islands. In the election of 1900, Roosevelt became McKinley's vice president and succeeded him when McKinley died of his wounds on September 14, 1901, after being shot by an anarchist. Following the surrender of the last of the major rebel leaders in April 1902,[50] Roosevelt issued a proclamation on July 4, 1902,[51] asserting that the insurrection had ended (with the exception of the Moros in the southern islands where a persistent insurgency continued for some time[52]) and granting amnesty to all prisoners.

Taft's goal in life had been to serve on the Supreme Court, and he even turned down Roosevelt's proffered nomination to continue his work in the Philippines.[53] Shortly thereafter, based on Roosevelt's urgent request, he returned to the United States to serve as secretary of war.[54] In 1907, Taft spoke at the first Philippine Assembly, which was the popularly elected branch of the government and the first freely elected parliament in Asia.[55] In his address, Taft acknowledged that the United States had made serious missteps but pointed to many advancements, such as the hundreds of thousands of children in school, new infrastructure, and formation of a civil service. He concluded by congratulating the assembly "upon the auspicious beginning of your legislative life."[56]

The United States began a slow embrace of eventual Philippine independence. For example, on July 4, 1904, Jacob G. Shurman, president of Cornell University, said in a speech that the Philippine people were ready for independence and that the retention of the islands was "abnormal and jarring to our principles."[57] By the end of his term, Roosevelt "came to believe that the United States could not sustain long-term imperialism because of its ideals of self-government and its party system."

President Taft, on July 4, 1910, said that the time would arrive when the Filipinos were ready for their own government and, at that time, the United States would withdraw or offer to do so, fulfilling the Declaration of Independence promise of a just government resting on the consent of the governed.[58] In 1916, Congress passed the Jones Law, which stated that the eventual independence of the Philippines was American policy, subject to the establishment of a stable government. The act created an elected senate, thus making the Philippine legislature a fully elected body. In 1934, Congress passed the Tydings–McDuffie Act, officially named the Philippine Independence Act, which established the process for the Philippines to become independent after a ten-year transitional period. Under the act, the 1935 Constitution of the Philippines was written and the Commonwealth of the Philippines established with a directly elected president. Thus, in 1935, the executive, national assembly, and a supreme court were entirely composed of Filipinos.

The Japanese invaded the Philippines in 1941, gaining full control of the islands by May 1942. The occupation continued for three years until the surrender of Japan, and the commonwealth government went into exile from 1942 to 1945. That occupation was shockingly brutal.

The Americans, under the command of General Douglas MacArthur, returned to the Philippines to expel the Japanese, who typically fought to the last man, causing extensive destruction and loss of life. The street-to-street contest in Manila resulted in devastation only exceeded in Berlin, and with brutality second to none, with an estimated one hundred thousand deaths in the city alone.[59]

After the war, the Americans and the reinstalled commonwealth government quickly moved to fulfill the promise of independence, fixing July 4, 1946, as the date. On that day, President Harry S. Truman issued Proclamation 2695,[60] officially recognizing the independence of the Philippines. As Truman stated at the time, it was "the first instance in history where a colony of a sovereign nation has been voluntarily given independence."[61] On that day, jubilant ceremonies in Manila were attended by three hundred thousand, and to "deafening applause," the American flag was lowered and the Philippine flag raised.[62] "Bands played 'The Star-Spangled Banner' and the 'Marcha Nacional,' the Philippine anthem. A warship fired a twenty-one gun salute, church bells pealed, sirens screamed and speakers tried to outshout the din."[63] The president of the Philippines, Manuel Roxas, took the oath of office and spoke:

> An historic drama has just been unfolded before our eyes. The American flag has been lowered from the flagstaffs in this land . . . not in defeat, not in surrender, not by compulsion, but by the voluntary act of the sovereign American Nation. The flag which was first raised in conquest here has been hauled down with even greater glory. The Stars and Stripes will no longer fly over this land; but in the hearts of 18,000,000 Filipinos and in the eyes of many millions more in this part of the world, the American flag flies more triumphantly today than ever before in history. Some hundreds of yards from here at Fort San Antonio Abad, the American flag was first planted in 1898. As its brave colors fluttered down from the flagstaff a moment ago, the cycle of history had completed a full turn. In the culmination today, America justified her destiny. For America, today's act of renunciation was the climax of triumph . . .

> for enlightenment, for democratic values, for liberty. We mark here today the forward thrust of the frontiers of freedom.
>
> I have raised the Philippine flag to wave henceforth alone and unshadowed over the entire Philippines. American sovereignty has been withdrawn. It has been transferred and is now possessed in full measure by the Filipino people.
>
> We have thus reached the summit of the mighty mountain of independence toward which we and our fathers have striven during the lifetime of our people.
>
> Long before the coming of America to the Philippines, our aspirations for nationhood had been influenced by thoughts and doctrines originating in the United States. The philosophers of our several revolutions were inspired by the Declaration of Independence, the Virginia Bill of Rights, and the Federal Constitution. Our patriots of those early days demanded the rights of free speech and of free press and of self-government. We well recall those who died here on the altar of religious freedom. When the first Philippine Republic was proclaimed, its constitution provided for a representative democracy. The Philippine Declaration of Independence borrowed even the language of the great American charter of liberty.
>
> When American troops landed on these shores in 1898, they found in full cry the yearning for freedom. American control had to be spread by force of arms throughout the Islands. But the conquerors spoke strange words into Filipino ears. They said that America had come not to exploit but to teach, not to tyrannize but to lead, not to own but to liberate. To our great surprise and to the wonder of the entire world this promise was kept. The benevolent stewardship was discharged with scrupulous regard. The successive spokesmen America sent here reiterated and emphasized the intentions of the United States to educate the Filipinos for freedom.[64]

It was a day to be gracious, and Roxas's address was well crafted to suit that purpose. He also pointed to the monumental rebuilding tasks ahead, thanking the United States for its continued support. General MacArthur also spoke, saying that the occasion foretold "the end of mastery over peoples by force alone—the end of empire as the political chain that binds the unwilling weak to the unyielding strong."[65] He added that the United States had promised the Philippines independence, and it was redeeming that pledge.[66] Thereafter, July Fourth was observed in the Philippines as Independence Day until 1962. In 1964, the name of the July 4 holiday was changed to Republic Day. United States involvement in and with the Philippines did not end on July 4, 1946, but that complex relationship has continued between two independent countries.

As was observed some time ago, "both Americans and Filipinos implicitly [have] understood that, however, lopsided, thorny and at times frustrating their 'special relationship' might be, it reflected a century of shared experience."[67]

PART III

Pursuing Happiness

The Declaration of Independence asserts that all men have an inalienable right to the "pursuit of happiness." Historians and legal scholars have long debated whether or not Jefferson's words had some specialized meaning. For example, Garry Wills wrote that the phrase, although it appears vague and indefinable, "acquires a rich background of specificity" as a "scientific concept for measuring the distributable quanta of public happiness," as a "moral concept," as a "political concept making for predictable laws of human behavior," and as a "sentimental basis for social life."[1] Others have different theories.[2] However, one distinguished historian has disputed the need for such quests, asserting that nothing in particular should be attributed to that phrase, stating that, for "anyone who bothers to look," references to "happiness as a political goal are everywhere in American political writings" of the era and earlier European writings.[3]

Jefferson apparently borrowed the phrase from George Mason's authorship of the Virginia Declaration of Rights, which was itself grounded in a history of the use of similar phrases, all of which had no specialized meaning.[4] Indeed, late in life, Jefferson maintained that, in writing that Declaration, "whether I had gathered my ideas from reading or reflection I do not know. I know only that I turned to neither book nor pamphlet while writing it. I did not consider it as any part of my charge to invent new ideas altogether and to offer no sentiment which had ever been expressed before."[5] The following chapters join in that view and have opted to set forth some of the myriad ways in which Americans *have* pursued happiness on the Fourth of July. Those pursuits have been in ways large and small, peculiar to the individual, and national in scope. Some have been quiet, others loud celebrations.

CHAPTER 9

Henry David Thoreau: A Personal Independence

On July 4, 1845, Henry David Thoreau began his two-year, two-month stay at his not-yet-completed cabin at Walden Pond in Concord, Massachusetts.[1] It was only a mile and a half walk from the village where he grew up. Thoreau would turn twenty-eight later that month.

Thoreau remains a major source of inspiration as a writer, naturalist, and philosopher. His writings have had important influences on political reformers such as Mahatma Gandhi and Martin Luther King, Jr., naturalists such as John Burroughs and John Muir, environmentalists, and countless other readers of his works. Poet Robert Frost wrote of Thoreau's *Walden*: "In one book (*Walden*) he surpasses everything we have had in America."[2] "Events that seem to be completely unrelated to his stay at Walden Pond have been influenced by it, including the national park system, the British labor movement, the creation of India, the civil rights movement, the hippie revolution, the environmental movement, and the wilderness movement. Today, Thoreau's words are quoted with feeling by liberals, socialists, anarchists, libertarians, and conservatives alike."[3]

Although Thoreau modestly stated in *Walden* that the date of his occupancy was accidental,[4] one can view that claim with some skepticism. Elsewhere in the book, he emphasized how deliberate he was:

> I went to the woods because I wished to live deliberately, to front only the essential facts of life, and see if I could not learn what it had to teach, and not, when I came to die, discover that I had not

> lived. I did not wish to live what was not life, living is so dear; nor did I wish to practice resignation, unless it was quite necessary. I wanted to live deep and suck out all the marrow of life, to live so sturdily and Spartan-like as to put to rout all that was not life, to cut a broad swath and shave close, to drive life into a corner, and reduce it to its lowest terms, and, if it proved to be mean, why then to get the whole and genuine meanness of it, and publish its meanness to the world; or if it were sublime, to know it by experience, and be able to give a true account of it in my next excursion.[5]

The independence that Thoreau sought and achieved at Walden Pond was not physical—it was intellectual and perhaps psychological. Prior to his residence at Walden and with the exception of his time attending Harvard College, Thoreau had lived all his life either with his father or with the Emerson family. The land he built on was owned by Ralph Waldo Emerson; he was, in his own words, "merely a squatter."[6] Even the axe he used to fell the trees was not his. As he stated in *Walden*: "It is difficult to begin without borrowing, but perhaps it is the most generous course thus to permit your fellow-men to have an interest in your enterprise. The owner of the axe, as he released his hold on it, said that it was the apple of his eye; but I returned it sharper than I received it."[7]

The Walden stay was an experiment in living simply—an experiment Thoreau carried beyond his tenancy at Walden and which lasted all his life. He spoke to his readers about it—the cost of his cabin, his bean field that yielded money for his expenses, his spare furnishings, his few needs. "Our life is frittered away by detail. . . . Simplicity, simplicity, simplicity."[8] And he spoke to any who would listen.

One day, he found shelter from a storm in the hut of John Field, an Irish immigrant who lived there along with his wife and children. Field was struggling to provide for his family, and it was clear that his circumstances were not the best. Thoreau described him as an "honest, hard-working, but shiftless man." Nonetheless, Thoreau said he spoke with him as if Fields were a philosopher on the benefits of a simple life. Fields, in response, merely sighed, and his wife "stared with arms a-kimbo."[9]

Thoreau's time at Walden was not a wilderness experience, eking out subsistence. Thoreau lived in nature, apart from society but not too distant. Train tracks could be seen from his cabin, and the trains ran regularly. He used the tracks to walk to the village and became a familiar figure to the men on the freight trains.[10] From his cabin, Thoreau could hear the "rattle of railroad cars,"[11] the distant sounds of farm animals, the clang of church bells, and the noise of wagons passing along a road. His purpose—his pursuit—did not require "a primitive setting on an actual frontier"; it was, instead, "an inner, personal attitude toward life."[12]

He created himself: the walker, the writer, the naturalist, and the independent thinker. Unlike Emerson, whose written works often sought to offer a structured view of the world, Thoreau's work turned personal: his relationship to nature, his observations of everyday natural events, and his personal maintenance of self-awareness. Emerson, in his essay on *The Transcendentalist*, defined the movement in which he and Thoreau have been identified as a form of idealism, with roots as deep as Plato and with his active acknowledgment of Kant as a source: It was, according to Emerson, a "class of intuitive thought." The senses gather "representations of things, but what are the things themselves, they cannot tell." The idealist, he contended, concedes that the senses do this but that the idealists, based on consciousness, "affirm facts not affected by the illusions of sense, facts which are of the same nature as the faculty which reports them, and not liable to doubt."[13]

Thoreau had no such aspirations—his was a personal philosophy about how to live, how one should relate to the state, and a view of the relation of each person to nature: "To be a philosopher is not merely to have subtle thoughts, nor even to found a school, but so to love wisdom as to live according to its dictates, a life of simplicity, independence, magnanimity, and trust. It is to solve some of the problems of life, not only theoretically, but practically."[14] Although Emerson was concerned with the origins of knowledge, Thoreau was concerned with knowledge of self. Thoreau's message was direct: "But I would say to my fellows, once for all, as long as possible live free and uncommitted. It makes but little difference whether you are committed to a farm or the county jail."[15]

And so he began every day: "Every morning was a cheerful invitation to make my life of equal simplicity, and may I say innocence, with Nature itself."[16] He would live in contrast to others "who live meanly, like ants."[17]

> Morning is when I am awake and there is dawn in me. Moral reform is the effort to throw off sleep. Why is it that men give so poor an account of their day if they have not been slumbering? . . . The millions are awake enough for physical labor; but only one in a million is awake enough for effective intellectual exertion, only one in a hundred millions to a poetic or divine life. To be awake is to be alive. I have never yet met a man who is quite awake. How could I have looked him in the face?[18]

Thoreau was not a hermit. He wrote of the chairs he had in his cabin: "I had three chairs in my house; one for solitude, two for friendship, three for society."[19] In *Walden,* he details numerous individuals with whom he had contact. There were the men on the train, the men who helped him raise the walls of his cabin, visitors, farmers, woodcutters, a poet, an old man, and companions. Rarely were various individuals named. Instead, he found solace in another companion—himself: "I never found the companion that was so companionable as solitude."[20]

Nature was the study for each day. Thoreau saw "nature as force, energy, and process, *and* as landscape, view, scene, or picture."[21] His reports in *Walden* were not scientific; he crafted simple but detailed observations that became a felt experience for the reader.

> Sometimes, in a summer morning, having taken my accustomed bath, I sat in my sunny doorway from sunrise til noon, rapt in a revery, amidst the pines and hickories and sumachs, in undisturbed solitude and stillness, while the birds sang around and flitted noiseless through the house, until by the sun falling in at my west window, or the noise of some traveler's wagon on the distant highway, I was reminded of the lapse of time. I grew in those seasons like corn in the night, and they were far better than any

> work of the hands would have been. They were not time subtracted from my life, but so much over and above my usual allowance.[22]

Thoreau's gaze ranged widely but returned often to the pond itself: "A lake is the landscape's most beautiful and expressive feature. It is the earth's eye; looking into which the beholder measures the depth of his own nature."[23] He measured the pond's size and depth.[24] But more pertinently, he observed the many daily and seasonal changes. By the beginning of September, he

> had seen two or three small maples turned scarlet across the pond, beneath where the white stems of three aspens diverged, at the point of a promontory, next the water. Ah, many a tale their color told! And gradually from week to week the character of each tree came out, and it admired itself reflected in the smooth mirror of the lake. Each morning the manager of this gallery substituted some new picture, distinguished by more brilliant or harmonious coloring, for the old upon the walls.[25]

One calm October day, while paddling his boat, a loon "betrayed himself" by "his wild laugh."[26] Thoreau "pursued with a paddle and he dived, but when he came up I was nearer than before." This pursuit and diving went on for quite some time, with Thoreau trying to determine where the loon would reappear. "I found that it was well for me to rest on my oars and wait his reappearing as to endeavor to calculate where he would rise; for again and again, when I was straining my eyes over the surface one way, I would suddenly be startled by his unearthly laugh behind me." Thoreau was convinced that the loon "laughed in derision of [Thoreau's] efforts, confident of his own resources." In late November, the pond reflected the "somber November colors of the surrounding hills."[27] Paddling that day, he found himself "surrounded by myriads of small perch, about five inches long, of a rich bronze color in the green water, sporting there, and constantly rising to the surface and dimpling it, sometimes leaving bubbles on it." Another day, when the ice had only hardened in the "shadiest and shallowest coves," he lay on the ice to observe the shallows, so he could study the bottom at his leisure.[28]

At the conclusion of *Walden*, he wrote:

> I learned this, at least, by my experiment; that if one advances confidently in the direction of his dreams, and endeavors to live the life which he has imagined, he will meet with a success unexpected in common hours. He will put some things behind, will pass an invisible boundary; new, universal, and more liberal laws will begin to establish themselves around and within him; or the old laws expanded, and interpreted in his favor in a more liberal sense, and he will live with the license of a higher order of beings. In proportion as he simplifies his life, the laws of the universe will appear less complex, and solitude will not be solitude, nor poverty poverty, nor weakness weakness. If you have built castles in the air, your work need not be lost; that is where they should be. Now put foundations under them.[29]

Walden is not merely a report of Thoreau's residence there. Although he made an initial draft of *Walden* at the cabin, he does not mention that effort in *Walden* itself. He worked and reworked the drafts seven times, and he did not finish the book for nine years. Thoreau returned to Concord and lived there until his death in 1862. He became an expert surveyor and helped in his family's business, which was making pencils. He walked daily, read widely, and traveled some, mostly in New England. He wrote almost constantly, including lectures, articles, book manuscripts, and an extensive journal.

Thoreau slowly became recognized as an important figure, including for his stand against slavery and for his now-famous essay *Civil Disobedience*. On July 4, 1854, he spoke of the evils of slavery, and that talk turned into the essay *Slavery in Massachusetts*.[30] Focused on the then-recent seizure in Massachusetts of an escaped slave, Anthony Brown, pursuant to the Fugitive Slave Act, and his shipment South, Thoreau emphasized the duty of each person to do what is right. Since the law was wrong, it should not be obeyed. He pointedly used strong rhetoric:

> The majority of the men of the North, and of the South and East and West, are not men of principle. If they vote, they do not send men to Congress on errands of humanity; but while their brothers and sisters are being scourged and hung for loving liberty, while—I might here insert all that slavery implies and is—it is the mismanagement of wood and iron and stone and gold which concerns them. Do what you will, O Government, with my wife and children, my mother and brother, my father and sister, I will obey your commands to the letter. It will indeed grieve me if you hurt them, if you deliver them to overseers to be hunted by bounds or to be whipped to death; but, nevertheless, I will peaceably pursue my chosen calling on this fair earth, until perchance, one day, when I have put on mourning for them dead, I shall have persuaded you to relent. . . .
>
> Rather than do thus, I need not say what match I would touch, what system endeavor to blow up; but as I love my life, I would side with the light, and let the dark earth roll from under me, calling my mother and my brother to follow. . . . I walk toward one of our ponds; but what signifies the beauty of nature when men are base? We walk to lakes to see our serenity reflected in them; when we are not serene, we go not to them. Who can be serene in a country where both the rulers and the ruled are without principle? The remembrance of my country spoils my walk. My thoughts are murder to the State, and involuntarily go plotting against her.[31]

Similar views were expressed in *Walden* itself: "But the only true America is that country where you are at liberty to pursue such a mode of life as may enable you to do without [tea, coffee, or meat each day], and where the state does not endeavor to compel you to sustain the slavery and war and other superfluous expenses which directly or indirectly result from the use of such things."[32]

Thoreau sought independence—for himself, for slaves, for immigrant Irishmen, for all who would advance confidently in the direction of their dreams. For those who would be awake. Emerson spoke at Thoreau's funeral and, in the printed version that followed, warmly observed: "The country knows not yet, or in the least part, how great a son it has lost. . . . His soul was made for the noblest society; wherever there is knowledge, wherever there is virtue, wherever there is beauty, he will find a home."[33]

Walt Whitman added this in 1888. Thoreau was "one of the native forces—stands for a fact, a movement, an upheaval: Thoreau belongs to America, to the transcendental, to the protesters. . . . He was a force—he looms up bigger and bigger: his dying does not seem to have hurt him a bit: every year has added to his fame."[34]

CHAPTER 10

Two Very Different Independence Days for a Union Private

Robert Knox Sneden was born in Nova Scotia but later moved to New York City, where, in the summer of 1861, he enlisted in the 40th New York Infantry Regiment. Later, with the Army of the Potomac, Sneden served as a map maker and topographical engineer. He was recognized for his abilities and sought after by various generals to serve on their staffs. In November 1863, Sneden was captured by Mosby's Rangers and spent the next thirteen months as a prisoner of war in various Confederate prisons, including Andersonville in Georgia.

Sneden, in his diary, detailed two very different Independence Day commemorations. The first was on July 4, 1862, at Harrison's Landing in Virginia, where he and the Army of the Potomac had retreated to after the Seven Days battles. The battles marked the end of General George B. McClellan's unsuccessful peninsula campaign to capture Richmond. The day featured an inspection of the troops, with "long lines of infantry with shining muskets and bayonets [making] a fine appearance." At noon on that day, Sneden recorded, "a national salute was fired by all the artillery in the army in honor of the day, and to let the enemy know that we had not been conquered quite yet." The guns in the "front line nearest the enemy were shotted and sent a storm of iron across the swamp and ravines into the woods." Regimental bands played as General McClellan and dozens of other generals, along with their staff officers, rode along the line. "The men cheered and put their caps on the bayonet points, all was the enthusiasm in the serried ranks, and the morale of the army was ascertained to be much better than supposed."

The gunboats fired a salute and the "roar of 300 guns made the earth tremble, and echoed far down the James [River]." After this, whiskey rations were issued. That evening, regimental bands played until midnight. Sneden noted that this was the first music they had heard for some time and it "was fully appreciated by all." Nonetheless, the reality of war persisted, with "great numbers" of hospital tents erected that day, soon to be filled with twelve thousand sick or wounded. Surgeons and their assistants were "hard at work amputating and probing for bullets," with many "dying hourly."[1]

Sneden was captured on November 27, 1863, in northern Virginia near Culpeper.[2] He was moved several times and eventually transferred to Andersonville Prison, also known as Camp Sumter, in Georgia. The prison was commanded by Captain Henry Wirz, who was tried and executed after the war for war crimes that occurred at the prison. To say that the prison is notorious for the horrific conditions under which the prisoners lived does not begin to describe it. To state that the food, water, and shelter were inadequate and the grounds unsanitary does not begin to characterize accurately the inhumane conditions. Private Sneden was among the first prisoners to arrive in late February 1864. Over the course of the next few months, approximately four hundred prisoners arrived daily. By June 1864, over twenty-six thousand prisoners had been confined in a stockade designed to house ten thousand. The largest number of prisoners held at one time was thirty-three thousand in August 1864. Of the approximately forty-five thousand Union prisoners held there, nearly thirteen thousand died and were buried in a cemetery created outside the prison walls. Sergeant Samuel Corthell, Company C, 4th Massachusetts Cavalry remembered:

> The camp was covered with vermin all over. You could not sit down anywhere. You might go and pick the lice all off of you, and sit down for a half a moment and get up and you would be covered with them. In between these two hills it was very swampy, all black mud, and where the filth was emptied it was all alive; there was a regular buzz there all the time, and it was covered with large white maggots.[3]

Sneden's recorded memory of the conditions was even more graphic. Yet, in the midst of all this misery, Sneden took note of the Fourth of July:

> Today being Independence Day several educated comrades made short speeches to small crowds of willing listeners. Our desperate condition was fully discussed and as there was no prospect of being exchanged and seeing our far off homes again we were advised to keep orderly and abide our time when Sherman's army might reach us, as it was known that he was marching with 100,000 men through Georgia. The fearful monthly death toll was commented on and prayer meetings would be held if any would attend. . . . Three rousing cheers from 200 or more prisoners were given for "The Old Flag," while hundreds of others sang "Rally round the flag boys" and "Star Spangled Banner." One of the sailors who was good at sewing made a small American flag from some red flannel and part of a white shirt. This was waved as the crowd sang, and cheers went up all over the northern part of the stockade. All was quiet and orderly again in a few minutes.[4]

Wirz, who was concerned about the singing and cheering by the prisoners and desertions by guards, reported his worries to higher authorities. General Cobb responded and gave a speech to the Confederate troops guarding the prison, seeking to encourage the Confederates and, at the same time, threatening to summarily execute deserters. Cobb was standing on a stump with the guards in a circle around him. According to Sneden, as Cobb spoke, the Union prisoners began singing:

> "The Star Spangled Banner," etc., and "Long may it wave," etc. As the chorus ended the speaker resumed. "Is there a man here who would so fail of his duty? Hear me, I announce in your hearing – and let no one be deceived by the hope of escape. The next and every other desert from this post, who is captured will be immediately tried by drum head court martial, and executed on the spot. And I announce further, that the commander of this

> post is fully vested with authority to carry out this order into execution."

Over the noise of the prisoners, General Cobb ordered Captain Wirz to have the prisoners stop. Nonetheless, the sound grew louder, as "from 10,000 to 20,000 voices were now singing." The Rebels stood still until the chorus had ended and then General Cobb "shouted sternly to have the prisoners 'stop that noise.'"

General Cobb tried to continue his speech, but the chorus resumed, drowning out his voice. The guards watched in "astonishment," and a sentry "on the stockade wall was so scared that he let his musket fall inside the stockade." Cobb stopped talking, and the Confederate troops were ordered to return to their camps. Sneden added that "the corpulent figure of Cobb was helped down from the tree stump and he with others walked up to Wirz's headquarters to get a drink probably." Sneden opined that

> the singing was very good considering that so many thousands voices without any leader [were] doing it. Good time was kept too throughout. Poor half starved prisoners, cripples and sick fellows caught at the comrades who helped them to stand, and waving their bony hands united their hollow voices with enthusiasm in vocation. This was about noon time.

After this, "every one quieted down. The sailors had managed to get some whiskey, and fiddle from somewhere outside and they kept up a noisy jubilee as long as the whiskey lasted. Singing and dancing until ration came in after 6 p.m. when all were hungry enough to eat some of the mule or rotten meat."[5]

After his exchange in December 1864, Private Sneden was discharged and returned to New York City. He never married and devoted much of his life to preserving his Civil War memories. He died at the Soldiers Home in Bath, New York, in 1918. Throughout the war, even as a prisoner, Private Sneden made detailed sketches and recorded the events in a diary, which he later expanded. To keep his sketches from being confiscated by prison guards, Sneden hid them in his shoes and sewed them into his clothes. This body of work was unknown to the public until 1994 when an art dealer approached the Virginia Historical Society about a Civil War archive that had languished in a Connecticut bank vault. Sneden's great-great-nephew also transferred a trove of Sneden's materials to the historical society. Together, the materials included almost five thousand pages of diary entries and memoirs, and nearly five hundred watercolors and maps.[6] In 2000, Sneden was introduced to the public in the *Eye of the Storm* exhibition and subsequent book,[7] which is a truly extraordinary account of his experiences accompanied by his exquisite art. According to the Virginia Historical Society, it is "the largest collection of Civil War soldier art ever produced."

CHAPTER 11

Theodore Roosevelt at Dickinson, North Dakota

Dickinson, in western Dakota territory, was near the Badlands, and had been founded in 1881. The area was uncrowded and untamed; it witnessed the closing acts of the Western Frontier.[1] The buffalo had almost vanished. The rugged and eroded land was and is starkly beautiful: the North Dakota Badlands feature stunning rock formations of multicolored layers of clay, sandstone, red "scoria" rock, and black coal veins. The horizon appears limitless. Now Dickinson is considered the gateway to Theodore Roosevelt National Park, but that was an unforeseen future. Back in 1886, only five years after its founding, the town of seven hundred inhabitants decided to hold its first Fourth of July celebration. As recorded in the newspaper account of the *Dickinson Press*, the town "made up its mind to 'spread itself.' From near and far eager crowds streamed into the little town, on foot and on horse back."[2]

Held on July 5 since the Fourth was a Sunday, the newspaper called the day "a grand success" and would "long be remembered." People came from around the region to participate and "by ten o'clock the largest crowd ever assembled in Stark County lined the principal streets." First came the parade:

> About ten o'clock everything was in readiness and the parade began to move, headed by the Dickinson Silver Cornet Band. Following the band were the lady equestriennes, a large number of ladies being in line. They were followed by the members of Fort Sumter Post G.A.R. and Onward Lodge R.R.B. Next came a beautifully

> decorated wagon drawn by four white horses, containing little girls dressed in white, representing the States of the Union. This was one of the most attractive features of the parade, and was followed by a display of reaping and other farm machinery. The "Invincibles" next in line and created considerable mirth by their fantastic and grotesque appearance. Citizens in carriages and on horseback brought up the rear. After parading through the principal streets the procession marched to the public square and were dismissed.

"'The trouble with the parade,' remarked Bill Dantz long after, 'was that every one in town was so enthusiastic they insisted on joining the procession, and there was no one to watch except two men who were too drunk to notice anything.'" After the parade came the ceremonies. Western Starr—his actual name—who was the justice of the peace, "read the Declaration of Independence in a clear, forcible tone." The audience then joined in singing "America." A free dinner was then served, followed by a prayer offered by the Reverand E. C. Dayton. After the band played music, two speeches followed.

John Rea was the first speaker, and all that is recorded of his talk was his opening joke—but it was a good one:

> This is a big country. At a dinner party of Americans in Paris during the Civil War this toast was offered by a New Englander: "Here's to the United States, bounded on the north by British America, on the south by the Gulf of Mexico, on the east by the Atlantic, and on the west by the Pacific Ocean."
>
> An Ohio man followed with a larger notion of our greatness: "Here's to the United States, bounded on the north by the North Pole, on the south by the South Pole, on the east by the rising sun, and on the west by the setting sun."
>
> It took the Dakota man, however, to rise to the greatness of the subject: "I give you the United States, bounded on the north by the Aurora Borealis, on the south by the precession of the equinoxes, on the east by primeval chaos, and on the west by the Day of Judgment."

Theodore Roosevelt was the second speaker. Roosevelt led a full, colorful life, including becoming the twenty-sixth president of the United States from 1901 to 1909; he is one of only four presidents whose face is depicted on Mount Rushmore. Born into money and privilege, he was sickly as a child, but he overcame his health problems by embracing what he called the "strenuous life." He entered politics as a young man and was elected to the New York State Assembly for the first time in 1882. After the tragic death of his mother and young wife on the same day in 1884, Roosevelt returned to North Dakota, where he embraced a "cowboy" lifestyle.

Roosevelt first visited the Dakota Territory in 1883 to hunt bison. Exhilarated by the frontier life it offered and with the cattle business booming in the territory, Roosevelt invested fourteen thousand dollars, seeking to become a prosperous cattle rancher. For the next several years, he shuttled between his home in New York and his ranch in Dakota. Beginning in 1884, Roosevelt built a second ranch named Elkhorn, which was thirty-five miles north of Medora. His dream of western riches based on raising cattle was soon to end with the return of harsh Dakota winters. The ranches later became Theodore Roosevelt National Park. Roosevelt had gained local notoriety in the territory for, among other things, tracking and arresting three men who had stolen his boat, covering three hundred miles to bring them back to jail in Medora.

For the Fourth of July celebration, Roosevelt, "accompanied by two New York friends, Lispenard Stewart and Dr. Taylor, and half the cowboys of Billings County, 'jumped' an east-bound freight" from Medora to travel to Dickinson. According to the newspaper account, Roosevelt "looked very slim and young and embarrassed." He was twenty-seven years old. But he gave a memorable speech. He began by reminding the audience of "the great gifts and blessings you enjoy" and belonging to "the greatest nation that has ever existed on this earth." But he wanted instead to

> say a few words to you about your duties. Much has been given to us, and so, much will be expected of us; and we must take heed to use aright the gifts entrusted to our care. . . .

> The Declaration of Independence derived its peculiar importance, not on account of what America was, but because of what she was to become; she shared with other nations the present, and she yielded to them the past, but it was felt in return that to her, and to her especially, belonged the future. It is the same with us here. We, grangers and cowboys alike, have opened a new land; and we are the pioneers, and as we shape the course of the stream near its head, our efforts have infinitely more effect, in bending it in any given direction, than they would have if they were made farther along. . . .
>
> We have rights, but we have correlative duties; none can escape them. We only have the right to live on as free men, governing our own lives as we will, so long as we show ourselves worthy of the privileges we enjoy. We must remember that the Republic can only be kept pure by the individual purity of its members; and that if it become once thoroughly corrupted, it will surely cease to exist. In our body politic, each man is himself a constituent portion of the sovereign, and if the sovereign is to continue in power, he must continue to do right. When you here exercise your privileges at the ballot box, you are not only exercising a right, but you are also fulfilling a duty; and a heavy responsibility rests on you to fulfill your duty well. If you fail to work in public life, as well as in private, for honesty and uprightness and virtue, if you condone vice because the vicious man is smart, or if you in any other way cast your weight into the scales in favor of evil, you are just so far corrupting and making less valuable the birthright of your children. The duties of American citizenship are very solemn as well as very precious; and each one of us here today owes it to himself, to his children, and to all his fellow Americans, to show that he is capable of performing them in the right spirit. It is not what we have that will make us a great nation; it is the way in which we use it.

Roosevelt said, "like all Americans, I like big things; big prairies, big forests and mountains, big wheat-fields, railroads,—and herds of cattle, too,—big factories, steamboats, and everything else." But all those riches would go away if "prosperity corrupted their virtue."

> We have fallen heirs to the most glorious heritage a people ever received, and each one must do his part if we wish to show that the nation is worthy of its good fortune. Here we are not ruled over by others, as in the case of Europe; we rule ourselves. All American citizens, whether born here or elsewhere, whether of one creed or another, stand on the same footing; we welcome every honest immigrant no matter from what country he comes, provided only that he leaves off his former nationality, and remains neither Celt nor Saxon, neither Frenchman nor German, but becomes an American, desirous of fulfilling in good faith the duties of American citizenship.

After the events, "a hilarious party of cowpunchers" rode the afternoon train back to Medora. A newspaperman named Arthur Packard sat with Roosevelt and discussed Roosevelt's speech. Afterward, Packard said:

> It was during this talk that I first realized the potential bigness of the man. One could not help believing he was in deadly earnest in his consecration to the highest ideals of citizenship. He had already made his mark in the New York Legislature. He was known as a fighter who dared to come out in the open and depend upon the backing of public opinion. He was reputed to be wealthy enough to devote his life to any work he chose, and I learned, on the return journey to the Bad Lands that day, that he believed he could do better work in a public and political way than in any other. My conclusion was immediate, and I said, "Then you will become President of the United States."

Packard could not recall Roosevelt's actual words in reply, but he did remember "distinctly that he was not in the least surprised at my statement. He gave me the impression of having thoroughly considered the matter and to have arrived at the same conclusion that I had arrived at. I remember only this of what he said, 'If your prophecy comes true, I will do my part to make a good one.'"[3]

Theodore Roosevelt traveled widely in his life, seeing and ultimately preserving many of the natural wonders in America. Roosevelt had many achievements and a wide range of interests, including being a Nobel Peace Prize winner, leader of the progressive movement, prolific author, Rough Rider, and champion of his "Square Deal" for the average American. His efforts to preserve our natural resources are unsurpassed by any president. Roosevelt oversaw the creation of five national parks, eighteen national monuments, and fifty-five wildlife preserves; he also created or expanded 150 national forests.[4]

Roosevelt traveled extensively in Africa, Europe, and elsewhere. But of all those spectacular locales, none was more important to him than North Dakota, where he repeatedly returned to replenish his mind and body. "The towering buttes and scarred escarpments told geological stories of the prehistoric upheavals, the deposits, the erosion of forgotten times. There was, [Roosevelt said], a sacredness to the Badlands silhouette against the oceanic sky that exuded a cosmic sense of God's Creation as described in Genesis."[5]

After his brother's death in 1894, Roosevelt again headed to North Dakota to recuperate. Hunting on the plains near Medora and absorbing the solitude of the Badlands, he said that he emerged after a "fortnight all the time in the open; and feel as rugged as a bull-moose."[6]

CHAPTER 12

Lou Gehrig and America's Pastime, Baseball

Lou Gehrig Day on July 4, 1939, was bittersweet. But his example, when facing certain death from the incurable disease named after him, offers insights into another aspect of the freedom we associate with Independence Day. Gehrig showed us freedom from fear—from fear of death and fear of disease. It is a different kind of freedom, or, if you prefer, courage, but it is shared with all of those in the other chapters of this book who stood up to kings, to enslavers, to men who denied women their rights, or who simply walked into the woods. All required courage in pursuit of their freedom.

Gehrig's story is also intimately connected to the pursuit of happiness that we celebrate on the Fourth of July, given that there is nothing more American than baseball. Many remember the highlight of the season as a Little Leaguer: It was not the hit you had, the strikeout that you pitched, touching home plate with the winning run, or stealing second base. No, it was going to the major league park with your Little League team for the once-a-year trip to the ball game. You got to wear your team hat and shirt (so the coach could find you if you got lost, but you did not know that). Your parents put up money for a hot dog, soda, and some cotton candy. The peanut vendor might throw you a brown paper bag of warm peanuts to share with your friends. He was calling: "Peanuts, peanuts, fresh roasted peanuts." You got to sit in the stands with your fellow teammates, your summer friends. You had your glove in the hope that a foul ball would be caught (not knowing that, in those cheap seats deep behind first or third base, only about one really bad swing a year brought a ball anywhere near). There was always a buzz emanating from the fans, a residual excitement even when there was no crack of a bat sending a ball so high and long that it might be out of the park. In the old days, in the old parks, you may have been stuck behind one of those steel girders—some of which still persist in parks like Fenway in Boston or Wrigley Field in Chicago. That did not matter: You got to be in the park, root for your team, and, together with your friends, create a lifetime memory. The coaches and parents who drove you to the game were the unsung heroes, only to be dimly noticed later.

America loved baseball and still does, as evidenced by the proliferation of minor league stadiums in the more recent decades and the millions of fans who return to the stands each year. It is true that football on Sundays eclipses television ratings for baseball, but in-person attendance of NFL games pales in comparison to baseball attendance: only 2%[1] of NFL fans have actually attended a game, while baseball attendance has averaged more than seventy million fans a year for the past two decades.[2] Football is a TV sport; baseball is a day or night at the ballpark.

Baseball, one dedicated observer has said, is not just about winning. It has a beauty, craftsmanship, and exactingness that makes it "an *activity* to be loved, as much as ballet or fishing, or politics, and loving it is a form of participation."[3] A baseball game seems almost synonymous with celebrating the Fourth of July.

Turning to an earlier era, baseball had no rival, and for many decades, the New York Yankees ruled. The Yankees have won the World Series twenty-seven times, including nineteen times from 1923 to 1962. Those teams had immortals, including Babe Ruth and Joe DiMaggio. Henry Louis Gehrig ("Lou Gehrig") was one of them. He was a member of the team for six of those titles, playing first base for the Yankees for seventeen seasons (1923–1939). He held the record for the most consecutive games played—2130—for fifty-six years until that record was broken by Cal Ripken Jr. Gehrig's streak earned him the title "The Iron Man," but he was also known as the "Pride of the Yankees," primarily due to the movie of that title starring Gary Cooper, made shortly after Gehrig's death. He was the first and last Yankee to wear the number four and the first to have his number retired by the Yankees.

A member of the Baseball Hall of Fame, Gehrig was an All-Star seven consecutive times, a Triple Crown winner, and twice the American League Most Valuable Player. He had a career .340 batting average, a .632 slugging average, and a .447 on-base average. He hit 493 home runs and had 1,995 runs batted in.[4] He is one of only six players to hit at least .350 in a season, have 150 RBIs, and hit 40 or more home runs; he did it four times, matched only by Babe Ruth.[5] He shares the record of twice hitting 100 or more extra-base hits in a season with one other player.[6] "In 1969, he was voted the greatest first baseman of all time by the Baseball Writers' Association of America. In 1989, on the fiftieth anniversary of the end of his streak, he was honored with a United States postage stamp. In 1999, he was the leading vote-getter for Major League Baseball's All-Century Team."[7]

Lou Gehrig was often overlooked, playing in the shadow of Babe Ruth, who was a larger-than-life figure (both literally and figuratively). Gehrig's numbers—hits, RBIs, and especially home runs—quickly started to approach those of the Babe after becoming a member of the Yankees. In 1931, Gehrig set the American League single-season RBI mark with 185, hitting after Ruth, who knocked in 162.[8] Reporters, seeking to fuel competition between the two sluggers, would ask Gehrig about Ruth. Gehrig would simply remark that there would "never be another guy like the Babe" or that "there is only one Babe Ruth."[9]

Gehrig was painfully shy; he "neither bragged nor fussed" and just enjoyed "making a living at play in a child's game."[10] Baseball was how he pursued happiness. Gehrig recalled that, as a kid, he would "get up and play baseball at six or seven o'clock in the morning" so that, before the day got hot, they would "have our fill of the game."[11] He overcame his shyness when playing, finding his "greatest joy" in physical play and "in the reassuring feel of a leather ball with raised stitches squeezed in his left hand."[12] As a professional baseball player, he seemed most comfortable "inside the straight white lines of the batter's box."[13] Gehrig, in his early playing days with the Yankees, would sometimes go home after a game and round up the neighborhood kids and play ball in the street until dark.[14] He led a quiet life before and after each game. He was devoted to his mother and married later in his short life, to Eleanor Grace Twitchell, in 1933.

Some time in 1938, although he did not recognize it at the time, Lou Gehrig contracted amyotrophic lateral sclerosis,[15] now commonly named after him—Lou Gehrig's disease. In his biography of Gehrig, Jonathan Eig summarized the effects of the disease, which is always fatal:

> In a healthy person, messages travel in an instant from the brain to the fingers and toes. But the messages travel a long way—through motor nerves running from the base of the skull down the spine. In a person with ALS, these motor nerves begin to die, with no warning and for no apparent reason. Messages can't get through. The disease begins shutting down the body's function one by one, like a night watchman switching off the factory-floor lights. Muscles waste away.[16]

Spring training in 1939 did not go well for Gehrig, and it was clear that he was not well.[17] Observers were shocked at his appearance. Gehrig told reporters that he never hit well in spring training and maintained that he felt fine.[18] Bill Hitchcock, trying to make the team as an infielder, had always idolized Gehrig, but he was shaken by what he saw: Gehrig could not field the ball; a grounder was by him before he could get a glove down, and then Gehrig "would hobble around, chasing after the ball—too late to make the play."[19] The 1939 regular season began on April 20. It was clear to teammates, fans, and reporters that something was wrong with Gehrig. On May 2, after traveling with the team to Detroit to begin a road trip, Gehrig met with Yankee manager Joe McCarthy in McCarthy's hotel room. Gehrig said he was ready to sit on the bench, noting he had to do it for the good of the team. McCarthy walked to the hotel lobby and asked the reporters to gather around: "'It's a black day for me,' he said, his voice choking. 'And for the Yankees.'"[20]

Gehrig's streak of consecutive games had ended at 2130. The Yankees won the game 22–2. In the seventh, eighth, and ninth innings, Babe Dahlgren, who had replaced Lou, asked Gehrig if he wanted to get into the game to keep his streak alive; he refused.[21] Gehrig stayed with the Yankees for the rest of the season but played only a couple of innings in one more game. In June, he finally went to the Mayo Clinic in Rochester,

Minnesota, to be examined and was diagnosed with the disease. He turned thirty-six a few days later.

The New York Yankees designated July 4, 1939, Lou Gehrig Appreciation Day. Yankee Stadium was packed with over sixty thousand fans. Many of Lou's old teammates were there. Officials planned to hold a ceremony between games of the doubleheader with the St. Louis Browns. The ever-reticent Gehrig wanted none of it, saying to Joe McCarthy that he'd give a month's pay to get out of it.[22] McCarthy did not answer.

Jonathan Eig describes the scene: The ceremony was held at home plate before a bank of microphones. Gehrig's wife and parents were in the stands. A brass band played. Politicians, dignitaries, and Babe Ruth spoke. Trophies and gifts were presented. Gehrig never looked up, and began to cry as the first speaker was introduced. As the ceremony continued, he twisted his baseball cap in his hands and pawed at the dirt with his cleats. He wiped tears with a handkerchief. When it came time to speak, Gehrig declined, shaking his head no. The crowd shouted as one repeatedly: "We want Lou." Gehrig began to move toward the dugout; McCarthy put his hand on his back and said something to him, evidently encouraging him to speak. He moved to the microphones. After a wave of excitement went through the crowd, it became deadly silent. Gehrig wiped his eyes, took a deep breath, and swallowed hard. "He was about to deliver one of the saddest and strongest messages an American audience had ever heard."[23] He came to home plate for the last time of his life and stood at the microphones: "Fans, for the past two weeks, you've been reading about a bad break." He paused. Then continued: "Today I consider myself the luckiest man on the face of the earth."

> I have been in ballparks for 17 years and have never received anything but kindness and encouragement from you fans.
>
> When you look around, wouldn't you consider it a privilege to associate yourself with such fine-looking men as are standing in uniform in this ballpark today? Sure, I'm lucky. Who wouldn't consider it an honor to have known Jacob Ruppert? Also, the builder of baseball's greatest empire, Ed Barrow? To have spent six years with that wonderful little fellow, Miller Huggins? Then to

> have spent the next nine years with that outstanding leader, that smart student of psychology, the best manager in baseball today, Joe McCarthy? Sure, I'm lucky.
>
> When the New York Giants, a team you would give your right arm to beat, and vice versa, sends you a gift—that's something. When everybody down to the groundskeepers and those boys in white coats remember you with trophies—that's something. When you have a wonderful mother-in-law who takes sides with you in squabbles with her own daughter—that's something. When you have a father and a mother who work all their lives so you can have an education and build your body—it's a blessing. When you have a wife who has been a tower of strength and shown more courage than you dreamed existed—that's the finest I know.
>
> So I close in saying that I might have been given a bad break, but I've got an awful lot to live for.—Thank you.[24]

The crowd stood and applauded for almost two minutes. Gehrig was visibly shaken as he stepped back from the microphone and wiped the tears away from his face with his handkerchief. Babe Ruth came over and hugged him as a band played "I Love You Truly," and the crowd chanted, "We love you, Lou." One sports writer summed him up as standing "for everything that makes sports important in the American scene."[25] Lou Gehrig, the Iron Horse known for his strength and quiet determination, died on June 2, 1941.

Jonathan Eig reflected on Gehrig for the ALS Association, writing in part:

> In his farewell speech at Yankee Stadium on July 4, 1939, Gehrig called himself the luckiest man on the face of the earth. He wasn't thinking of himself, though. He was thanking those who had helped him in life. He was helping his family, his friends, and his fans get through the ordeal of his illness. The letters he wrote to his doctor showed that Gehrig did the same thing in private. He showed no self-pity, no denial, only grace. All his life, Gehrig was taken for granted. The sportswriters called him boring. It wasn't

> until he came to the end that those same writers realized that they had overlooked him. Gehrig never boasted. He never wrote a memoir. [H]e felt no need to explain himself. He lived the way he played the game, with resolution, decency, and selflessness. He showed his strength in the way he fought ALS. He showed his kindness in the way he cared for the loved ones when he faced his greatest challenge. Gehrig's quiet courage speaks louder than ever.[26]

It is worth emphasizing that Gehrig's speech did more than thank people. It offered them hope by hearing not just his words but a look at the man behind those words, the individual who had the courage in the most dire of conditions to be thankful and gracious. He not only said he was lucky and thankful but that he had a lot to live for. Gehrig lived the remaining years of his life on his own terms, turning down lucrative offers that traded on his name.[27] Now, through the Lou Gehrig Society and with the support of Major League Baseball's annual Lou Gehrig Day,[28] those affected by the disease and many others can find strength in that man's life.

CHAPTER 13

From Fireworks to Hot Dogs: Celebrations from 1776 to 2026

The Fourth of July has been celebrated continuously since 1776. Many of the features of those celebrations are familiar ones: parades, speeches, public readings of the Declaration of Independence, cookouts, music, toasts, fireworks, sporting events, ringing the Liberty Bell and church bells, flag waving, battle reenactments, setting cornerstones, and dedicating new projects, statues, and monuments. Since 1819, each new state has been admitted to the Union on July 4, beginning with Illinois and ending in 1960 with Hawaii, the fiftieth state.[1] In 1870, Congress made July 4 a federal holiday, which became a paid holiday for all federal employees in 1938.[2] Along the way, there have been protests and dissent. Not surprisingly, honoring the birthday of our nation disappeared from the seceding Southern states and did not return for many years after the conclusion of the Civil War in those states. Some years have seen muted celebrations, such as during World War II when fireworks were banned, during the COVID pandemic when many parades and other festivities were canceled, and often in various locations when under the threat of wildfires and droughts.

This chapter highlights celebrations and other events through the years. It is not comprehensive—there have been too many events throughout the United States over the course of history to do that.[3] Instead, it is illustrative, showing how we have acknowledged independence in so many ways in so many locations for so long. The material selected here ranges from humorous to serious, poignant to patriotic, and just plain fun. As an example of the latter, in 2015, Matt "Megatoad" Stonie, in an upset, defeated eight-time hot-dog-eating champion Joey "Jaws" Chestnut at Nathan's annual contest at Coney Island, consuming sixty-two hot dogs.[4] Chestnut, however, set a new world record of seventy-six hot dogs in 2021.[5] The contest has been held almost annually since 1916.

In 1801, Thomas Jefferson became the first president to celebrate the Fourth of July at the White House. He opened the house and greeted diplomats, civil and military officers, citizens, and Cherokee chiefs in the center of the oval saloon (today's Blue Room). The Marine Band played in the Entrance Hall while, on the north grounds, a festival took place—complete with horse races, parades, and food and drink. The tradition of an annual reception at the White House continued for much of the nineteenth century. The north grounds of the President's Park—the "common"—came alive at daybreak with the raising of tents and booths, soon followed by crowds of people. A festival took place just for the day. Food and drink and cottage goods of all types were sold. There were horse races and cockfights and parades of the Washington militia and other military companies. A bare-headed Jefferson with his "grey locks waving in the air" watched from the steps of the White House. Then he invited everyone in to partake of his hospitality and his thanksgiving for the preservation of independence.[6]

Some events are unique. Boxing champion Jack Johnson, the first African American to hold the world heavyweight boxing title, kept his title on July 4, 1910, knocking out Jim Jeffries, dubbed "The Great White Hope," in an outdoor arena in Reno, Nevada. In 1948, 362 U.S. and British planes airlifted nearly three thousand tons of food into Berlin, which constituted the highest tonnage carried and the largest number of planes used since the beginning of the effort to thwart the Soviet blockade of the city.

The town of George, Washington, since 1959, has held a Fourth of July celebration, which attracts twenty times the town's population. Among its features are a "cherry bomb" run, parade, VFW band, floats, flag raising, breakfast by the senior club, concessions, stage show, and fireworks. George reports that it also features the world's largest cherry pie.[7]

FIREWORKS AND CANNONS

John Adams wrote in 1776 that, in addition to "Pomp and Parade," Independence Day should be celebrated with "Guns, Bells, Bonfires and Illuminations." The tradition of setting off fireworks on the Fourth of July had begun by at least 1777 in Philadelphia. The *Pennsylvania Evening Post* reported: "at night there was a grand exhibition of fireworks (which began and concluded with thirteen rockets) on the Commons, and the city was beautifully illuminated."

That same night, patriots set off fireworks over the Boston Common.[8] Pikes Peak in Colorado was the site of a "volcano-like" explosion of rockets and kerosene in 1890.[9]

As time progressed, the sale and distribution of fireworks became a major business.[10] Although individuals throughout the land continue to set off individual displays—legal and illegal—towns and cities offer them every Fourth of July.[11] Two of the largest celebrations, The Capital Fourth in Washington, D.C. and The Boston Pops in Boston, are nationally televised each year and draw large crowds to the events.[12] Then there was the 2012 fireworks show in San Diego. In less than a minute, all seven thousand fireworks, which were intended for a seventeen-minute display, discharged simultaneously from four barges and the pier. The premature discharge was blamed on a corrupted computer file. Needless to say, the video went viral on the internet.[13]

Explosives are dangerous, and many accidents have been recorded over the years. A Fourth of July firecracker in 1866 started the Great Portland Fire in Maine. The conflagration burned 1,800 buildings, left ten thousand homeless, and killed two. Boys threw fireworks into a carpenter's shop in Allegheny City, Pennsylvania, on July 4, 1874, causing a fire that resulted in a large number of buildings being destroyed.[14] A church was burned in Trenton, New Jersey, in 1879.[15] Most of Benton, Pennsylvania, was burned to the ground in 1910 after a firecracker "lodged" in a barn.[16] A forest fire on French Mountain, New York, was started by fireworks in 1913. Near Yosemite National Park in 1988, 2,200 acres were burned, with illegal fireworks the suspected cause.[17] Over the years, countless injuries—minor, serious, and fatal—have been caused by exploding fireworks.[18] States have long regulated and sometimes outright banned the use of fireworks by private citizens.[19] It takes no citation to observe that those bans are often ignored.

Even official events have seen tragedy, with rockets falling and exploding into the crowds, along with the destruction of nearby buildings. For instance, in Geneva, New York, the 1842 fireworks included some large rockets weighing six pounds. After several had been successfully launched, a spark ignited a box of them. The rockets were lying in a horizontal position, and they flew into the celebrants, seriously injuring eight and killing one.[20] In 1903 alone, according to the *Journal of the American Medical Association*, 466 people died and 4,449 people were injured from holiday-related accidents. Infections from tetanus precipitated a large swath of those deaths, triggered by shrapnel from fireworks and toy guns that got into a person's skin. From 1903 to 1909, a full two-thirds of July 4 deaths connected to explosive incidents were tetanus deaths.[21] In 2017, 12,900 people were hospitalized, and several died from fireworks-related accidents.[22]

The tradition of cannon and artillery salutes is long. Typical early salutes consisted of the firing of thirteen cannons for each of the original thirteen states, as was done in Philadelphia in 1777.[23] George Washington ordered "discharging thirteen pieces of cannon" in 1779.[24] During other wars, military salutes of a different kind were conducted: 1942 saw the first American bombing mission over Nazi-occupied Europe. In 1944, 1,100 artillery rounds were fired at German lines in Normandy. For the Centennial, one-hundred-gun salutes were ordered.[25]

A unique blast occurred on July 4, 2005, when NASA's spacecraft *Deep Impact* slammed into the comet Tempel 1 at 23,000 mph.[26] In 1893, a gunner in New York who miscounted the number for a twenty-one-gun salute was arrested after twenty-three guns were fired instead. Artillery accidents became common after the Revolution.[27] "It was not uncommon that scores of persons each year lost limbs and had other injuries while others lost their lives. One of the earliest instances of a tragic ending to an artillery salute occurred at Fort Constitution in Portsmouth, New Hampshire, on July 4, 1809." Two chests of powder and some loose cartridges ignited, resulting in the death of 14 to 20 people.[28]

TOASTS AND ALCOHOL

In 1778, General George Washington ordered rum to be distributed to his troops. The next year, however, he did not, writing in his order: "I wish we had it in our power to distribute a portion of rum to the Soldiers, to exhilarate their spirits upon the occasion; but unfortunately our stock is too scanty to permit."[29] During the Continental Convention in 1787, the delegates joined the Fourth of July celebrations in Philadelphia. The festivities included church bells, fireworks, and artillery salutes. "Pennsylvania militia officers drank thirteen toasts, beginning with one for the Congress, then to the Convention, to Louis XVI of France, all the way down to the wish that 'Rhode Island be excluded [from] the union until they elect honest men to rule them.'"[30]

The combination of alcohol and explosives has never been a good one. Coincident in part with the temperance movement of the nineteenth and early twentieth centuries, attempts were made to exclude alcohol and fireworks from celebrations. The movement was called the "Safe and Sane" celebration of the Fourth. Alternative events included parades, pageants, sporting events, and concerts.[31] Numerous state and local laws have been passed to make celebrations safer. President William Howard Taft wrote in 1909 that he was "heartily in sympathy with the movement to rid the celebration of our country's natal days of these distressing accidents." A year later, Taft attended a Safe and Sane Fourth of July march in Boston.[32] The idea persists to this day in communities across the nation. Not surprisingly in today's world, its name has been appropriated by fireworks manufacturers, who label their products as such: "'Safe and sane' are not a brand but are types of fireworks that include: fountains, sparklers, smokeballs, snake-type fireworks, ground-spinning fireworks, pinwheels, most novelty fireworks, toytrick noisemakers, and some crackling items—basically anything that doesn't leave the ground."[33]

CORNERSTONES, DEDICATIONS, AND MARKING NEW BEGINNINGS

July Fourth has often been used as a day for beginning new projects. The ceremonial laying of the cornerstone of the Massachusetts State House by Samuel Adams and Paul Revere occurred in 1795. Work on the Ohio Canal, the Farmington Canal, and the Chesapeake and Ohio Canal all began on July Fourth in various years. In 1828, the last surviving signer of the Declaration, Charles Carroll, turned the first earth for the Baltimore and Ohio Railroad on that day.[34] The day often saw dedications of Liberty poles. In 1848, the cornerstone of the Washington Monument was laid before a large crowd, including President James K. Polk. Washington's face on Mount Rushmore was unveiled on Independence Day in 1930. Three Liberty ships were launched in Baltimore in 1942. The next year, a crowd of twenty thousand saw the Liberty ship named the *George Cohan* launched, as a band played his famous songs, including "Yankee Doodle Dandy" and "It's a Grand Old Flag." In 1950, Radio Free Europe began its first broadcasts, transmitting thirty minutes of American programming to Czechoslovakia from a 7,500-watt shortwave transmitter located at Lampertheim in West Germany. In 1997, Pathfinder landed on Mars on July Fourth. In 2004, the cornerstone of the Freedom Tower was laid at the site of the World Trade Center in New York City. The Statue of Liberty's crown reopened in 2009 to the public after eight years of closure due to security concerns following the September 11 attacks.

Another kind of new beginning has been immigrants becoming American citizens on Independence Day. Large numbers have done so over the years. In 1976, for example, 7,320 took the oath of citizenship at the Miami Beach Convention Center.[35] One tradition began at Monticello, the home of Thomas Jefferson, in 1963. "A typical ceremony includes 'a concert of American patriotic music; the petitioners for naturalization, their family, friends and guests" and an "invited guest who reads the preamble to the Declaration of Independence; and a guest speaker delivers remarks before the new citizens take the oath of citizenship."[36]

THE CENTENNIAL, SESQUICENTENNIAL, BICENTENNIAL, AND SEMIQUINCENTENNIAL

As discussed previously, the fiftieth anniversary of the Declaration of Independence has been forever marked in history by the deaths of John Adams and Thomas Jefferson on that day. The Centennial, with its focus on the Centennial Exhibition in Philadelphia, similarly has faded into history except for the actions of the suffragettes protesting the lack of women's rights. At the time, it attracted millions to the exhibition over the course of several months. On the Fourth, wide-ranging events occurred throughout the country to mark the Centennial. For example, San Francisco hosted a four-mile parade with ten thousand participants.[37] "In Bristol, Rhode Island, a parade float named 'Triumphal Car' saw 38 ladies and a 'Goddess of Liberty' waving to the crowds along the streets."[38] In Port Richmond, New York, five hundred children sang "Hail Columbia" and the "Star-Spangled Banner."[39] Although the states of the former Confederacy did not resume celebrations until many years after the conclusion of the Civil War, freed slaves did celebrate. In 1876, in Hamburg, South Carolina, a conflict arose between the races during a parade of local black militia, resulting in the massacre of numerous African American men.[40] That year, in Richmond, Virginia, the American flag was raised on the state capitol for the first time on the Fourth of July in sixteen years.[41] Given the era and the importance of the Centennial, grand oratory was expected and many words said.[42]

The Sesquicentennial—1926—also had its full share of speeches. Once again, Philadelphia held a fair, and President Calvin Coolidge gave an address marking the 150th anniversary of the Declaration of Independence.[43] Not known for his oratory—he was called "Silent Cal" for a reason—he nonetheless rose to the occasion (perhaps because he was born on July 4, 1872). He said in part:

> It was not because [the Declaration of Independence] was proposed to establish a new nation, but because it was proposed to establish a nation on new principles, that July 4, 1776, has come to be regarded as one of the greatest days in history. Three very definite propositions were set out in its preamble regarding the nature of

> mankind and therefore of government. These were the doctrine that all men are created equal, that they are endowed with certain inalienable rights, and that therefore the source of the just powers of government must be derived from the consent of the governed.
>
> About the Declaration there is a finality that is exceedingly restful. It is often asserted that the world has made a great deal of progress since 1776, that we have had new thoughts and new experiences which have given us a great advance over the people of that day, and that we may therefore very well discard their conclusions for something more modern. But that reasoning can not be applied to this great charter. If all men are created equal, that is final. If they are endowed with inalienable rights, that is final. If governments derive their just powers from the consent of the governed, that is final. No advance, no progress can be made beyond these propositions. If anyone wishes to deny their truth or their soundness, the only direction in which he can proceed historically is not forward, but backward toward the time when there was no equality, no rights of the individual, no rule of the people. Those who wish to proceed in that direction can not lay claim to progress. They are reactionary. Their ideas are not more modern, but more ancient, than those of the Revolutionary fathers.

The Bicentennial coincided with a wave of patriotism and nostalgia that swept the nation following the divisiveness of the previous decades, which were marked in part by the Civil Rights Movement, the Vietnam War, vast social changes, and the Watergate scandal of 1974. Red, white, and blue paint was used throughout the nation to decorate mailboxes, fire hydrants, and train cars. More than "5,000 colorful and memorable events were staged across the nation."[44] In Philadelphia on July 6, Queen Elizabeth II presented the Bicentennial Bell on behalf of the British people. It is a replica of the Liberty Bell, cast at the same foundry, and bears the inscription "For the People of the United States of America from the People of Britain 4 July 1976 LET FREEDOM RING." Congress, by joint resolution, posthumously appointed George Washington to the grade of General of the Armies of the United States, with the effective date of July 4, 1976. Perhaps the most memorable event was "Operation Sail" in waters off of New York City, which was then the "largest assemblage ever of tall ships, representing twenty-two nations."[45] President Gerald Ford, on board the USS *Forrestal*, presided over the review of ships.[46]

The United States Semiquincentennial (also called Sestercentennial or Quarter Millennial) will be the 250th anniversary of the Declaration of Independence in 2026. Planning is underway by a variety of governmental and nongovernmental organizations.[47] The United States Semiquincentennial Commission Act of 2016 directed the United States Government to issue commemorative coins and postage stamps and commission appropriately named naval vessels. Specific activities—both officially organized and independently created—are being planned. The commission wisely calls the celebration "America 250," rather than Semiquincentennial. The commission's goals are lofty: "engaging all Americans in the largest and most inclusive celebration and commemoration in our nation's history." It seeks to "inspire the American spirit to deepen understanding of our history and the democratic process" and "foster unity." It seeks to produce more than 100,000 programs over a multi-year period, "reaching its peak on the Fourth of July 2026."[48]

PROTESTS, DEMONSTRATIONS, AND OCCASIONAL UNITY

Protests, demonstrations, disagreements, and disturbances are a common feature of July Fourth throughout history. In 1788, in Albany, New York, there was a fight between those in favor of and those opposing the adoption of the proposed Constitution. A full-length portrait of Alexander Hamilton, painted by John Trumbull, was revealed at City Hall in New York on July 4, 1792.[49] On the same day, the "slanderous hyperbole of Philip Freneau's *National Gazette* now soared to a new pitch," running a front-page article attacking Secretary Hamilton's Treasury Department programs as the "most effective means" of "'changing limited republican government into an unlimited hereditary one."[50] In 1794, John Jay negotiated a treaty with Great Britain that did little to satisfy American concerns about issues unresolved since independence. The adverse reaction in the states upon learning its details was intense. On July 4, 1795,

Jay was "burned in effigy in so many cities that he said he could have walked the length of America by the glow from his own flaming figure."[51]

The Vietnam War era saw many anti-war demonstrations on the Fourth. A protest of another kind, *Born on the Fourth of July*, written by Ron Kovic, focused on a Vietnam veteran who was paralyzed from the chest down.[52] The Fourth of July has been the occasion to proclaim alternative versions of the Declaration of Independence: the suffragettes did so in 1876; that same year, socialists distributed their own version. Other years have seen flag burning, riots, and other forms of dissent. William Lloyd Garrison, a famous abolitionist, burned a copy of the Constitution in 1854 in Farmington, Massachusetts. Yippies, for many years, held an annual march in Washington, D.C., seeking the repeal of marijuana laws.

Unusual unity prevailed on July 4, 2002, the year after the terrorist attacks of September 11, 2001. Despite heightened security throughout the country, celebrations large and small were seen across the land. In Philadelphia, Secretary of State Colin Powell was awarded the Philadelphia Freedom Medal for his leadership in the War on Terror, his efforts in the Middle East, and his human rights concerns. Powell said: "The terrorists thought they could keep us from celebrating the Fourth of July. They were wrong. We are here, and we will remain."[53]

CHAPTER 14

Why We Celebrate

During the Revolution, many of the American sailors captured by the British were housed on prison ships in New York Harbor. The conditions varied, but as many as eleven thousand prisoners died over the course of the war, often from rampant diseases spreading among the men, poor diets, and filthy, fetid, and overcrowded confinements.[1] Apparently, all of the prisoners were sailors.[2] One prisoner, Philip Freneau, left a poem about his experiences, which was in part:

> Conveyed to York we found, at length, too late,
> That Death was better than the prisoner's fate,
> There doomed to famine, shackles, and despair,
> Condemned to breathe a foul, infected air,
> In sickly hulks, devoted while we lay,
> Successive funerals gloomed each dismal day.[3]

"The most infamous British prison ship was the HMS *Jersey* or *Old Jersey*, referred to by its inmates simply as 'Hell.' More than 1,000 men were kept aboard the *Jersey* at any one time, and about a dozen died every night from diseases such as small pox, dysentery, typhoid and yellow fever, as well as from the effects of starvation and torture."[4] The *Jersey* was a decommissioned British Royal Navy vessel, at one point mounting sixty guns and a crew of four hundred, but had become a leaky old hulk[5] moored in the Wallabout, a sheltered bay on the Long Island shore.[6] It was abandoned by the British at the end of the war, where it eventually rotted and sank.[7]

Thomas Dring was a masters-mate on board a privateer named the *Chance*, which mounted twelve 6-pound cannon, with a crew of sixty-five.[8] Within a few days of sailing out of Providence, Rhode Island, in May 1782, the ship proved unlucky—it was captured and the crew imprisoned on the *Jersey.* Dring, in later life, recalled the horrors of the confinement, which rivaled those of Private Robert Knox Sneden in Andersonville Prison during the Civil War. Like those prisoners of war, the sailors imprisoned on the *Jersey* were determined to celebrate the Fourth of July.

Dring recounted that, as soon as he and other prisoners were allowed on deck that day, they displayed thirteen "little national flags" in a row on the boom. The guards ordered them to remove the flags, and, when the prisoners did not, the guards "triumphantly demolished and trampled them under foot."[9] The men then sang patriotic songs, accompanied by occasional cheers. More guards were ordered out, and the prisoners were driven below deck at the point of bayonets. Dring recalled that they continued to be noisy and sing patriotic songs despite orders to stop. That evening, the guards descended among the prisoners with lanterns and drawn cutlasses, which they used to cut and wound anyone within reach. After the assault, in total darkness, Dring heard the "groans and lamentations" of the wounded. Adding to the misery, the men had been driven below deck without water, and the heat below deck was extreme. The cries and "supplications" for water were ignored by the guards. All of this combined to form "a combination of horrors which no pen can describe."[10] The night seemed endless; Dring managed to find his way to the grating of the main hatchway, where, to distract himself from the "terrible sounds," he watched the progress of the stars in the east. About eight to ten men died that night.

Dring was part of a prisoner exchange on July 27, 1782. Of the sixty-five sailors from the *Chance* that had been imprisoned, only thirty-five or thirty-nine survived to be exchanged.[11] Dring went on to be a ship captain. Said he later in life:

> Since that time I have often, while standing on the deck of a good ship under my command, and viewing the rising stars, thought upon the horrors of that night, when I stood watching their

> progress through the gratings of the Old Jersey, and when I now contrast my former wretchedness with my present situation, in the full enjoyment of liberty, health, and every earthly comfort, I cannot but muse upon the contrast, and bless the good and great Being from whom my comforts have been derived.[12]

***

Declaring independence was not the same as achieving it. On July 4, 1776, the United States issued its Declaration, but it was not until September 3, 1783, that the Treaty of Paris was signed, in which Great Britain recognized the United States as independent. There have been other, longer roads to freedom, equality, and the pursuit of happiness since that time. The road remains difficult as we seek to better approximate the Declaration's promises. It is right—and necessary—to celebrate what has been achieved and to seek new variations of the promises that remain unfulfilled or are still unknown.

America's story, highlighted often from events occurring on the Fourth of July, is a story of perseverance within the context of an expanding understanding of freedom. It is about independence: of the country, of races, of gender, of self. We should and do celebrate it. We may celebrate the date, but we should celebrate the ideas and the ideals represented by what occurred that day and on the many subsequent Fourth of Julys. The success of those ideas and ideals was the result of many individuals persevering and striving, sometimes for decades, sometimes for centuries, many times with their lives, to expand the promise of freedom. None of this was preordained. We should celebrate those individuals who have dedicated their lives to the document's ideals, who have sacrificed so much.

There have been landmarks along the way: words, actions, people, and events that underscore the day's importance. John Adams, a chief agitator for independence, observed how hard the road to freedom was going to be, and his life is a testament to that observation.

One man, Henry David Thoreau, merely walked into the woods on Independence Day to begin his personal pursuit of happiness. But that physical act was not the hard part; the quest for a dignified life on his own terms was the essential challenge.

Frederick Douglass, after physically freeing himself from slavery, used his voice on another July day celebrating independence to point to the vast number of Americans who were not free and to underscore the hypocrisy of the promise of the Declaration of Independence to those in slavery. Douglass pursued a life of agitating for freedom and equality for his race long after his physical safety had been assured.

Susan B. Anthony and her fellow suffragettes used the day to protest the unequal treatment of her gender. Anthony, the drafter of the Nineteenth Amendment guaranteeing women the right to vote, did not live to see it adopted, but she committed her entire life to securing the vote.

Lincoln, speaking of the Union victories at Vicksburg and Gettysburg, gave modern meaning to the promise of the Declaration of Independence, eventually polishing his views in the speech at Gettysburg, dedicating the National Cemetery. He strove toward a new birth of equality and liberty within an enduring Union.

The dedication and sacrifices of so many in the Civil War (and in the many other conflicts of the United States that fell on many July Fourths) is given voice through the Union Private Robert Knox Sneden, who celebrated Independence Day after a significant Union defeat and later as a captive in the most horrid conditions at Andersonville Prison. Sneden, who saw more than his share of misery, could still celebrate. So could Thomas Dring aboard the *Jersey* as the country struggled to be recognized as independent.

The determination of Grant to take Vicksburg and the steady bravery of the Union lines at Gettysburg are underlined examples of the importance of the date in American history and the sacrifices of so many in the service of their country. Others, such as young Theodore Roosevelt and eulogist Daniel Webster, have reminded us of our own responsibilities to help ensure that the promises of life, liberty, and the pursuit of happiness endure.

Some events are poignant reminders of personal courage, such as Lou Gehrig's farewell address at Yankee Station as he suffered the devastating effects of the disease named after him.

There are deep flaws in our history. George Washington was one of Virginia's largest slaveholders, growing his plantation throughout his life through that slave labor. So did Thomas Jefferson. The deaths, injuries, and sufferings of hundreds of thousands of Americans—North and South—occurred within the span of time that included the four July Fourths during the Civil War. Slavery and the denial of equal rights based on race and gender were highlighted by Frederick Douglass in one great Fourth of July speech and in the actions of Susan B. Anthony and her fellow suffragettes at the Centennial. The aftermath of the Spanish-American War saw the country in possession of new lands and new peoples. It took many years and much conflict before acknowledging the independence of the Philippines and granting self-determination to Puerto Rico.

There has been an evolution to America's vision of freedom and independence, often with July the Fourth as a hinge for events. The risks have been great, the challenges daunting, and the reward often delayed. But the story of America continues. While writing in 1790, Thomas Jefferson observed: "the ground of liberty is to be gained by inches, that we must be contented to secure what we can get from time to time, and eternally press forward for what is yet to get."[13] Hence, even if that flawed man did not fully understand the reach of his chosen language in the Declaration of Independence, its enduring promise continues to be more fully appreciated. There are more Fourth of July celebrations to come as the promise evolves.

Acknowledgments

I thank my wife, Sally, for her extensive proofreading of this book as it evolved. Several individuals helped me rethink the structure of the manuscript, including Mike Magner and Sally. The Honorable Daniel J. Crothers of the Supreme Court of North Dakota offered valuable comments for the chapter about the celebration in that state on July 4, 1886.

Readers and writers of American history are extremely fortunate to live in this time because there are so many high-quality biographies and history books written by eminent historians and biographers. This book certainly benefited from those sources, which are cited in the various notes in each chapter. We are lucky for the additional reason that many original sources are now available online and can be accessed by anyone who so chooses. Sites such as Founders Online, Library of Congress, and the Massachusetts Historical Society have made researching the historical record so accessible, offering a wealth of information. For example, George Washington's entire diary is online, giving me a very different perspective on him than I previously held. The extensive letters between John Adams and Thomas Jefferson are similarly available. The organizations that have done all of this detailed work enrich us all.

Finally, I thank Sunbury Press and its publisher, Lawrence Knorr, for agreeing to publish this book and for all the advice that made it better. In particular, I thank Sarah Peachey for her detailed and outstanding editorial work on the manuscript.

Notes

Quotations in this book are often edited, including changes to paragraph breaks, capitalization, spelling, and similar material. There have been no substantive changes to the content. Occasionally, the original spelling and sentence structure are left unedited for effect.

Preface

1. Robert Leckie, Vol. I, *The Wars of America* (New York: Harper & Row 1968), 105.

Chapter 1: The Separation from Great Britain

1. Pauline Maier, *American Scripture: Making the Declaration of Independence* (New York: Knopf, 1997), 38.

2. Garry Wills, *Inventing America: Jefferson's Declaration of Independence* (Garden City: Doubleday & Company 1978), 54–57.

3. Ibid., 64.

4. Robert M. Calhoon, "Loyalism and neutrality," in A Companion to the American Revolution, edited by Jack P. Greene and J. R. Pole (Malden, MA: Blackwell Publishers Ltd, 2000), 235.

5. Letter to H. Niles, February 13, 1818, Works of John Adams, ed. Charles Frances Adams (Boston: Little, Brown & Co., 1865) 10:282.

6. Ibid., 282–83 (letter to H. Niles, February 13, 1818). Ibid., 183-84 (letter to Dr. Morse on November 29, 1815) (stating that the "revolution in the principles, views, opinions, and feelings of the American people" began with Otis's argument).

7. Ibid., 172 (letter to Thomas Jefferson on August 24, 1815).

8. Ibid., 283 (letter to H. Niles, February 13, 1818).

9. The British came to regret that neglect as troubles with the colonies multiplied in the years before the Revolution, with one source characterizing the colonials as been "bred up almost in Independency." John C. Miller, Origins of the American Revolution (Boston: Little Brown & Co. 1943), 207–08. From their point of view, "it seemed more likely that the troubles of the mother country came from sparing the rod and spoiling the child." Professor Miller details that the British viewpoint was one of "innate British superiority" that emphasized both political and economic subordination of the colonies. Ibid., 204. Contributing to that period of "salutary neglect" was the influence of the frontier and the vast expanse of ocean separating the colonies from Britain. Ibid., 30, 37–38.

10. For detailed discussion of the Writs case and its impact on the development of the Fourth Amendment, which regulates governmental searches and seizures, see Thomas K. Clancy, "The Framers' Intent: John Adams, His Era, and the Fourth Amendment," Indiana Law Journal 86 (2011): 979.

11. Significant aspects of Otis's arguments later became elements of Fourth Amendment structure and jurisprudence. They include: identifying the right to be "secure" as the interest implicated by a search or seizure; listing the home as a protected place; utilizing the common law search warrant as a model for when warrants may issue; defining unjustified intrusions as "unreasonable;" and indicating that probable-cause-based searches and seizures are proper. More broadly, Otis's concerns about the need for certain procedures, the scope of intrusions, and the arbitrary use of authority, have had continued importance in search and

seizure jurisprudence to this day. Underlying all of those arguments and principles was a quest for objective criteria to measure the legitimacy of a search or seizure. Ibid.

12. A principal import of the time was molasses, from which rum was made. John Adams observed late in life: "Wits may laugh at our fondness for molasses, and we ought all to join in the laugh. . . . I know not why we should blush to confess that molasses was an essential ingredient in American independence." Letter to William Tudor, August 11, 1818, Works of John Adams, 10:345.

13. Josiah Quincy, Jr., Reports of Cases Argued and Adjudged in the Superior Court of Judicature of the Province of Massachusetts Bay, Between 1761 and 1772 (1865), 489.

14. Diary and Autobiography of Adams, ed. L.H. Butterfield (Cambridge, MA: Harvard University Press, 1961), 3:276.

15. Letter to Abigail Adams, 3 July 1776, Works of John Adams 9:418.

16. Letter to Mr. Calkoen dated October 4, 1780, Works of John Adams, 9:266–67.

17. Letter to William Tudor, March 29, 1817, Works of John Adams, 10:247–48.

18. Letter to William Tudor, February 25, 1818, 10 Works of John Adams, 291.

19. John Adams diary 6, 2 December 1760 - 3 March 1761 [electronic edition]. https://www.masshist.org/digitaladams/archive/doc?id=D6 (last accessed October 16, 2024).

20. Letter to J. Morse, November 29, 1815, Works of John Adams, 10:183.

21. Letter to Thomas McKean, August 31, 1831, Works of John Adams, 10:63. Letter to Benjamin Waterhouse, February 6, 1818, Works of John Adams, 10:281 (expressing his love for Otis).

22. Letter to William Tudor, February 25, 1818, Works of John Adams, 10:291. Note that Adams's comment covers only the ten-year period ending in 1770. After that time, Otis's mental health deteriorated and his influence waned. Adams, in his diary entry for January 16, 1770, observed that Otis did not appear to be "in his perfect mind," that he "loses himself," and was in confusion. He concluded: "I never saw such an object of admiration, reverence, contempt and compassion all at once as this. I fear, I tremble, I mourn the man, and for his Country. Many others mourn him with tears in their eyes."

23. For a detailed examination of Samuel Adams's roles as a propagandist and organizer, see John C. Miller, Sam Adams: Pioneer in Propaganda (Stanford: Stanford University Press, 1964); Stacy Schiff, The Revolutionary: Samuel Adams (New York: Little Brown, 2022).

24. John C. Miller, Sam Adams: Pioneer in Propaganda (Stanford: Stanford University Press, 1964), 343.

25. Stacy Schiff, The Revolutionary: Samuel Adams (New York: Little Brown, 2022), 157–61, 362n159.

26. The acting governor of Massachusetts, Thomas Hutchinson, described Samuel Adams as having "talents beyond any other persons on the globe at misrepresentation." Stacy Schiff, The Revolutionary, Samuel Adams, 177.

27. Stacy Schiff, The Revolutionary: Samuel Adams, 296.

28. John C. Miller, Sam Adams, 40.

29. John C. Miller, Sam Adams, 40.

30. Founders Online, "From John Adams to Hezekiah Niles, 13 February 1818," National Archives, https://founders.archives.gov/documents/Adams/99-02-02-6854 (last accessed October 16, 2024).

31. Pauline Maier, The Old Revolutionaries (New York: Knopf, 1980), 12.

32. John C. Miller, Origins of the American Revolution, 101–06.

33. Historian John C. Miller characterized this pattern of "alternate coercion and appeasement" as convincing Americans "that they had little to fear from the Ministry, however it might bluster and threaten. The mother country began to appear an impotent old shrew with an uncommonly evil temper but quite unable to bring her unruly children overseas to book." Origins of the American Revolution, 285.

34. Letter to Richard Jackson, October 22, 1765, quoted in John C. Miller, Origins of the American Revolution, 167.

35. John C. Miller, Origins of the American Revolution, 218.

36. Ibid., 121–22.

37. Ibid., 25.

38. Pauline Maier, American Scripture, xx.

39. John C. Miller, Origins of the American Revolution, 122–23.

40. Ibid., 131–32.

41. Ibid., 130.

42. Ibid., 137–39.

43. John Adams diary 11, 18 December 1765, www.masshist.org/digitaladams/archive/doc?id=D11.

44. Johns Adams diary, 19-21 December, 1765, www.masshist.org/digitaladams/archive/doc?id=D11 .
45. David McCullough, John Adams (New York, NY: Simon & Schuster, 2001), 61.
46. Ibid., 60.
47. He returned to this theme of reciprocity late in life: "believing allegiance and protection to be reciprocal, when protection was withdrawn, [the colonists] thought allegiance dissolved." Letter to H. Niles, February 13, 1818, Works of John Adams, 10:282. Adams, also late in life, maintained that he had some "distant thoughts of an independency from Great Britain" as early as 1755 to 1757. Letter to William Tudor, March 7, 1819, Works of John Adams, 10:368.
48. The mob's actions have been described as "remarkable for its savagery," smashing and destroying everything within the house, working throughout the night and only leaving at daylight. Bernard Bailyn, The Ordeal of Thomas Hutchinson (Cambridge: Belknap Press, 1974), 35.
49. John Adams diary for January 2, 1766, https://www.masshist.org/digitaladams/archive/doc?id=D12&bc=%2Fdigitaladams%2Farchive%2Fbrowse%2Fdiaries_by_number.php (last accessed October 16, 2024).
50. John Adams diary, December 23, 1765, https://www.masshist.org/digitaladams/archive/doc?id=D12&bc=%2Fdigitaladams%2Farchive%2Fbrowse%2Fdiaries_by_number.php (last accessed October 16, 2024).
51. In June 1768, John Hancock's ship Liberty was seized in Boston Harbor after unloading a cargo of uncustomed wines, causing more riots and chaos. John Adams represented Hancock in the litigation stemming from the seizure; Adams's diary recorded that he viewed it as an "odious cause" and "painful drudgery" that was only suspended permanently after the battle at Lexington, which ended all such prosecutions. John Adams autobiography, part I, through 1776, sheet 16. One tragic incident on February 22, 1770, involved the shooting of a child named Christopher Seider by Ebenezer Richardson, a Tory, stemming from a protest against merchants who were violating the nonimportation agreement. John Adams attended the funeral the next day and recorded that it was also attended by "a vast number of women and men. . . . My eyes never beheld such a funeral." He believed that it showed that "there were many more lives to spend if wanted in the service of their country." John Adams diary, February 26 "or thereabouts," 1770.
52. John C. Miller, Origins of the American Revolution, 278.
53. For a detailed account of the trial, see Hiller B. Zobel, The Boston Massacre (New York: W.W. Norton & Co., 1970). For Samuel Adams's efforts to characterize the events as a "horrid massacre," see Stacy Schiff, The Revolutionary, Samuel Adams, 188; John C. Miller, Sam Adams, 166–92. John Adams was widely criticized for defending the soldiers but was, nonetheless, elected to the Massachusetts legislature in 1770.
54. John Adams diary, December 29, 1772, https://www.masshist.org/digitaladams/archive/doc?id=D19 (last accessed October 16, 2024).
55. Diary and Autobiography of John Adams, 2:79.
56. Founders Online, "From John Adams to Benjamin Rush, 21 May 1807," National Archives, https://founders.archives.gov/documents/Adams/99-02-02-5186 (last accessed October 16, 2024).
57. Legal Papers of John Adams, ed. L. Kinvin Wroth and Hiller B. Zobel (Cambridge, MA: Harvard University Press, 1965), 2:105.
58. Legal Papers of John Adams, 2:105.
59. John C. Miller, Origins of the American Revolution, 294.
60. Stacy Schiff, The Revolutionary: Samuel Adams, 239–42.
61. John C. Miller, Origins of the American Revolution, 277.
62. Ibid., 290–94.
63. John Adams diary, January 17, 1773.
64. Henry S. Commager and Richard B. Morris, eds., "Lord Frederick North Calls for Swift Punishment," The Spirit of 'Seventy-Six: The Story of the American Revolution as Told by Participants, (New York: Da Capo Press, 1958), 13–14.
65. Richard Henry Lee, letter to Arthur Lee, in The Letters of Richard Henry Lee, 1762–1778, vol. 1, ed. James Curtis Ballagh (1911), 114.
66. John Adams's diary is the main source for this material. The online version, hosted by the Massachusetts Historical Society, is helpfully supplemented by other sources and this summary utilizes all of that material. See www.masshist.org/publications/adams-papers/index.php/view/ADMS-01-02-02-0004-0005-0001 (last accessed October 16, 2024).
67. Founders Online, "From John Adams to Timothy Pickering, 6 August 1822," National Archives, https://founders.archives.gov/documents/Adams/99-02-02-7674 (last accessed October 16, 2024). Although

the details differ, the fact that the Massachusetts delegation was cautioned to avoid attempting to dictate and that other colonies had delegates with "very worthy, learned men." Joseph Hawley to John Adams, July 25, 1774, quoted in Henry S. Commager and Richard B. Morris, eds., The Spirit of 'Seventy-Six.

68. John Adams diary, September 6, 1774, www.masshist.org/digitaladams/archive/doc?id=D22A (last accessed October 16, 2024).

69. John Adams autobiography, part 1, through 1776, sheet 18 of 53, September 1774 - May 1775, www.masshist.org/digitaladams/archive/doc?id=A1_18 (last accessed October 16, 2024).

70. Works of John Adams, 3:22.

71. David McCullough, John Adams, 96.

72. Pauline Maier, American Scripture, 79.

73. Jefferson letter to Roger C. Weightman, June 24, 1826, available at https://www.loc.gov/exhibits/declara/rcwltr.html (last accessed October 16, 2024).

74. John C. Miller, Sam Adams, 339.

75. John Adams autobiography, part 1, "John Adams," through 1776, sheet 24 of 53 [electronic edition]. Adams Family Papers: An Electronic Archive. Massachusetts Historical Society. https://www.masshist.org/digitaladams/archive/doc?id=A1_24 (last accessed October 16, 2024).

76. www.masshist.org/publications/adams-papers/index.php/view/DJA03d298 (last accessed October 16, 2024).

77. Founders Online, "From Thomas Jefferson to Henry Lee, 8 May 1825," National Archives, https://founders.archives.gov/documents/Jefferson/98-01-02-5212 (last accessed October 16, 2024). Historian Pauline Maier details that the Declaration was one among many declarations of independence at that time from various localities and states. Her work confirms what Jefferson wrote—that the sentiments and ideas Jefferson set forth were widespread regarding the causes and justification for independence. See generally Pauline Maier, American Scripture. While surveying the various declarations, she observed:

A sense of shared grievances and the repeated efforts to coordinate opposition and to secure redress helped establish this common identity, but it also owed much to the colonists' experience of belonging to an entity larger than their separate provinces, the British Empire. As affection for the Mother Country faded, it was transferred to that jerry-built institution, the Second Continental Congress, and the fledgling nation it struggled to lead.

Ibid., 76.

78. The draft was almost exclusively Jefferson's but some details of interactions with the other members of the drafting committee before submitting it to Congress are disputed among historians. Pauline Maier, American Scripture, 99–105.

79. Letter to James Madison, 30 August 1823.

80. David McCullough, John Adams, 126.

81. "Notes on a Conversation with Thomas Jefferson," in The Papers of Daniel Webster: Correspondence, ed. Charles M. Wiltse (Hanover, NH: The University Press of New England, 1974), 1:375.

82. Walter Isaacson, Benjamin Franklin (New York: Simon and Schuster, 2004), 313.

83. "Thomas Jefferson's Anecdotes of Benjamin Franklin, [ca. 4 December 1818]," Founders Online, National Archives, https://founders.archives.gov/documents/Jefferson/03-13-02-0407 (last accessed October 16, 2024). [Original source: The Papers of Thomas Jefferson, Retirement Series, vol. 13, 22 April 1818 to 31 January 1819, ed. J. Jefferson Looney. Princeton: Princeton University Press, 2016, 462–465.]

84. Walter Isaacson, Benjamin Franklin, 313.

85. Founders Online, "To John Adams from Benjamin Rush, 20 July 1811," National Archives, https://founders.archives.gov/documents/Adams/99-02-02-5659 (last accessed October 16, 2024).

86. David McCullough, John Adams, 129.

87. Founders Online, "John Adams to Abigail Adams, 3 July 1776," National Archives, https://founders.archives.gov/documents/Adams/04-02-02-0016 (last accessed October 16, 2024). [Original source: The Adams Papers, Adams Family Correspondence, vol. 2, June 1776–March 1778, ed. L. H. Butterfield. Cambridge, MA: Harvard University Press, 1963, pp. 29–33.].

88. David McCullough, John Adams, 136.

89. Pauline Maier, American Scripture, 154.

90. David McCullough, John Adams, 136–37.

91. Founders Online, "General Orders, 9 July 1776," National Archives, https://founders.archives.gov/documents/Washington/03-05-02-0176 (last accessed October 16, 2024). [Original source: The Papers of

George Washington, Revolutionary War Series, vol. 5, 16 June 1776 – 12 August 1776, ed. Philander D. Chase. Charlottesville: University Press of Virginia, 1993, pp. 245–247.]

92. Ron Chernow, Alexander Hamilton (New York: Penguin Books, 2004), 77.

93. Ron Chernow, Washington: A Life (New York: Penguin Books, 2010), 237; Founders Online, "From George Washington to John Hancock, 10 July 1776," National Archives, https://founders.archives.gov/documents/Washington/03-05-02-0188 (last accessed October 16, 2024). [Original source: The Papers of George Washington, Revolutionary War Series, vol. 5, 16 June 1776 – 12 August 1776, ed. Philander D. Chase. Charlottesville: University Press of Virginia, 1993, pp. 258–261.].

94. Founders Online, "From George Washington to John Hancock, 10 July 1776," National Archives, https://founders.archives.gov/documents/Washington/03-05-02-0188 (last accessed October 16, 2024). [Original source: The Papers of George Washington, Revolutionary War Series, vol. 5, 16 June 1776 – 12 August 1776, ed. Philander D. Chase. Charlottesville: University Press of Virginia, 1993, pp. 258–261.]

95. Chernow, Alexander Hamilton, 77–78.

96. Ron Chernow, Washington: A Life (New York: Penguin Books 2010), 237.

97. Chernow, Alexander Hamilton, 77–78.

98. Pauline Maier, American Scripture, 156. Later celebrations typically focused on the act of independence rather than the details of the document declaring independence. Historian Maier has observed: "The Declaration was at first forgotten almost entirely, then recalled and celebrated by Jeffersonian Republicans, and later elevated into something akin to holy writ, which made it a prize worth capturing on behalf of one cause after another." Pauline Maier, American Scripture, 154. In contrast, Garry Wills maintained that the document became associated with the Federalists during the war and, by end of the eighteenth century had become "a Federalist preserve." Garry Wills, Inventing America, 338.

99. Pauline Maier, American Scripture, 157.

100. Ibid., 157.

101. Henry S. Commager and Richard B. Morris, eds. The Spirit of 'Seventy-Six, 322–23.

102. Letter to William Tudor, September 18, 1818, Works of John Adams, 10:359. This was consistent with views he expressed as early as 1766 in his diary, writing that the colonies were "allies rather than subjects" of Britain and that the settlement of the colonies were not national acts. Diary of John Adams, January 1, 1766.

103. Mellen Chamberlain, "Remarks Before the Sons of the American Revolution, Concord, April 19, 1884," John Adams: Statesman of the American Revolution (Boston: Houghton, Mifflin & Co., 1899), 248.

104. Ibid., 249–50; "Why Captain Levi Preston Fought: An Interview with One of the Survivors of the Revolution by Hon. Mellen Chamberlain of Chelsea," 8 Danvers Historical Collections (1920), 68–70. Other published versions of Chamberlain's interview of Preston have Preston answering: "we always had been free, and we meant to be free always."

Chapter 2: George Washington: From an Inauspicious Prelude to an Emblem of Perseverance

1. Ron Chernow, Washington: A Life, 31.

2. Founders Online, "Journey to the French Commandant: Narrative," National Archives, https://founders.archives.gov/documents/Washington/01-01-02-0003-0002 (last accessed October 16, 2024). [Original source: The Diaries of George Washington, vol. 1, 11 March 1748 – 13 November 1765, ed. Donald Jackson. Charlottesville: University Press of Virginia, 1976, pp. 130–161.]

3. For Washington's brief account, see Founders Online, "Expedition to the Ohio, 1754: Narrative," National Archives, https://founders.archives.gov/documents/Washington/01-01-02-0004-0002 (last accessed October 16, 2024). [Original source: The Diaries of George Washington, vol. 1, 11 March 1748 – 13 November 1765, ed. Donald Jackson. Charlottesville: University Press of Virginia, 1976, pp. 174–210.]

4. Chernow, Washington: A Life, 42.

5. Ibid., 43.

6. Founders Online, "From George Washington to Robert Dinwiddie, 27 May 1754," National Archives, https://founders.archives.gov/documents/Washington/02-01-02-0053 (last accessed October 16, 2024). [Original source: The Papers of George Washington, Colonial Series, vol. 1, 7 July 1748 – 14 August 1755, ed. W. W. Abbot. Charlottesville: University Press of Virginia, 1983, pp. 104–106.]

7. Fort Necessity National Battlefield, National Park Service, https://www.nps.gov/fone/index.htm (last accessed October 16, 2024).

8. Chernow, Washington: A Life, 44.

9. Ibid., 47.

10. Ibid., 47.

11. Ibid. 48. The document in full is at Founders Online, "II., 3 July 1754," National Archives, https://founders.archives.gov/documents/Washington/02-01-02-0076-0003 (last accessed October 16, 2024). [Original source: The Papers of George Washington, Colonial Series, vol. 1, 7 July 1748 – 14 August 1755, ed. W. W. Abbot. Charlottesville: University Press of Virginia, 1983, pp. 165–168.]

12. Founders Online, "I., 19 July 1754," National Archives, https://founders.archives.gov/documents/Washington/02-01-02-0076-0002 (last accessed October 16, 2024). [Original source: The Papers of George Washington, Colonial Series, vol. 1, 7 July 1748 – 14 August 1755, ed. W. W. Abbot. Charlottesville: University Press of Virginia, 1983, pp. 159–164.]

13. Chernow, Washington: A Life, 48.

14. Walter Isaacson, Benjamin Franklin, 168. As he lay dying, Braddock whispered to an aide: "Who would have thought it?" Ibid.

15. Chernow, Washington: A Life, 58–59.

16. Founders Online, "From George Washington to John Augustine Washington, 18 July 1755," National Archives, https://founders.archives.gov/documents/Washington/02-01-02-0169 (last accessed October 16, 2024). [Original source: The Papers of George Washington, Colonial Series, vol. 1, 7 July 1748 – 14 August 1755, ed. W. W. Abbot. Charlottesville: University Press of Virginia, 1983, p. 343.]

17. Chernow, Washington: A Life, 61.

18. Ibid., 124.

19. James Thacher, Military Journal During the American Revolutionary War, July 1775 to February 17, 1777 (Boston: Richardson & Lord, 2d Ed., 1827), 33.

20. John Adams to Abigail Adams, June 11, 1775, www.masshist.org/digitaladams/archive/doc?id=L17750611ja#:~:text=I%20begin%20to%20hope%20We,him%2C%20in%20a%20great%20Degree (last accessed October 16, 2024).

21. Abigail Adams to John Adams, July 16, 1775, www.masshist.org/digitaladams/archive/doc?id=L17750716aa&bc=%2Fdigitaladams%2Farchive%2Fbrowse%2Fletters_1774_1777.php (last accessed October 16, 2024)

22. David McCullough, 1776 (New York: Simon & Schuster, 2005), 42.

23. Founders Online, "From George Washington to Bryan Fairfax, 4 July 1774," National Archives, https://founders.archives.gov/documents/Washington/02-10-02-0075 (last accessed October 16, 2024). [Original source: The Papers of George Washington, Colonial Series, vol. 10, 21 March 1774 – 15 June 1775, ed. W. W. Abbot and Dorothy Twohig. Charlottesville: University Press of Virginia, 1995, pp. 109–110.]

24. Founders Online, "Address to the Massachusetts Provincial Congress, 4 July 1775," National Archives, https://founders.archives.gov/documents/Washington/03-01-02-0029 (last accessed October 16, 2024). [Original source: The Papers of George Washington, Revolutionary War Series, vol. 1, 16 June 1775 – 15 September 1775, ed. Philander D. Chase. Charlottesville: University Press of Virginia, 1985, pp. 59–60.]

25. Founders Online, "General Orders, 4 July 1775," National Archives, https://founders.archives.gov/documents/Washington/03-01-02-0027 (last accessed October 16, 2024). [Original source: The Papers of George Washington, Revolutionary War Series, vol. 1, 16 June 1775 – 15 September 1775, ed. Philander D. Chase. Charlottesville: University Press of Virginia, 1985, pp. 54–58.]

26. Chernow, Washington: A Life, 194–95.

27. From George Washington to Colonel Adam Stephen, 20 July 1776, Founders Online, National Archives, https://founders.archives.gov/documents/Washington/03-05-02-0298 (last accessed October 16, 2024). [Original source: The Papers of George Washington, Revolutionary War Series, vol. 5, 16 June 1776 – 12 August 1776, ed. Philander D. Chase. Charlottesville: University Press of Virginia, 1993, pp. 408–409.] Washington returned to the scene of Fort Necessity in 1784. He then owned the property and seemed concerned only about the meadow's commercial value and ordered his local agent to rent it. Chernow, Washington, 480; "Diary entry: 12 September 1784," Founders Online, National Archives, https://founders.archives.gov/documents/Washington/01-04-02-0001-0001-0011. [Original source: The Diaries of George Washington, vol. 4, 1 September 1784 – 30 June 1786, ed. Donald Jackson and Dorothy Twohig. Charlottesville: University Press of Virginia, 1978, pp. 18–20.].

28. Founders Online, "General Orders, 3 July 1778," National Archives, https://founders.archives.gov/documents/Washington/03-16-02-0020 (last accessed October 16, 2024). [Original source: The Papers of

George Washington, Revolutionary War Series, vol. 16, 1 July–14 September 1778, ed. David R. Hoth. Charlottesville: University of Virginia Press, 2006, p. 15.]

29. Founders Online, "General Orders, 4 July 1778," National Archives, https://founders.archives.gov/documents/Washington/03-16-02-0020 (last accessed October 16, 2024). [Original source: The Papers of George Washington, Revolutionary War Series, vol. 16, 1 July–14 September 1778, ed. David R. Hoth. Charlottesville: University of Virginia Press, 2006, pp. 19–20.]

30. Crossroads of the American Revolution, www.revolutionarynj.org/americas-first-official-independence-day-fete-new-jersey-event/ (last accessed October 16, 2024).

31. Founders Online, "From George Washington to Major General Alexander McDougall, 4 July 1779," National Archives, https://founders.archives.gov/documents/Washington/03-21-02-0287 (last accessed October 16, 2024). [Original source: The Papers of George Washington, Revolutionary War Series, vol. 21, 1 June–31 July 1779, ed. William M. Ferraro. Charlottesville: University of Virginia Press, 2012, p. 351.]

32. Founders Online, "General Orders, 4 July 1779," National Archives, https://founders.archives.gov/documents/Washington/03-21-02-0282 (last accessed October 16, 2024). [Original source: The Papers of George Washington, Revolutionary War Series, vol. 21, 1 June–31 July 1779, ed. William M. Ferraro. Charlottesville: University of Virginia Press, 2012, pp. 342–345.]

33. Founders Online, "General Orders, 4 July 1780," National Archives, https://founders.archives.gov/documents/Washington/03-26-02-0488 (last accessed October 16, 2024). [Original source: The Papers of George Washington, Revolutionary War Series, vol. 26, 13 May–4 July 1780, ed. Benjamin L. Huggins and Adrina Garbooshian-Huggins. Charlottesville: University of Virginia Press, 2018, p. 639.]; "General Orders, 3 July 1782," Founders Online, National Archives, https://founders.archives.gov/documents/Washington/99-01-02-08824.

34. Founders Online, "General Orders, 4 July 1781," National Archives, https://founders.archives.gov/documents/Washington/99-01-02-06284 (last accessed October 16, 2024).

35. David McCullough, 1776, 45.

36. David McCullough, John Adams, 533.

37. Founders Online, "From George Washington to the States, 8 June 1783," National Archives, https://founders.archives.gov/documents/Washington/99-01-02-11404 (last accessed October 16, 2024).

38. National Constitution Center, "Farewell Address (1796)" National Constitution Center, https://constitutioncenter.org/the-constitution/historic-document-library/detail/george-washington-farewell-address-1796 (last accessed October 16, 2024).

39. David McCullough, 1776, 44.

40. Founders Online, "From George Washington to Joseph Reed, 4 July 1780," National Archives, https://founders.archives.gov/documents/Washington/03-26-02-0499 (last accessed October 16, 2024). [Original source: The Papers of George Washington, Revolutionary War Series, vol. 26, 13 May–4 July 1780, ed. Benjamin L. Huggins and Adrina Garbooshian-Huggins. Charlottesville: University of Virginia Press, 2018, pp. 649–651.]

41. Chernow, Washington: A Life, 433.

42. Ibid., 435.

43. Ibid.

44. www.mountvernon.org/library/digitalhistory/quotes/article/gentlemen-you-will-permit-me-to-put-on-my-spectacles-for-i-have-grown-not-only-gray-but-almost-blind-in-the-service-of-my-country/

45. https://constitutioncenter.org/blog/george-washington-calms-down-the-newburgh-conspiracy

46. Founders Online, "[Diary entry: 18 May 1769]," National Archives, https://founders.archives.gov/documents/Washington/01-02-02-0004-0013-0018 (last accessed October 16, 2024). [Original source: The Diaries of George Washington, vol. 2, 14 January 1766 – 31 December 1770, ed. Donald Jackson. Charlottesville: University Press of Virginia, 1976, pp. 152–153.]

47. Chernow, Washington: A Life, 145–46.

48. Founders Online, "[Diary entry: 4 July 1768]," National Archives, https://founders.archives.gov/documents/Washington/01-02-02-0003-0019-0004 (last accessed October 16, 2024). [Original source: The Diaries of George Washington, vol. 2, 14 January 1766 – 31 December 1770, ed. Donald Jackson. Charlottesville: University Press of Virginia, 1976, p. 74.]

49. Founders Online, "[March 1768]," National Archives, https://founders.archives.gov/documents/Washington/01-02-02-0003-0007 (last accessed October 16, 2024). [Original source: The Diaries of George Washington, vol. 2, 14 January 1766 – 31 December 1770, ed. Donald Jackson. Charlottesville: University Press of Virginia, 1976, pp. 44–47.]

50. David McCullough, 1776, 47.

51. Founders Online, "From George Washington to Joseph Thompson, 2 July 1766," National Archives, https://founders.archives.gov/documents/Washington/02-07-02-0300 (last accessed October 16, 2024). [Original source: The Papers of George Washington, Colonial Series, vol. 7, 1 January 1761 – 15 June 1767, ed. W. W. Abbot and Dorothy Twohig. Charlottesville: University Press of Virginia, 1990, pp. 453–454.]

52. Founders Online, "From George Washington to Henry Lee, Jr., 4 February 1787," National Archives, https://founders.archives.gov/documents/Washington/04-05-02-0008 (last accessed October 16, 2024). [Original source: The Papers of George Washington, Confederation Series, vol. 5, 1 February 1787 – 31 December 1787, ed. W. W. Abbot. Charlottesville: University Press of Virginia, 1997, pp. 10–11.]

53. Chernow, Washington: A Life, 801-02.

54. Ibid., 202.

55. Founders Online, "[Diary entry: 4 July 1785]," National Archives, https://founders.archives.gov/documents/Washington/01-04-02-0002-0007-0004 (last accessed October 16, 2024). [Original source: The Diaries of George Washington, vol. 4, 1 September 1784 – 30 June 1786, ed. Donald Jackson and Dorothy Twohig. Charlottesville: University Press of Virginia, 1978, pp. 159–160.]

56. Founders Online, "April 1787," National Archives, https://founders.archives.gov/documents/Washington/01-05-02-0002-0004 (last accessed October 16, 2024). [Original source: The Diaries of George Washington, vol. 5, 1 July 1786 – 31 December 1789, ed. Donald Jackson and Dorothy Twohig. Charlottesville: University Press of Virginia, 1979, pp. 126–146.]

57. Founders Online, "[July 1787]," National Archives, https://founders.archives.gov/documents/Washington/01-05-02-0002-0007 (last accessed October 16, 2024). [Original source: The Diaries of George Washington, vol. 5, 1 July 1786 – 31 December 1789, ed. Donald Jackson and Dorothy Twohig. Charlottesville: University Press of Virginia, 1979, pp. 173–179.]

58. Founders Online, "From George Washington to Benjamin Harrison, 24 September 1787," National Archives, https://founders.archives.gov/documents/Washington/04-05-02-0316 (last accessed October 16, 2024). [Original source: The Papers of George Washington, Confederation Series, vol. 5, 1 February 1787 – 31 December 1787, ed. W. W. Abbot. Charlottesville: University Press of Virginia, 1997, pp. 339–340.]

59. Founders Online, "[July 1788]," National Archives, https://founders.archives.gov/documents/Washington/01-05-02-0004-0007 (last accessed October 16, 2024). [Original source: The Diaries of George Washington, vol. 5, 1 July 1786 – 31 December 1789, ed. Donald Jackson and Dorothy Twohig. Charlottesville: University Press of Virginia, 1979, pp. 353–371.]

60. Founders Online, "From George Washington to the Society of the Cincinnati, 4 July 1789," National Archives, https://founders.archives.gov/documents/Washington/05-03-02-0055 (last accessed October 16, 2024). [Original source: The Papers of George Washington, Presidential Series, vol. 3, 15 June 1789–5 September 1789, ed. Dorothy Twohig. Charlottesville: University Press of Virginia, 1989, pp. 114–116.]

61. Founders Online, "[Diary entry: 5 July 1790]," National Archives, https://founders.archives.gov/documents/Washington/01-06-02-0001-0007-0005 (last accessed October 16, 2024). [Original source: The Diaries of George Washington, vol. 6, 1 January 1790 – 13 December 1799, ed. Donald Jackson and Dorothy Twohig. Charlottesville: University Press of Virginia, 1979, pp. 85–86.]

62. Founders Online, "From George Washington to the People of South Carolina, 5 July 1790," National Archives, https://founders.archives.gov/documents/Washington/05-06-02-0011 (last accessed October 16, 2024). [Original source: The Papers of George Washington, Presidential Series, vol. 6, 1 July 1790 – 30 November 1790, ed. Mark A. Mastromarino. Charlottesville: University Press of Virginia, 1996, pp. 16–19.]

63. Founders Online, "[July 1791]," National Archives, https://founders.archives.gov/documents/Washington/01-06-02-0002-0006 (last accessed October 16, 2024). [Original source: The Diaries of George Washington, vol. 6, 1 January 1790 – 13 December 1799, ed. Donald Jackson and Dorothy Twohig. Charlottesville: University Press of Virginia, 1979, pp. 167–169.]

64. Founders Online, "From George Washington to Anthony Whitting, 4 July 1792," National Archives, https://founders.archives.gov/documents/Washington/05-10-02-0350 (last accessed October 16, 2024). [Original source: The Papers of George Washington, Presidential Series, vol. 10, 1 March 1792 – 15 August 1792, ed. Robert F. Haggard and Mark A. Mastromarino. Charlottesville: University of Virginia Press, 2002, pp. 517–518.]

65. Founders Online, "From George Washington to the Citizens of Alexandria, Virginia, 1 July 1793," National Archives, https://founders.archives.gov/documents/Washington/05-13-02-0116 (last accessed October 16, 2024). [Original source: The Papers of George Washington, Presidential Series, vol. 13, 1 June–

31 August 1793, ed. Christine Sternberg Patrick. Charlottesville: University of Virginia Press, 2007, pp. 167–168.]

66. Founders Online, "From George Washington to Buchan, 4 July 1797," National Archives, https://founders.archives.gov/documents/Washington/06-01-02-0193 (last accessed October 16, 2024). [Original source: The Papers of George Washington, Retirement Series, vol. 1, 4 March 1797 – 30 December 1797, ed. W. W. Abbot. Charlottesville: University Press of Virginia, 1998, pp. 235–237.]

67. In his diary for that day, Washington recorded the weather and noted that he celebrated Independence Day near Alexandria. He failed to note that he had been escorted into town by a detachment of troops while dressed in full uniform. He reviewed the troops, followed by a dinner for four hundred or five hundred people. Founders Online, "July—1798," Founders Online, National Archives, https://founders.archives.gov/documents/Washington/01-06-02-0007-0007 (last accessed October 16, 2024). [Original source: The Diaries of George Washington, vol. 6, 1 January 1790 – 13 December 1799, ed. Donald Jackson and Dorothy Twohig. Charlottesville: University Press of Virginia, 1979, pp. 303–311.]

68. Founders Online, "From George Washington to James McHenry, 4 July 1798," National Archives, https://founders.archives.gov/documents/Washington/06-02-02-0295 (last accessed October 16, 2024). [Original source: The Papers of George Washington, Retirement Series, vol. 2, 2 January 1798 – 15 September 1798, ed. W. W. Abbot. Charlottesville: University Press of Virginia, 1998, pp. 376–382.]

69. Founders Online, "To John Adams from George Washington, 13 July 1798," National Archives, https://founders.archives.gov/documents/Adams/99-02-02-2724 (last accessed October 16, 2024).

70. David McCullough, John Adams, 519.

71. Founders Online, "[Diary entry: 4 July 1799]," National Archives, https://founders.archives.gov/documents/Washington/01-06-02-0008-0007-0004 (last accessed October 16, 2024). [Original source: The Diaries of George Washington, vol. 6, 1 January 1790 – 13 December 1799, ed. Donald Jackson and Dorothy Twohig. Charlottesville: University Press of Virginia, 1979, pp. 355–356.]

72. Founders Online, "December [1799]," National Archives, https://founders.archives.gov/documents/Washington/01-06-02-0008-0012 (last accessed October 16, 2024). [Original source: The Diaries of George Washington, vol. 6, 1 January 1790 – 13 December 1799, ed. Donald Jackson and Dorothy Twohig. Charlottesville: University Press of Virginia, 1979, pp. 377–380.]

73. Chernow, Washington: A Life, 806–09.

Chapter 3: The Last of the Revolutionary Giants

1. Founders Online, "Thomas Jefferson to John Adams, 21 January 1812," National Archives, https://founders.archives.gov/documents/Jefferson/03-04-02-0334 (last accessed October 16, 2024). [Original source: The Papers of Thomas Jefferson, Retirement Series, vol. 4, 18 June 1811 to 30 April 1812, ed. J. Jefferson Looney. Princeton: Princeton University Press, 2007, pp. 428–430.]

2. Founders Online, "To John Adams from Thomas Jefferson, 21 January 1812," National Archives, https://founders.archives.gov/documents/Adams/99-02-02-5743 (last accessed October 16, 2024).

3. Jon Meacham, Thomas Jefferson: The Art of Power (New York: Random House, 2013), 306.

4. Ibid., 318–19.

5. Ibid., 323; David McCullough, John Adams, 578.

6. Jon Meacham, Thomas Jefferson, 208, 300, 322–23.

7. Jefferson had noteworthy Fourth of Julys during his presidency. In 1807, after an attack of the USS Chesapeake by a British warship on June 22, 1807, resulting in the death of three sailors and the wounding of the captain and seventeen others, Federalist lawmakers made it a point to attend Jefferson's Fourth of July levee as a show of solidarity. The very next year, he called on Congress impose an embargo of all American shipping, which resulted in widespread dissatisfaction with him. He was burned in effigy on July 4, 1808. Ibid., 425–33.

8. Founders Online, "To John Adams from Benjamin Rush, 17 October 1809," National Archives, https://founders.archives.gov/documents/Adams/99-02-02-5450 (last accessed October 16, 2024).

9. Founders Online, "From John Adams to Benjamin Rush, 25 October 1809," National Archives, https://founders.archives.gov/documents/Adams/99-02-02-5454 (last accessed October 16, 2024).

10. Founders Online, "To John Adams from Benjamin Rush, 16 December 1811," National Archives, https://founders.archives.gov/documents/Adams/99-02-02-5725 (last accessed October 16, 2024).

11. Founders Online, "From John Adams to Benjamin Rush, 25 December 1811," National Archives, https://founders.archives.gov/documents/Adams/99-02-02-5731 (last accessed October 16, 2024).

12. Founders Online, "Resumption of Correspondence with John Adams, followed by John Adams to Thomas Jefferson, 1 January 1812," National Archives, https://founders.archives.gov/documents/Jefferson/03-04-02-0296-0002 (last accessed October 16, 2024).

13. Founders Online, "Thomas Jefferson to John Adams, 21 January 1812," National Archives, https://founders.archives.gov/documents/Jefferson/03-04-02-0334 (last accessed October 16, 2024).

14. Founders Online, "To John Adams from Benjamin Rush, 17 February 1812," National Archives, https://founders.archives.gov/documents/Adams/99-02-02-5758 (last accessed October 16, 2024).

15. Founders Online, "Resumption of Correspondence with John Adams, followed by John Adams to Thomas Jefferson, 1 January 1812," National Archives, https://founders.archives.gov/documents/Jefferson/03-04-02-0296-0002 (last accessed October 16, 2024).

16. Founders Online, "To John Adams from Thomas Jefferson, 21 January 1812," National Archives, https://founders.archives.gov/documents/Adams/99-02-02-5743 (last accessed October 16, 2024).

17. Founders Online, "From John Adams to Thomas Jefferson, 3 February 1812," National Archives, https://founders.archives.gov/documents/Adams/99-02-02-5749 (last accessed October 16, 2024).

18. Founders Online, "From John Adams to Thomas Jefferson, 1 May 1812," National Archives, https://founders.archives.gov/documents/Adams/99-02-02-5781 (last accessed October 16, 2024).

19. Founders Online, "To John Adams from Thomas Jefferson, 27 June 1813," National Archives, https://founders.archives.gov/documents/Adams/99-02-02-6076 (last accessed October 16, 2024).

20. Founders Online, "From John Adams to Thomas Jefferson, 2 March 1816," National Archives, https://founders.archives.gov/documents/Adams/99-02-02-6585 (last accessed October 16, 2024).

21. Founders Online, "To John Adams from Thomas Jefferson, 8 April 1816," National Archives, https://founders.archives.gov/documents/Adams/99-02-02-6590 (last accessed October 16, 2024).

22. Founders Online, "From John Adams to Thomas Jefferson, 22 June 1819," National Archives, https://founders.archives.gov/documents/Adams/99-02-02-7158 (last accessed October 16, 2024).

23. Founders Online, "To John Adams from Thomas Jefferson, 9 July 1819," National Archives, https://founders.archives.gov/documents/Adams/99-02-02-7176 (last accessed October 16, 2024).

24. Founders Online, "To John Adams from Thomas Jefferson, 15 August 1820," National Archives, https://founders.archives.gov/documents/Adams/99-02-02-7391 (last accessed October 16, 2024).

25. Founders Online, "From John Adams to Thomas Jefferson, 3 February 1821," National Archives, https://founders.archives.gov/documents/Adams/99-02-02-7460 (last accessed October 16, 2024).

26. Founders Online, "From John Adams to Thomas Jefferson, 25 February 1825," National Archives, https://founders.archives.gov/documents/Adams/99-02-02-7962 (last accessed October 16, 2024).

27. David McCullough, John Adams, 632.

28. Ibid., 605.

29. Founders Online, "To John Adams from Thomas Jefferson, 21 January 1812," National Archives, https://founders.archives.gov/documents/Adams/99-02-02-5743 (last accessed October 16, 2024).

30. David McCullough, John Adams, 605.

31. "Founders Online, To John Adams from Thomas Jefferson, 21 January 1812," National Archives, https://founders.archives.gov/documents/Adams/99-02-02-5743 (last accessed October 16, 2024).

32. Founders Online, "To John Adams from Thomas Jefferson, 27 May 1813," National Archives, https://founders.archives.gov/documents/Adams/99-02-02-6041 (last accessed October 16, 2024).

33. Founders Online, "From John Adams to Thomas Jefferson, 11 June 1813," National Archives, https://founders.archives.gov/documents/Adams/99-02-02-6060 (last accessed October 16, 2024)

34. Founders Online, "To John Adams from Thomas Jefferson, 9 July 1819," National Archives, https://founders.archives.gov/documents/Adams/99-02-02-7176 (last accessed October 16, 2024).

35. Pauline Maier, American Scripture, 172–74.

36. Founders Online, "From John Adams to Thomas Jefferson, 21 July 1819," National Archives, https://founders.archives.gov/documents/Adams/99-02-02-7194; Founders Online, "From John Adams to Thomas Jefferson, 28 July 1819," National Archives, https://founders.archives.gov/documents/Adams/99-02-02-7203 (last accessed October 16, 2024).

37. Founders Online, "From John Adams to Thomas Jefferson, 30 July 1815," National Archives, https://founders.archives.gov/documents/Adams/99-02-02-6497 (last accessed October 16, 2024).

38. Founders Online, "To John Adams from Thomas Jefferson, 10 August 1815," National Archives, https://founders.archives.gov/documents/Adams/99-02-02-6502 (last accessed October 16, 2024).

39. Founders Online, "From John Adams to Thomas Jefferson, 24 August 1815," National Archives, https://founders.archives.gov/documents/Adams/99-02-02-6507 (last accessed October 16, 2024).

40. Founders Online, "From John Adams to Thomas Jefferson, 29 May 1818," National Archives, https://founders.archives.gov/documents/Adams/99-02-02-6900 (last accessed October 16, 2024).
41. Founders Online, "To John Adams from Thomas Jefferson, 21 January 1812," National Archives, https://founders.archives.gov/documents/Adams/99-02-02-5743 (last accessed October 16, 2024).
42. Founders Online, "From John Adams to Thomas Jefferson, 3 February 1821," National Archives, https://founders.archives.gov/documents/Adams/99-02-02-7460 (last accessed October 16, 2024).
43. Founders Online, "From John Adams to Thomas Jefferson, 3 February 1821," National Archives, https://founders.archives.gov/documents/Adams/99-02-02-7460 (last accessed October 16, 2024).
44. Founders Online, "From John Adams to Thomas Jefferson, 5 July 1813," National Archives, https://founders.archives.gov/documents/Adams/99-02-02-6092 (last accessed October 16, 2024).
45. Founders Online, "From John Adams to Thomas Jefferson, 21 December 1819," National Archives, https://founders.archives.gov/documents/Adams/99-02-02-7287 (last accessed October 16, 2024).
46. Founders Online, "From John Adams to Thomas Jefferson, 3 February 1821," National Archives, https://founders.archives.gov/documents/Adams/99-02-02-7460 (last accessed October 16, 2024).
47. Founders Online, "To John Adams from Thomas Jefferson, 28 October 1813," National Archives, https://founders.archives.gov/documents/Adams/99-02-02-6189 (last accessed October 16, 2024).
48. Founders Online, "To John Adams from Thomas Jefferson, 1 August 1816," National Archives, https://founders.archives.gov/documents/Adams/99-02-02-6618 (last accessed October 16, 2024).
49. Founders Online, "To John Adams from Thomas Jefferson, 12 September 1821," National Archives, https://founders.archives.gov/documents/Adams/99-02-02-7544 (last accessed October 16, 2024).
50. Founders Online, "From John Adams to Thomas Jefferson, 25 February 1825," National Archives, https://founders.archives.gov/documents/Adams/99-02-02-7962 (last accessed October 16, 2024).
51. Founders Online, "From John Adams to Thomas Jefferson, 2 March 1816," National Archives, https://founders.archives.gov/documents/Adams/99-02-02-6585 (last accessed October 16, 2024).
52. Founders Online, "To John Adams from Thomas Jefferson, 8 April 1816," National Archives, https://founders.archives.gov/documents/Adams/99-02-02-6590 (last accessed October 16, 2024).
53. Founders Online, "To John Adams from Thomas Jefferson, 1 August 1816," National Archives, https://founders.archives.gov/documents/Adams/99-02-02-6618 (last accessed October 16, 2024).
54. Founders Online, "From John Adams to Thomas Jefferson, 1 December 1825," National Archives, https://founders.archives.gov/documents/Adams/99-02-02-8005 (last accessed October 16, 2024).
55. David McCullough, John Adams, 643.
56. Founders Online, "From Thomas Jefferson to John Adams, 25 March 1826," National Archives, https://founders.archives.gov/documents/Jefferson/98-01-02-5983 (last accessed October 16, 2024).
57. Letter from Thomas Jefferson to Roger C. Weightman, Library of Congress, www.loc.gov/exhibits/declara/rcwltr.html (last accessed October 16, 2024).
58. David McCullough, John Adams, 645.
59. Ibid., 646.
60. Ibid.
61. Meacham, Thomas Jefferson, 493.
62. Ibid., 494; David McCullough, John Adams, 646.
63. Pauline Maier, American Scripture, 189. On July 4, 1831, James Monroe, the fifth president of the United States, died at the age of seventy-three at his son-in-law's home in New York City. Monroe, the last of the founding fathers to hold the presidency, worked closely with his secretary of state, John Quincy Adams, who succeeded him as president. See Tim McGrath, James Monroe: A Life (New York: Dutton, 2020). Among many observations at that time of Monroe's death were those of the Boston Traveler, which wondered: "Again our national anniversary has been marked by one of those events, which it may be scarcely permitted to ascribe the chance."
64. Nancy Isenberg and Andrew Burstein, The Problem of Democracy: The Presidents Adams Confront the Cult of Personality (New York: Viking, 2019), 360.
65. 65. Daniel Webster, *Discourse in Commoration of the Lives and Services of John Adams and Thomas Jefferson* (Boston: Cumming, Hilliard and Company 1826), 6–10, 59–60.

Chapter 4: The Promises of Freedom and Equality

1. "By using the word 'sacred,' Jefferson had asserted, intentionally or not, that the principle in question—the equality of men and their endowment by their creator with inalienable rights—was an assertion of

religion." Franklin's edit, it has been argued, "turned it instead into an assertion of rationality." Walter Isaacson, Benjamin Franklin, 312.

2. The Papers of Thomas Jefferson, 1760-1776, ed. Julian P. Boyd (Princeton: Princeton University Press, 1950), 1:243–247 (italics and punctuation in original).

3. Jon Meacham, Thomas Jefferson, 48.

4. Ibid., 218.

5. Ibid., 454–55.

6. Ibid., 55.

7. David McCullough, John Adams, 133.

8. Thomas Hutchinson, Strictures Upon the Declaration of the Congress at Philadelphia (London 1776), 9–10.

9. David McCullough, John Adams, 134.

10. Ibid., 132.

11. Garry Wills, Inventing America, 67.

12. Ibid., 72.

13. Ibid., 74.

14. Ibid., 306.

15. Dred Scott v. Sandford, 60 U.S. 393 (1857).

16. Pauline Maier, American Scripture, 191.

17. Ibid., 197.

18. Ibid., 198.

19. Ibid., 199–201.

20. Ibid., 202.

21. Doris Kearns Goodwin, Team of Rivals (New York: Simon & Schuster, 2005), 202–04, 585.

22. Pauline Maier, American Scripture, 204–05.

23. Ibid., 205.

24. Doris Kearns Goodwin, Team of Rivals, 203.

25. "June 26 , 1857 - SPEECH IN SPRINGFIELD, ILLINOIS," Abraham Lincoln, Complete Works, ed. John G. Nicolay & John Hay (New York: The Century Company, 1920), 1:232.

26. Goodwin, Team of Rivals, 585.

27. Garry Wills, Inventing America: Jefferson's Declaration of Independence, xiv.

28. Pauline Maier, American Scripture, xx.

29. Ibid., 207.

30. Founders Online, "Abigail Adams to John Adams, 31 March 1776," National Archives, https://founders.archives.gov/documents/Adams/04-01-02-0241 (last accessed October 16, 2024). [Original source: The Adams Papers, Adams Family Correspondence, vol. 1, December 1761 – May 1776, ed. Lyman H. Butterfield. Cambridge, MA: Harvard University Press, 1963, pp. 369–371.]

31. Founders Online, "John Adams to Abigail Adams, 14 April 1776," National Archives, https://founders.archives.gov/documents/Adams/04-01-02-0248 (last accessed October 16, 2024). [Original source: The Adams Papers, Adams Family Correspondence, vol. 1, December 1761 – May 1776, ed. Lyman H. Butterfield. Cambridge, MA: Harvard University Press, 1963, pp. 381–383.]

32. Founders Online, "Abigail Adams to John Adams, 7 May 1776," National Archives, https://founders.archives.gov/documents/Adams/04-01-02-0259 (last accessed October 16, 2024). [Original source: The Adams Papers, Adams Family Correspondence, vol. 1, December 1761 – May 1776, ed. Lyman H. Butterfield. Cambridge, MA: Harvard University Press, 1963, pp. 401–403.]

33. Founders Online, "From John Adams to James Sullivan, 26 May 1776," National Archives, https://founders.archives.gov/documents/Adams/06-04-02-0091 (last accessed October 16, 2024). [Original source: The Adams Papers, Papers of John Adams, vol. 4, February–August 1776, ed. Robert J. Taylor. Cambridge, MA: Harvard University Press, 1979, pp. 208–213.]

34. Letter to Hannah Corbin from Richard Henry Lee, March 17, 1778, https://leefamilyarchive.org/9-family-papers/362-richard-henry-lee-to-hannah-lee-corbin-1778-march-18#:~:text=I%20am%20illy%20able%20by,in%20a%20few%20hours%20conversation (last accessed October 16, 2024).

35. Minor v. Happerssett, 88 U.S. 162 (1874).

36. Jon Meacham, Thomas Jefferson, 225.

37. Abraham Lincoln, Speech at Chicago, Illinois (July 10, 1858), in The Collected Works of Abraham Lincoln, ed. Roy P. Basler (1953) 2:499–500. The Collected Works of Abraham Lincoln are available online

from a website maintained by the Abraham Lincoln Association. See The Collected Works of Abraham Lincoln, The Abraham Lincoln Ass'n, http://quod.lib.umich.edu/l/lincoln/ (last accessed October 16, 2024).

38. Abraham Lincoln, Speech at Lewistown, Illinois (Aug. 17, 1858), in The Collected Works of Abraham Lincoln, at 2:544, 546.

39. Abraham Lincoln, Speech at Peoria, Illinois (Oct. 16, 1854), in The Collected Works of Abraham Lincoln, 2:266.

40. Abraham Lincoln, Speech at Philadelphia, Pennsylvania (February 22, 1861), in The Collected Works of Abraham Lincoln, 4:240-41.

41. Abraham Lincoln, Message to Congress in Special Session (July 4, 1861), in The Collected Works of Abraham Lincoln, 4:438.

Chapter 5: Frederick Douglass: Agitating for Freedom

1. He became legally free in 1846 after being purchased from his slave master by supporters.

2. Frederick Douglass, Narrative of the Life of Frederick Douglass: An American Slave (Dolphin Books Edition, 1963), 30.

3. Ibid., 29–30, 32, 36.

4. Ibid., 36–37, 41–42, 44–46.

5. Ibid., 65.

6. Ibid., 106–07.

7. The full text of the speech is readily available from multiple sources on line. E.g., https://masshumanities.org/files/programs/douglass/speech_abridged_med.pdf

8. Douglass also maintained that there was nothing in the Constitution that supported the institution of slavery: "In that instrument I hold there is neither warrant, license, nor sanction of the hateful thing; but interpreted, as it ought to be interpreted, the Constitution is a GLORIOUS LIBERTY DOCUMENT. Read its preamble, consider its purposes. Is slavery among them? Is it at the gateway? or is it in the temple? it is neither." Indeed, he asserted that the Constitution had "principles and purposes, entirely hostile to the existence of slavery."

9. John Stauffer, Giants: The Parallel Lives of Frederick Douglass and Abraham Lincoln (Twelve, 2008), 217–19.

10. The speech in full, hosted by the Frederick Douglass Papers Project, is at: https://frederickdouglasspapersproject.com/s/digitaledition/item/10537.

11. Ibid.

12. Ibid.

13. Ibid.

14. John Stauffer, Giants: The Parallel Lives, 243.

15. Ibid., 246.

16. Doris Kearns Goodwin, Team of Rivals, 207, 407–08, 551–52.

17. Ibid., 550–51.

18. Ibid., 483.

19. Ibid., 650.

20. Ron Chernow, Grant (New York: Penguin Press, 2017), 565. As Reconstruction was coming to an end and fearing its abandonment after the presidency of Grant ended, Douglass lamented what good abolition had been if, "having been freed from the slaveholder's lash, he is to be subject to the slaveholder's shotgun?" Ibid., 828.

21. One memorable speech was on, July 6, 1863, in Philadelphia, urging black men to serve in the Union Army: "Young men of Philadelphia, you are without excuse. The hour has arrived, and your place is in the Union army. Remember that the musket—the United States musket with its bayonet of steel—is better than all mere parchment guarantees of liberty. In your hands that musket means liberty; and should your constitutional right at the close of this war be denied, which, in the nature of things, it cannot be, your brethren are safe while you have a Constitution which proclaims your right to keep and bear arms." https://frederickdouglasspapersproject.com/s/digitaledition/item/9183.

22. Frederick Douglass Papers Project, https://frederickdouglasspapersproject.com/s/digitaledition/item/8695 (last accessed October 16, 2024).

23. Joseph W. Holley, You Can't Build a Chimney from the Top (New York: William Frederick Press 1949), 23.

Chapter 6: Two Important Union Victories: Contrasting Words of Dissent and Affirmation

1. Christopher R. Gabel, *The Vicksburg Campaign* (Center of Military History, U.S. Army: Washington D.C., 2013), 13.

2. Early on, Lincoln favored General John McClernand for the task, but, after much bureaucratic maneuvering, Grant secured authority to lead the campaign. Ron Chernow, Grant, 236–38, 241. McClernand, who served under Grant during the campaign as commander of the Thirteenth Army Corps, was relieved of command by Grant on June 22 for violating war department orders; McClernand had released for publication a misleading—and unduly favorable—account of his own actions. Ulysses S. Grant, "The Vicksburg Campaign," Battles and Leaders of the Civil War: The Tide Shifts, vol. 3, ed. Robert Underwood Johnson and Clarence Clough Buel (New York: The Century Co. 1884, 1888), 526.

3. For a detailed account of the campaign, see Christopher R. Gabel, The Vicksburg Campaign.

4. Ron Chernow, Grant, 248.

5. Ibid., 254.

6. B.H. Liddell Hart, Sherman: Soldier, Realist, American (New York: Da Capo, 1993), 191.

7. Christopher R. Gabel, The Vicksburg Campaign, 31.

8. Chernow, Grant, 255–56.

9. Ibid., 255–56.

10. Christopher R. Gabel, The Vicksburg Campaign, 34.

11. Ibid., 259–68, 294.

12. Ibid., 37.

13. Hart, Sherman: Soldier, Realist, American, 189.

14. Ibid., 189.

15. Ibid., 192.

16. Christopher R. Gabel, The Vicksburg Campaign, 61–62.

17. Ibid., 59.

18. Chernow, Grant, 286–88. At Vicksburg 31,600 soldiers were surrendered, together with 172 cannon, about sixty thousand muskets, and a large amount of ammunition. Battles and Leaders of the Civil War, 537.

19. Grant later wrote:

On the 19th [of May], just twenty days after the crossing, the city [of Vicksburg] was completely invested and an assault had been made: five distinct battles—besides continuous skirmishing—had been fought and won by the Union forces; the capital of the State had fallen, and its arsenals, military manufactories, and everything useful for military purposes had been destroyed; an average of about 180 miles had been marched by the troops engaged; but 5 days' rations had been issued, and no forage; over 6000 prisoners had been captured, and as many more of the enemy had been killed or wounded; 27 heavy cannon and 61 field-pieces had fallen into our hands; 250 miles of the river, from Vicksburg to Port Hudson, had become ours. The Union force that had crossed the Mississippi River up to this time was less than 43,000 men. . . . The enemy had at Vicksburg, Grand Gulf, Jackson, and on the roads between these places, over sixty thousand men. They were in their own country, where no rear-guards were necessary. The country is admirable for defense, but difficult to conduct an offensive campaign in. All their troops had to be met. We were fortunate, to say the least, in meeting them in detail: at Port Gibson, 7000 or 8000; at Raymond, 5000; at Jackson, from 8000 to 11,000; at Champion's Hill, 25,000; at the Big Black, 4000. A part of those met at Jackson were all that were left of those encountered at Raymond. They were beaten in detail by a force smaller than their own, upon their own ground. Grant, "The Vicksburg Campaign," *Battles and Leaders of the Civil War*, 518–19.

20. Grant, "The Vicksburg Campaign," Battles and Leaders of the Civil War, 534.

21. Hart, Sherman: Soldier, Realist, American, 197.

22. Doris Kearns Goodwin, Team of Rivals, 533.

23. Grant, "The Vicksburg Campaign," Battles and Leaders of the Civil War, 534.

24. Hart, Sherman: Soldier, Realist, American, 196.

25. Christopher R. Gabel, The Vicksburg Campaign, 60–61.

26. Personal Memoirs of Ulysses Simpson Grant, Vol. 1 (2d ed. 1895), 475.

27. Geoffrey C. Ward, et al., The Civil War: an Illustrated History (New York: Alfred A Knopf, 1990), 232.

28. Ibid., 230.

29. Bruce Cotton, The Civil War (New York: Fairfax Press, 1984), 416–17.

30. Ibid., 416–19.
31. Lincoln's announcement stated:

The President announces to the country that news from the Army of the Potomac, up to 10 p.m. of the 3rd. is such as to cover that Army with the highest honor, to promise a great success to the cause of the Union, and to claim the condolence of all for the many gallant fallen. And that for this, he especially desires that on this day, He whose will, not ours, should ever be done, be everywhere remembered and reverenced with profoundest gratitude.

Basler, Roy, et.al., *The Collected Works of Abraham Lincoln* (1953), 6:314.
32. Diary of Gideon Welles, vol. 1 (Boston: Houghton Mifflin Co., 1911), 364–65.
33. Goodwin, Team of Rivals, 534.
34. Diary of Gideon Welles, vol. 1, 364-65.
35. Basler, Roy, et.al., The Collected Works of Abraham Lincoln (1953), 6:319–20.
36. Speech at Academy of Music, New York, July 4, 1863, in Public Record of Horatio Seymour from 1856 to 1868, ed. Thomas M. Cook and Thomas W. Knox (New York: I.W. England, 1868), 118–24.
37. Geoffrey C. Ward, et al., The Civil War, 243–44.
38. Ibid., 244–45.
39. Speech to Rioters, New York Times Report, July 15, 1863 in Public Record of Horatio Seymour from 1856 to 1868, 127.
40. John G. Nicolay and John Hay, Abraham Lincoln: A History, vol. 7 (New York: Century Co., 1917), 23.
41. Diary of Gideon Welles, Vol. 1, 372–73.
42. Basler, Roy, et.al., The Collected Works of Abraham Lincoln. 6:332–33.
43. Geoffrey C. Ward, et al., The Civil War, 262; Doris Kearns Goodwin, Team of Rivals, 586.
44. Goodwin, Team of Rivals, 586.

Chapter 7: The Centennial and Suffrage

1. Www.wikipedia.org/wiki/Centennial_Exposition (last accessed October 16, 2024).
2. Www.wikipedia.org/wiki/Centennial_Exposition (last accessed October 16, 2024).
3. J.S. Ingram, The Centennial Exposition, Described and Illustrated (Philadelphia: Hubbard Bros. 1876), 652.
4. Ibid., 652–53.
5. Ibid., 654–55.
6. Ibid., 657–58.
7. Elizabeth Cady Stanton et. al., History of Woman Suffrage, vol. 1 (New York: Fowler & Wells, 1881), 67–71.
8. Faye E. Dudden, Fighting Chance: The Struggle Over Woman Suffrage and Black Suffrage in Reconstruction America (Oxford, England: Oxford University Press, 2011), 21.
9. Faye E. Dudden, Fighting Chance, 12.
10. Ibid., 49.
11. See generally Faye E. Dudden, Fighting Chance.
12. Ibid., 8, 62–63.
13. Elizabeth Cady Stanton et. al., History of Woman Suffrage, vol. 1, 94; Faye E. Dudden, Fighting Chance, 61–87.
14. Faye E. Dudden, Fighting Chance, 76.
15. Anthony described Truth as having the combination of "the two most hated elements of humanity. She was black and she was a woman, and all the insults that could be cast upon color and sex were together hurled at her." Lynn Sherr, Failure is Impossible: Susan B. Anthony in Her Own Words (New York: Times Books, 1995), 31.
16. Elizabeth Cady Stanton et. al., History of Woman Suffrage, vol. 2 (New York: Fowler & Wells, 1881), 193–94.
17. Ibid., vol. 2, 382–83.
18. Faye E. Dudden, Fighting Chance, 165.
19. Elizabeth Cady Stanton et. al., History of Woman Suffrage, vol. 2, 384.
20. Ibid., vol. 2, 91–92.
21. Ibid., vol. 2, 513.

22. Ibid., vol. 2, 586–88.
23. Lynn Sherr, Failure is Impossible, 109.
24. Elizabeth Cady Stanton et. al., History of Woman Suffrage, vol. 2, 647.
25. Ibid., vol. 2, 680; Lynn Sherr, Failure is Impossible, 109.
26. Elizabeth Cady Stanton et. al., History of Woman Suffrage, vol. 2, 687–89.
27. Pennsylvania was not an aberration. Under the common law, when a woman married, she became one with her husband and that one was him. Lynn Sherr, Failure is Impossible, xviii.
28. Elizabeth Cady Stanton et. al., History of Woman Suffrage, vol. 3 (Rochester, NY: Charles Mann Printing Co., 1886), 20–21.
29. Ibid., 22.
30. Ibid., 27.
31. Ibid., 27–28.
32. Ibid., vol. 3, 28.
33. Ibid., 29.
34. Ibid., 30.
35. Ibid., 41 (Letter of Lewise Oliver, dated July 13, 1876).
36. Ibid., 45 (Letter to Lucretia Mott, dated July 19, 1876).
37. Lynn Sherr, Failure is Impossible, xxvi.
38. The Woman Suffrage Year Book 1917 (NY: National Woman Suffrage Publishing Co., 1917), 45.
39. The Nineteenth Amendment provides:

The right of citizens of the United States to vote shall not be denied or abridged by the United States or by any State on account of sex.

Congress shall have power to enforce this article by appropriate legislation.

40. Lynn Sherr, Failure is Impossible, xii.
41. Ibid., xxv–xxvi.
42. Ibid., 64–65.
43. Ibid., 301.
44. Ibid., 306.
45. Ibid., 327.
46. Ibid., 324.

Chapter 8: Island Expansions: A Mixed Legacy

1. Robert W. Merry, President McKinley (New York: Simon & Schuster, 2017), 172–78, 204–10.
2. Robert Leckie, The Wars of America, vol. II (New York: Harper & Row, 1968), 42.
3. Daniel Immerwahr, How to Hide an Empire (New York: Picador, 2019), 65.
4. Robert Merry, President McKinley, 169–70.
5. Alfred Thayer Mahan, The Interest of America in Sea Power, Present and Future (Boston: Little Brown & Co., 1897), 21–22.
6. Evan Thomas, The War Lovers (New York: Little Brown & Co., 2010).
7. Robert Leckie, The Wars of America, vol. II, 24.
8. Evan Thomas, The War Lovers, 71.
9. Robert Merry, President McKinley, 341.
10. Evan Thomas, The War Lovers, 100–07.
11. Robert Leckie, The Wars of America, vol. II, 21.
12. Evan Thomas, The War Lovers, 160–61.
13. Robert Merry, President McKinley, 4.
14. Ibid., 485.
15. Evan Thomas, The War Lovers, 364.
16. H. W. Brands, Bound for Empire (New York: Oxford University Press, 1992), 21–22.
17. Robert Leckie, The Wars of America , vol. II, 25–26.
18. Ibid., 23–31.
19. On April 19, 1898, Senator Henry M. Teller proposed an amendment to the declaration of war against Spain that specified that the United States "disclaims any disposition of intention to exercise sovereignty, jurisdiction, or control over said island except for pacification thereof, and asserts its determination, when that is accomplished, to leave the government and control of the island to its people." After Spanish troops

left the island in 1898, the United States occupied Cuba until 1902. Cuban insurgents had fought in conjunction with the Americans during the war but were shut out of the peace negotiations, although the peace treaty recognized the independence of Cuba. In 1901, the Platt Amendment, introduced in Congress by Senator Orville Platt, was passed; it provided that the United States had the "right to intervene for the preservation of Cuban independence, the maintenance of a government adequate for the protection of life, property, and individual liberty." Hence, before withdrawing from Cuba, the United States obtained several concessions from the Cubans, including obtaining a naval base at Guantanamo Bay. (The Platt Amendment was abrogated on May 29, 1934.) The subsequent history of Cuba's troubled relationship with the United States does not coincide with any significant Fourth of July events.

20. Guam was placed under the control of the navy and remained under that control until the Guam Organic Act of 1950 (48 U.S.C. § 1421, enacted August 1, 1950), which made the island an unincorporated territory of the United States; established executive, legislative, and judicial branches; and transferred federal jurisdiction to the Department of the Interior. The island, in the western Pacific Ocean, has a total area of 212 square miles. Its unofficial motto is "Where America's Day Begins" due to its proximity to the International Date Line. It is home to large American military bases.

21. Treaty of Paris, Art. 9, Dec. 10, 1898, 30 Stat. 1759.

22. Puerto Rico v. Sánchez Valle, 579 U.S. 1863 (2016).

23. In 1900, the Foraker Act provided for presidential appointment (with Senate confirmation) of Puerto Rico's governor, the heads of departments, the legislature's upper house, and the justices of its high court. Organic Act of 1900, §§ 17, 18, 33, 31 Stat. 81, 84. It also provided for the popular election of a lower legislative house. The Jones Act in 1917 established an elected Senate and made Puerto Ricans citizens of the United States. Organic Act of Puerto Rico, ch. 145, 39 Stat. 951. Congress in 1947 provided for an elected governor of Puerto Rico and granted that governor the power to appoint cabinet officials. Act of Aug. 5, 1947, ch. 490, §§ 1, 3, 61 Stat. 770, 771.

24. Puerto Rico v. Sánchez Valle, 579 U.S. 1863 (2016).

25. Examining Bd. of Engineers, Architects and Surveyors v. Flores de Otero, 426 U.S. 572, 597 (1976).

26. Rodriguez v. Popular Democratic Party, 457 U.S. 1, 8 (1982).

27. Nationalists seeking independence through the years have occasionally resorted to violence and revolts. Some Puerto Ricans, notably the Nationalists, opposed the 1950 law and resorted to violence. A few Nationalists unsuccessfully attempted to assassinate Gov. Muñoz Marín, and there were Nationalist uprisings in several island towns. On November 1, 1950, two Puerto Rican nationalists attempted to kill Truman. David McCullough, Truman (New York: Simon & Schuster, 1992). 810. The last major armed event by the Nationalists occurred in 1954 when four party members shot and wounded five Congressmen at the U.S. House of Representatives.

28. Robert Merry, President McKinley, 331.

29. Daniel Immerwahr, How to Hide an Empire, 88–89.

30. Ibid., 89.

31. Robert Merry, President McKinley, 332.

32. Ibid., 290-91.

33. Ibid., 327.

34. H. W. Brands, Bound for Empire (New York: Oxford University Press, 1992), 24.

35. Robert Merry, President McKinley, 326–34.

36. Ibid., 347.

37. H. W. Brands, Bound for Empire, 49–51; Robert Merry, President McKinley, 366–67.

38. A particularly vicious massacre of American soldiers at a small outpost in Samar occurred on September 27, 1900, showing that the rebellion still had adherents willing to engage in horrific actions; the American military responded in kind, with wanton killing of civilians. Doris Kearns Goodwin, The Bully Pulpit: Theodore Roosevelt, William Howard Taft, and the Golden Age of Journalism (New York: Simon & Schuster, 2013), 288–89.

39. Robert Leckie, The Wars of America, vol. II 47–48; Thomas, The War Lovers, 386.

40. Ibid., 51.

41. Robert Merry, President McKinley, 363–64.

42. Ibid., 398–99.

43. Ibid., 274–75.

44. The American Presidency Project, www.presidency.ucsb.edu/documents/proclamation-483-granting-pardon-and-amnesty-participants-insurrection-the-philippines (last accessed October 17, 2024).

45. Daniel Immerwahr, How to Hide an Empire, 132.
46. Robert Merry, President McKinley, 400–01.
47. Doris Kearns Goodwin, The Bully Pulpit, 264.
48. Ibid., 269.
49. Ibid., 269–74.
50. H. W. Brands, Bound for Empire, 66.
51. The American Presidency Project, www.presidency.ucsb.edu/documents/proclamation-483-granting-pardon-and-amnesty-participants-insurrection-the-philippines (last accessed October 17, 2024).
52. Daniel Immerwahr, How to Hide an Empire, 103–07.
53. Ibid., 387–89.
54. Ibid., 389–91.
55. Ibid., 525.
56. Ibid., 526.
57. James R. Heintze, Fourth of July Encyclopedia (North Carolina: McFarland & Co., 2007), 221.
58. Ibid., 222.
59. Stanley Karnow, In Our Image: America's Empire in the Philippines (New York: Ballatine Books 1989), 323.
60. www.archives.gov/federal-register/codification/proclamations/02695.html
61. Daniel Immerwahr, How to Hide an Empire, 237.
62. Ibid., 237-38.
63. Stanley Karnow, In Our Image, 323.
64. Studoc, Inaugural Address of President Roxas on the Independence of the Philippines, www.studocu.com/ph/document/mindanao-state-university/history-of-the-philippines/inaugural-address-of-president-roxas-on-the-independence-of-the-philippines/90965932 (last accessed October 17, 2024).
65. Stanley Karnow, In Our Image, 323–24.
66. For short newsreel of the ceremony, including excerpts of MacArthur's speech, see https://en.wikipedia.org/wiki/Manuel_Roxas (last accesed October 17, 2024).
67. Stanley Karnow, In Our Image, 434.

Part III: Pursuing Happiness

1. Garry Wills, Inventing America, 368.
2. Carli N. Conklin, Origins of the Pursuit of Happiness, 7 Wash. U. Jurisprudence Rev. 195 (2015) ("This article concludes that "the pursuit of happiness"—which was understood to be both a public duty and a private right—evoked an Enlightenment understanding of the first principles of law by which the natural world is governed, the idea that those first principles were discoverable by humans, and the belief that to pursue a life lived in accordance with those principles was to pursue a life of virtue, with the end result of happiness, best defined in the Greek sense of eudaemonic or human flourishing."); Patrick J. Charles, Restoring "Life, Liberty, and the Pursuit of Happiness" in Our Constitutional Jurisprudence: an Exercise in Legal History, 20 Wm. & Mary Bill Rts. J. 457 (2011) (collecting views).
3. Pauline Maier, American Scripture, 134.
4. Ibid., 126–28, 134–35.
5. Founders Online "To James Madison from Thomas Jefferson, 30 August 1823," National Archives, https://founders.archives.gov/documents/Madison/04-03-02-0113. [Original source: The Papers of James Madison, Retirement Series, vol. 3, 1 March 1823 – 24 February 1826, ed. David B. Mattern, J. C. A. Stagg, Mary Parke Johnson, and Katherine E. Harbury. Charlottesville: University of Virginia Press, 2016, pp. 114–116.]

Chapter 9: Henry David Thoreau: A Personal Independence

1. Henry David Thoreau, "Walden," in *The Works of Henry David Thoreau* (New York: Avenel Books, 1981), 49.
2. Robert Frost, Letter to Wade Van Dore, June 24, 1922, Twentieth Century Interpretations of Walden, ed. Richard Ruland (Englewood Cliffs, NJ: Prentice Hall, 1968), 8.
3. Ken Keifer, "Analysis and Notes on Walden: Henry Thoreau's Text with Adjacent Thoreauvian Commentary" KenKifer.com, https://www.phred.org/~alex/kenkifer/www.kenkifer.com/thoreau/index.htm (last accessed October 17, 2024).

4. Thoreau, Walden, 94.
5. Ibid., 100–01.
6. Ibid., 60.
7. Ibid., 45.
8. Ibid., 102.
9. Ibid., 226–29.
10. Ibid., 127–28.
11. Ibid., 127.
12. Robert D. Richardson, Jr., Henry Thoreau, A Life of the Mind (Berkeley: University of California Press, 1986), 171.
13. Ralph Waldo Emerson, "The Transcendentalist," in Selected Writings of Emerson (New York: Random House, 1950), 87, 93.
14. Thoreau, "Walden," 16.
15. Ibid., 93.
16. Ibid., 98.
17. Ibid., 101.
18. Ibid., 100.
19. Ibid., 155.
20. Ibid., 150.
21. Robert D. Richardson, Henry Thoreau, 266.
22. Henry David Thoreau, Walden, 123–24.
23. Ibid., 206–07.
24. Ibid., 195.
25. Ibid., 265.
26. Ibid., 259–60.
27. Ibid., 210.
28. Ibid., 272.
29. Ibid., 356.
30. Robert D. Richardson, Henry Thoreau, 314–317.
31. Henry David Thoreau, "Slavery in Massachusetts," University of Pennsylvania – African Studies Center, www.africa.upenn.edu/Articles_Gen/Slavery_Massachusetts.html (last accessed October 17, 2024).
32. Henry David Thoreau, Walden, 228.
33. Ralph Waldo Emerson, "Thoreau," in Selected Writings of Emerson (New York: Random House, 1950), 913–14.
34. Robert D. Richardson, Henry Thoreau, 348–49.

Chapter 10: Two Very Different Independence Days for a Union Private

1. Private Robert Knox Sneden, The Eye of the Storm: A Civil War Odyssey, ed. Charles F. Bryan, Jr., and Nelson D. Landford (New York: The Free Press, 2000), 102–03.
2. Ibid., 148–49.
3. National Park Service, "History of the Andersonville Prison," National Park Service, www.nps.gov/ande/learn/historyculture/camp_sumter_history.htm (last accessed October 17, 2024).
4. Private Robert Knox Sneden, The Eye of the Storm, 238–39.
5. Ibid., 238–41.
6. The maps are available online from the Library of Congress at www.loc.gov/search/?fa=contributor%3Asneden%2C+robert+knox (last accessed October 17, 2024).
7. Private Robert Knox Sneden, The Eye of the Storm: A Civil War Odyssey, ed. Charles F. Bryan, Jr., and Nelson D. Landford (New York: The Free Press, 2000).

Chapter 11: Theodore Roosevelt at Dickinson, North Carolina

1. In 1870, North Dakota had 2,405 people; by 1890, the population had grown to more than 190,000. It became a state, along with South Dakota, in 1889. The 1890 census officially declared that the frontier was closed.

2. The events and the newspaper account are set out in Herman Hagedorn, Roosevelt in the Bad Lands (Boston: Houghton Mifflin Co., 1921), 405–11. The printed version of the speech is at: https://www.theodorerooseveltcenter.org/Research/Digital-Library/Record?libID=o273668. Some additional information is contained in Clay S. Jenkinson, Theodore Roosevelt in the Dakota Badlands (Dickinson: Dickinson State University Press, 2006), 79–87.

3. Herman Hagedorn, Roosevelt in the Bad Lands, 405–11.

4. Douglas Brinkley, The Wilderness Warrior: Theodore Roosevelt and the Crusade for America (Harper 2009), Appendix. In all, he placed under public protection approximately 230 million acres. www.nps.gov/thro/learn/historyculture/theodore-roosevelt-and-conservation.htm

5. Douglas Brinkley, The Wilderness Warrior: Theodore Roosevelt and the Crusade for America (New York: Harper Perennial, 2009), 156.

6. Ibid., 273–74.

Chapter 12: Lou Gehrig and America's Pastime, Baseball

1. George F. Will, *Men at Work* (New York: Harper, 1990, 2010), xvii.
2. Ibid., xvii-xviii.
3. Ibid., 4.
4. National Baseball Hall of Fame, https://baseballhall.org/hall-of-famers/gehrig-lou (last accessed October 17, 2024).
5. George F. Will, Men at Work, 297–98.
6. Jonathan Eig, Luckiest Man: The Life and Death of Lou Gehrig (New York: Simon & Schuster, 2005), 297.
7. National Baseball Hall of Fame, https://baseballhall.org/hall-of-famers/gehrig-lou (last accessed October 17, 2024).
8. Ibid.
9. Jonathan Eig, Luckiest Man, 96, 160.
10. Ibid., 89.
11. Ibid., 13.
12. Ibid.
13. Ibid., 99.
14. Ibid., 95.
15. Ibid., 233.
16. Ibid., 233.
17. Ibid., 268–70.
18. Ibid., 270–71.
19. Ibid., 269.
20. Ibid., 287–88.
21. RUMORINTOWN, www.youtube.com/watch?v=VkviK4to-Xw (interview of Babe Dahlgren in 1989) (last accessed October 17, 2024).
22. Jonathan Eig, Luckiest Man, 314.
23. Ibid., 2.
24. The text is based on the official written version published on www.LouGehrig.com. Available snippets of the speech actually given are online. E.g., www.youtube.com/watch?v=Bak7WAHW_iQ The YES Network's Yankeeography of Lou Gehrig includes extensive footage of the day and of Gehrig's career: www.youtube.com/watch?v=0FC3QAEBf58 (last accessed October 17, 2024).
25. Jonathan Eig, Luckiest Man, 318.
26. Jonathan Eig, writing for the ALS Association at http://web.alsa.org/site/PageNavigator/blog_061820.html (last accessed October 17, 2024).
27. Jonathan Eig, Luckiest Man, 325.
28. ALS Association, https://www.als.org/4ALS (last accessed October 17, 2024).

Chapter 13: From Fireworks to Hot Dogs: Celebrations from 1776 to 2026

1. James R. Heintze, *Fourth of July Encyclopedia*, 271.
2. In 1941, the paid holiday was extended to employees of the government of the District of Columbia.

3. For extensive treatment, see James R. Heintze, Fourth of July Encyclopedia.

4. USA and the World, www.youtube.com/watch?v=XBKHjB1_uiQ (last accessed October 17, 2024).

5. NBC News (July 4, 2021), https://www.youtube.com/watch?v=gISd-Q7uH9I (last accessed October 17, 2024).

6. White House History.org., www.whitehousehistory.org/the-first-fourth-of-july-celebration-at-the-presidents-house (last accessed October 17, 2024).

7. The George Community Hall.com, www.georgecommunityhall.com/fourth-of-july-at-george-wa/ (last accessed October 17, 2024).

8. Heintze, Fourth of July Encyclopedia, 97.

9. Ibid., 223.

10. Ibid., 97–99.

11. Ibid., 233–34.

12. Ibid., 37–23, 47–48, 232.

13. E.g., NBC News & San Diego (July 2, 2020), www.nbcsandiego.com/news/local/missing-big-bay-boom-look-back-at-2012-blowout/2358457/ (last accessed October 17, 2024).

14. Heintze, Fourth of July Encyclopedia, 13.

15. Ibid., 282.

16. Ibid., 33.

17. Ibid., 103–04.

18. Ibid., 97–99.

19. Ibid., 99–100.

20. Ibid., 234.

21. Smithsonian Magazine (July 2, 2019), www.smithsonianmag.com/history/1900s-reform-movement-made-fourth-july-safe-and-sane-180972537 (last accessed October 17, 2024).

22. Ibid.

23. Heintze, Fourth of July Encyclopedia, 22.

24. Founders Online, "From George Washington to Major General Alexander McDougall, 4 July 1779," National Archives, https://founders.archives.gov/documents/Washington/03-21-02-0287 (last accessed October 17, 2024).. [Original source: The Papers of George Washington, Revolutionary War Series, vol. 21, 1 June–31 July 1779, ed. William M. Ferraro. Charlottesville: University of Virginia Press, 2012, p. 351.]

25. Heintze, Fourth of July Encyclopedia, 22.

26. Ibid., 195.

27. Ibid., 20–22.

28. Ibid., 20.

29. Founders Online, "From George Washington to Major General Alexander McDougall, 4 July 1779," National Archives, https://founders.archives.gov/documents/Washington/03-21-02-0287 (last accessed October 17, 2024). [Original source: The Papers of George Washington, Revolutionary War Series, vol. 21, 1 June–31 July 1779, ed. William M. Ferraro. Charlottesville: University of Virginia Press, 2012, p. 351.]

30. David O. Stewart, The Summer of 1787 (New York, Simon & Schuster, 2007), 113.

31. Heintze, Fourth of July Encyclopedia, 246–47.

32. Ibid., 276.

33. https://blog.jakesfireworks.com/blog/whats-the-difference-between-safe-and-sane-and-other-fireworks

34. Pauline Maier, American Scripture, 178.

35. Heintze, Fourth of July Encyclopedia, 201.

36. Ibid., 187.

37. Ibid., 50.

38. Ibid.

39. Ibid., 51.

40. Ron Chernow, Grant, 839–40.

41. Heintze, Fourth of July Encyclopedia, 51.

42. Ibid., 52.

43. .www.presidency.ucsb.edu/documents/address-the-celebration-the-150th-anniversary-the-declaration-independence-philadelphia

44. Heintze, Fourth of July Encyclopedia, 34.

45. Ibid.
46. Ibid., 294.
47. America 250.org., https://america250.org/discover/what-is-america-250/ (last accessed October 17, 2024).
48. Report to the President by America250 Commission (January 31, 2022), https://america250.org/wp-content/uploads/2023/06/Report-to-the-President-II-FINAL-2.16.22.pdf (last accessed October 17, 2024).
49. Ron Chernow, Alexander Hamilton (New York: Penguin Books, 2004), 384.
50. Ibid., 402. On July 4, 1804, seven days before he was shot and killed by Aaron Burr in a duel, Alexander Hamilton composed a farewell letter to his wife. In that letter, he said that it was not to be delivered to her "unless I shall first have terminated my earthly career." He maintained that it was not possible to avoid the duel "without sacrifices which would have rendered me unworthy of your esteem." He urged her to find consolation in religion: "Fly to the bosom of your God and be comforted." Hamilton expressed hope that he would meet her again in a "better world" and bid her "adieu best of wives and best of women. Embrace all my darling children for me." Ibid., 709.
51. Ibid., 487.
52. Heintze, Fourth of July Encyclopedia, 298.
53. Ibid., 323.

Chapter 14: Why We Celebrate

1. Commander Louis H. Roddis, *The New York Prison Ships in the American Revolution, 61* United States Naval Institute Proceedings 385 (March 1935), reproduced at www.usni.org/magazines/proceedings/1935/march/new-york-prison-ships-american-revolution
2. Ibid.
3. Danske Dandridge, American Prisoners of the Revolution (Charlottesville: The Michie Co., 1911), 227.
4. History.com, www.history.com/topics/american-revolution/the-hms-jersey#section_2 (last accessed October 17, 2024).
5. Danske Dandridge, American Prisoners of the Revolution, 239.
6. Ibid., 27.
7. Ibid., 243.
8. Ibid., 336.
9. Ibid., 372.
10. Ibid., 373.
11. Ibid., 388–93.
12. Ibid., 375–76.
13. Letter to Reverend Charles Clay, quoted in Jon Meacham, Thomas Jefferson, 225.

About the Author

Thomas K. Clancy is a nationally recognized expert on the Fourth Amendment (search and seizure) and on cyber crime and is the author of two law books: *Cyber Crime and Digital Evidence* (4th ed. 2023) and *The Fourth Amendment: Its History and Interpretation* (3d ed. 2017). He has been called the leading Fourth Amendment historian. With this book, he expands his historical perspective to other aspects of the founding era and to the evolution of the concept of freedom, highlighted repeatedly on our national holiday. Clancy is a Professor Emeritus from the University of Mississippi School of Law and graduated from Vermont Law School and the University of Notre Dame. He now lives on Cape Cod.

www.ingramcontent.com/pod-product-compliance
Lightning Source LLC
Chambersburg PA
CBHW011159090426
42740CB00020B/3408

* 9 7 9 8 8 8 8 1 9 2 5 4 2 *